Music and the Novel

Alex Aronson

Music and the Novel

A Study in
Twentieth-Century Fiction

Rowman and Littlefield
Totowa, New Jersey

Copyright © 1980 by Rowman and Littlefield

First published in The United States of America, 1980,
by Rowman and Littlefield, Totowa, New Jersey.

Library of Congress Cataloging in Publication Data

Aronson, Alex, 1912–
    Music and the novel.

    Bibliography: p.
    Includes index.
    1. Fiction—20th century—History and
criticism.   2. Music and literature.
I. Title.
PN3503.A76   809.3'3   79-4611
ISBN 0-8476-6170-9

Printed in the United States of America

Contents

Preface

The creation of a world of fiction and the composition of a work of music operate on different levels of experience. The novelist, by the very nature of his art, calls for a suspension of disbelief. Chronological time may be dispensed with when duration itself becomes a fiction. Plot and character, structure and texture, speech and silence are all equally illusory depending as much on the novelist's as on the reader's imaginative recreation of reality. Whether fiction is "true to life" matters only insofar as the reader can recognize in it the universe he inhabits. In this sense the reader is the sole arbiter of the "truth" of the story. Fictitious reality may or may not be founded on historically valid premisses. It may be hidden outside or beyond plot and character, in some inner time where speech is replaced by silence, character description by a descent into individual consciousness, and verbal by non-verbal texture.

This is especially true of the first half of the twentieth century when novelists became increasingly aware of the need of conveying the working of the human mind outside any definable historical context. The novelist began by questioning the criterion of historical reality itself as applied to the language used in the writing of a work of fiction. In his search for a language of the imagination which would correspond to the fictitious universe he created he was soon enough forced to acknowledge the lack of linguistic tools which alone would justify his disregard of chronological time. It is when his attention was drawn towards music, among all the arts, that he became aware of the existence of a non-verbal reality more expressive than speech and conforming to the dictates of inner time beyond anything that the novelist's language could communicate.

For the composer's sole preoccupation with sound and musical patterns shifts the emphasis from the fictitious back to the real, from life as metaphor to the demonstration of some irreversible truth as "heard" by the composer and projected outside himself into nature. The music thus composed acquires a temporal dimension only when it is being performed. Only when it is heard in "time" does it become available to the novelist as raw material for his representation of human life. Placed within a human setting, be it church or concert hall, the privacy of a drawing room or even the greater seclusion of individual memory, it creates amorphous states of consciousness originating in musical modulation, rhythm, pitch and volume. Though such a response may or may not be of musicological interest it acquires increasing literary significance in the modern novelist's creation of a fictitious reality.

How, then, does the novelist proceed when he incorporates a musical experience into his novel? The encounter between auditory stimuli and the visual associations or mental processes they evoke is, as this book sets out to show, of growing concern to the novelist who no longer acknowledges any uniform division between what is past or passing or to come. For the musical experience frequently occurs at the still point where memory and desire meet. While the novel, as a rule, assumes its shape in a given world of time and space this encounter between the uncontaminated purity of sound and the framework of individual beliefs, memories, and rationalizations which express the novelists' concern with specific human situations frequently invests the novel with progressively metaphysical overtones.

That music and the musical experience may have a truth to communicate which lies beyond any specific cultural context within a given social group is a theme repeatedly hinted at by contemporary novelists. For what music, at its deepest level, communicates transcends the self which listens and responds. It dwarfs the present moment into insignificance and reveals aspects of consciousness of which the listener had previously been unaware. To some of the novelists dealt with in this study the discipline of the contemplative life which the musical experience fosters is, in effect, the nearest approach to a realization of transcendence in our time. Other, more socially oriented, novelists saw in the portrayal of the clash between individual self-awareness and social compulsion the main function of the musical experience in a work of fiction.

It is with these observations in mind that a coherent framework was found necessary within which the ten chapters of this book would acquire meaning and continuity. Thus, the first chapter attempts a survey of various experiments with musical analogies in the past leading up to the twentieth-century novelist's concern with the musical experience as a linguistic challenge. The first chapter, therefore, serves as an introduction to the main problem this study is concerned with, the function of the musical experience in contemporary works of fiction written in the first half of the twentieth century. Chapter II is devoted to an analysis of the work of James Joyce in terms of its musical texture, while chapter III develops the theme of the listener to music in the modern novel as "character" and as a member of a given social group. Chapters IV and V recount the story of the clash between the composer's morally uncommitted art and the novelist's concern with the effect his music has on the listener's ability to apply moral criteria to his own life and to that of society at large. Chapters VI, VII, and VIII provide further evidence for the novelist's striving to incorporate the musical experience within a framework of attitudes and beliefs, here no longer determined by conformist moral or esthetic standards but intended to provide the individual with a musical equivalent for personal integration. The novelists whose attempts in this direction call for particular attention are Aldous Huxley and E.M. Forster in England, Proust in France, and Thomas Mann and Hermann Hesse in Germany. Lastly, chapter IX is devoted to the study of two of Patrick White's novels with particular emphasis on the part that the musical experience plays in his portrayal of the outsider's search for wholeness. This study would have been incomplete without a concluding chapter on Patrick White's more recent attempts to relate the musical experience to the humble and anonymous quest for individual integration which lies at the core of all his major novels. Chapter X is a summing up of some of the significant themes, literary as well as musical, which called for special and detailed treatment in this study.

Most of the novels dealt with here have, in the course of the past decades, been subjected to exhaustive critical comment.

The novelists' preoccupation with art and especially with music
has frequently and adequately been stressed, particularly in the
case of Proust, Joyce, Mann, and Hesse. Structural analogies between musical composition and various forms of fiction writing
have been established before this. Nowhere, to the best of my
knowledge, has a final assessment been made which would make
the musical experience an essential component of the novelist's
frame of reference regardless of the very different backgrounds,
temperaments and ideologies which went to the making of their
works of fiction. It was with this aim in view that I set out on my
task to establish a common denominator, deriving from the novelist's obsessive concern with music, which these novels might
be expected to share.

Considering the intensely emotional nature of the musical experience and the highly idiosyncratic response it evokes, its
place in the novel stresses individual commitment rather than
social consensus. Composer, performer, and listener are shown
to be solitary figures, frequently agonizingly aware of their social isolation, at times deliberately shunning contact with their
contemporaries. This is especially true of Vinteuil and Adrian
Leverkühn, the two fictitious composers in Proust's and Mann's
work. It is equally evident when the emphasis shifts from creator
to performer. Lucy playing a Beethoven sonata in Forster's
novel, Aaron performing on the flute in Lawrence's mature mas-
terpiece, Moraïtis embracing his cello during the performance
of a concerto for cello and orchestra in Patrick White's novel,
all alike enclose themselves in an inner space into which no
stranger nor friend is admitted. This is particularly the case
when they perform in public and are exposed to popular acclaim
which they despise. The listener is shown to be in search of solitude no less than composer and performer. Whether in a concert hall, a drawing room, or in front of a record player, the very
act of listening isolates the hearer from his accustomed environment, renders him oblivious of personal attachments and social
obligations, and reduces the outside world to a meaningless
conglomeration of sights and sounds. This applies to Stephen
Dedalus as a listener to the inner music of his imagination, to
Marcel and Swann listening to Vinteuil's "little phrase", to
Spandrell's spiritual revelation while absorbed in Beethoven's
Dankgesang, to Hans Castorp in the music room of the T.B. San-

atorium in Davos, to Roquentin listening to his favourite jazz-record in a seedy coffeehouse in some provincial French city, and, even more emphatically, to the early heroes in Hesse's novels, Sinclair and the Steppenwolf, encountering the musical experience at a moment in their lives when they have lost all purposeful contact with the outside world. The spinster Theodora, in Patrick White's novel, is the most socially isolated among them. The musical experience is her last support in her ambivalent struggle for survival. In our novels it is music, among all the arts, that isolates the individual from the society of his contemporaries, makes him aware of his separateness and, finally, provides a personal significance to his life regardless of his social or even personal loyalties. It is the one measure of survival which never fails and which all the novelists in this study share.

A.A.

Tel-Aviv University

Music and the Novel

I
Musical
Correlatives

1

In Aldous Huxley's *Point Counter Point*, published in 1928, there occurs a description of a concert at the house of Lord and Lady Tantamount before an audience of invited guests. The orchestra is playing Bach's suite in B-minor, for flute and strings. It is a festive occasion. Conductor, soloists and orchestra perform with gusto and precision. Some of the listeners present respond to the musical ritual by closing their eyes and by a willing surrender to visual associations of a vaguely disturbing though not unwelcome ambiguity. Others, less given to musical rapture, are irritated by what they consider to be either hypocrisy or self-indulgence or both and pass their time observing their variously entranced neighbors. It is a heterogeneous audience portrayed with considerable ironic detachment.

The reader is disconcertingly aware of this sense of aloofness when Huxley comes to describe the music itself. Evidently realizing the inadequacies of language to say anything of any validity whatever about the emotional content of the music, he is being facetiously scientific about it. The flautist "blew across the mouth hole and a cylindrical air column vibrated." The violinists produced a similar kind of vibration in the air when they "drew their rosined horse-hair across the stretched intestines of lambs." While Bach, in Huxley's words, was meditating on the beauty, goodness, and oneness of things, Huxley meditates on music or rather on "the universal concert of things."

The meditation takes place in the mind of Lord Edward who knows a great deal about chemistry and biology and the mathematical relation between them and is not without musical erudition. As an expert in osmosis he is especially interested in, if not actually obsessed, by the problem of "natural harmony" of which musical harmony may be said to be only a small part. In the "total life of the universe", as he likes to call it, the individual life of man or beast is being compared to a melody whose modulations are open to chemical and mathematical analysis. "It's all like music," meditates Lord Edward in his laboratory while performing an experiment on a newt and listening to Bach being played downstairs, "harmonies and counterpoint and modulations."

The composer who creates these melodies is equally exposed to this disconcerting osmotic process. When he dies he is, predictably, "transformed into grass and dandelions, which in their turn had been transformed into sheep" whose intestines, in due time, will be made into strings of various lengths on which these melodies are going to be played all over again. It is an alarming and inhuman prospect. In the course of this osmotic process music is being reduced to air vibrations which in turn shake the *membrana typani*, the interlocked *malleus*, *incus* and stirrup bones of the ear, "raise an infinitesimal storm in the fluid of the labyrinth", and finally make the hairy endings of the auditory nerve "shudder like weeds in a rough sea." All these complex auditory phenomena, the result of Bach's variously solemn or gay meditations on life can be summed up—and Huxley has no compunctions about doing so—by referring to "Euclidian axioms" which "made holiday with the formulae of elementary statistics. Arithmetic held a wild saturnalian kermesse; algebra cut capers". When, finally, the *Badinerie* with which the suite in B-minor ends reaches its joyful conclusion the music terminates "in an orgy of mathematical merry-making."[1]

Huxley, who had had a scientific education and possessed considerable musical knowledge, sets his osmotic description of biochemistry, translated into musical terms, and the music of Bach, explored in statistical terms, at the beginning of his novel. It is one of his counterpoints. There will be other forms of osmosis in his novel, based on the relationships between human beings, between the various arts, between the individual and the society he inhabits, between moral compulsions and the political life. The "universal concert of things," defined in parodied scientific terms, but understandable to the lay reader and applied to a well-known piece of music with which most educated readers may be assumed to be familiar, acquires comic dimensions. For what Huxley attempts in this episode, deliberately assuming the role of the all-knowing scientist who rejects the imaginative appeal of music for biochemical formulas, is to shock the reader out of his smug acceptance of music as a convenient release for repressed emotions and irrelevant mental or visual associations, and as a form of exuberant self-indulgence.

The reader is startled as he might well be. He does not know that Huxley's detached objectivity when portraying composer, musician and listener "osmotically" is founded upon a theory of numbers as old as humanity itself and that "the vibrating air columns" in the flute and "the stretched intestines of lambs" had been used for scientific measurements by Pythagoras two thousand five hundred years ago. The reader, ignorant of Pythagoras's discovery that the perceived harmony of musical intervals is paralleled by the simple numerical ratios of spatial distance on the string and the flute, to which may be added the presentday knowledge of the simple relations between the wave frequencies of musical sound, is thus liable to miss the ironic implications inherent in Huxley's veiled reference to ancient theories of measurable harmony in the absurd upper-class setting of twentieth-century London.

Pythagoras's theory of proportion is equally applicable to mathematical measurements, to the movement of stars and to the definition of musical harmony. It may not help the reader of Huxley's novel to achieve a deeper insight into the novelist's concern with osmosis. But it may open up revealing perspectives into the history of ideas—of special interest to the reader puzzled by the recurrent metaphor of harmonious music in the art and literature of all times. For in the language of symbols, created by Pythagoras and the Pythagoreans, harmony is determined by the mathematical relation between numbers and tones, made visible by diagrams and, when recreated on strings of various lengths, translated into chords.

One further dimension is added to this definition of harmony when this system of auditory and visual proportions is found to be embodied in certain planetary constellations and the motions of the spheres with which each planet follows its predetermined course. The belief that this movement of the spheres produces harmonious sound remained intact throughout the Renaissance, accepted as an unquestioned axiom by scientist, musician, artist and poet.

Huxley who by temperament and innate gifts was better qualified for scientific than literary explorations knew all this. He must also have known that his "universal concert of things," meditated upon first by Bach and than by Lord Edward Tantamount, was a parody of the humanist revival in the belief in Pythagoras's "music of the spheres." What he so mockingly resurrected were ancient and medieval analogies according to which scientist and artist alike were assumed to share a common body of musical knowledge and experience.

Huxley thus adds an ironic dimension to the tradition of past great masters of literature among whom Shakespeare comes to mind first of all. Shakespeare's preoccupation with the "universal concert of things" is of the very stuff of which his plays are made. By a curious coincidence he was equally startled at the apparently incongruous relation between the intestines of sheep and the creation of harmony in the soul of man. "Is it not strange," exclaims Benedick, "that sheeps' guts should hale souls out of men's bodies?"[2] Shakespeare, in all likelihood, knew a good deal less about Pythagoras than Aldous Huxley. But from Boethius or possibly Montaigne he had acquired a general, if vague, knowledge of the movement of the planets which, says Montaigne, "in their rolling motion, touching and rubbing against another, must of necessitie produce a wonderful harmonie."[3] Shakespeare also knew that this music of the spheres remained inaudible to men's ears and, thus, could not directly affect their souls. Though constantly reaching out towards harmony man's soul remained insensible—except by indistinct reflection—to those heavenly chords which, according to contemporary belief, determined the "Nativitie of Mortals."[4]

In *The Merchant of Venice*, Lorenzo, an otherwise unprepossessing figure, is heard meditating on music and, in six lines of impassioned poetry, sums up the Pythagorean system of spherical music. Harmony, he declares—and this is quite in line with Pythagorean ways of thinking—is confined to "immortal souls" only. As long as the soul of man is closed in by "this muddy vesture of decay"(V, 1, 64-5), harmony as a universal musical chord, may be at best an aspiration, a spiritual ideal beyond the reach of man. In very exceptional circumstances an echo reaches mortal ears when it may be heard in the speaking voice of a particularly well-integrated person. When Cleopatra describes Antony's voice as being "propertied as all the tuned spheres"[5] she communicates to those around her a sense of personal completeness derived from what, at a later stage, Huxley will rather more prosaically call "the universal concert of things."

In Shakespeare's vision of the harmonious relation between animate and inanimate elements in nature, only man constitutes a sometimes perplexing but mostly agonizing discord. It is man's propensity to think evil and to do evil which is taken as a pretext for "planetary" explanations. Ulysses, in *Troilus and Cressida*, in his speech on degree, blames the planets when they "in evil mixture to disorder wander"(I, 3, 94-5) for political and social upheavals. Jaques's melancholy in *As You Like It*, which threatens the prevailing harmony among the exiles in the Forest of Arden is compared to "discord in the spheres"(II, 7, 6). Iago blames "some planet" that has "unwitted men" (II, 3, 182) for the quarrel which woke Othello and tore him from Desdemona's side. Leontes, in *The Winter's Tale*, in search for a rational motive to justify his sudden and inexplicable fit of jealousy, ominously points at "a bawdy planet that will strike/When 'tis predominant."(I, 2, 201) The most explicit of them, Edmund, in *King Lear*, dismisses any sort of "spherical predominance" as a mere excuse for "knaves, thieves, and treachers" to indulge in their crimes as if, he mockingly observes, they acted "by heavenly compulsion", while "drunkards, liars, and adulterers" consider themselves at liberty to commit their sins "by an enforc'd obedience of planetary influence."(I, 2, 127)

Aldous Huxley who felt at home in Shakespeare's plays no less than in biochemistry knew that the drawing of musical analogies—whether in terms of planetary motion or simple mathematical measurements—was a commonly accepted practice among writers and artists throughout the Renaissance. Both concord and discord could be conceived visually in keeping with Pythagoras's diagrams. They could also be recreated, as it were, by painters who, assuming the existence of the universal harmony of things, might and indeed did attempt a reflection of it through the application of color and design on canvas. Thus, in Ficino's theory of the image, the Pythagorean belief in the music of the spheres is being transposed from the realm of music to that of art. For according to Ficino, "the number and proportions of a thing preserved in the image something of the power of the spiritual essence which it embodies."[6]

The artist in search of visual perfection frequently looked in music for valid analogies. Pythagorean theories provided the mathematical foundation. Spherical music stood for a symbolic representation of the essence of harmony. All that could be measured and divided into numbers and proportions, whether of visual or auditory import, became part of the universal harmony. If, as Shakespeare implied, man is the only discordant element in nature, then it is the artist's business to recreate harmony in the very teeth of man's attempts at self-destruction. Leonardo da Vinci, in one of his *Notebooks*, establishes this analogy between painting and music in terms of measurement and proportion. "Although objects observed by the eye touch one another as they recede, I shall nevertheless found my rule on a series of intervals measuring 20 *braccia* [about 28 inches] each, just as the musician who, though his voices are united and strung together, has created intervals according to the distance from voice to voice, calling them unison, second, third, fourth, and fifth, and so on, until numbers have been given to the various degrees of pitch proper to the human voice . . . If you say that music is composed of proportion, then I have used similar meanings in paintings, as I shall show."[7]

Such analogies abound in the history of art and art criticism. Each age developed a different musical criterion appropriate to the new cultural context. Thus, Poussin in the seventeenth century relates his paintings to Greek "modes" of musical composition and, in a well-known letter, promises his friend that "before a year is out I hope to paint a subject in [this] Phrygian mode" which, he believes, is particularly suitable for "horrible subjects."[8] Whistler, some two centuries later, insists on designating his works as "arrangements" or "harmonies" and, finally, decides to call them "symphonies" or "nocturnos."[9] In more recent times abstract painters found no difficulty in establishing even closer analogies between the abstract patterns of sound and design by merely calling a painting by the name of a musical composition. Familiarity with the music, represented on the canvas as an abstract configuration of lines, shapes, and colors, would enable the spectator to respond in a predictable and desirable way. When Mondrian labelled a painting *Broadway Boogie-Woogie* (painted in 1942/43) he aimed at an "orchestration" effect with its popular dance rhythm, pitch, and volume. However, the music remains unheard. Shapes and colors cannot be made to sing. The spectator who has never witnessed the playing of a boogie-woogie may conceivably associate this painting with the first of Bach's Brandenburg Concertos. The deliberate avoidance of any actual likeness leaves all aesthetic options open.[10] Similar doubts arise when one looks at Kandinsky's abstract paintings which were supposed to be attempts at translating Wagner's music into visual terms.

Pythagoras's system of numbers and proportions continues to haunt the artist in his search for harmonious structure. More even than the painter, the architect may discover analogies "in depth" between his planning an edifice and musical composition. Both arts assume the existence of a "third" dimension which in music is called an interval and in architecture free, unused space. This relation between mass and intervals establishes a criterion of harmony depending on spatial measure very close to the original Pythagorean assumption of a "universal concert of things." Le Corbusier who came from a family of musicians accepts the Renaissance view that architects should go to school to study science as well as music. "More than these thirty years past," he wrote, "the sap of mathematics has flown through the veins of my work, both as an architect and painter; for music is always present within me."[11] The somewhat baffling realization that architecture exists in space while music exists in time is no obstacle to analogical thinking of this kind. In mathematical terms both interval and silence are alike measurable. Music has been called "architectural" on more than one occasion. And if the analogy is not extended into extravagant absurdity (as in Huxley's novel which started this whole train of thought), the listener to music, responsive to geometric form and algebraic progression, may indeed receive an auditory image of some harmonious essence beyond anything that ordinary everyday life can provide. Within the context of the history of ideas the Pythagorean concept of harmony—though modified by modern scientific thought—is still with us.

2

Color and sound as used by the artist have this in common that they tend away from reality as a mere sense impression. A painting which does not go beyond a true-to-life imitation of reality ceases to be art however exact the measurements and proportions. Sound which merely imitates nature is not music even if pitch, volume, and interval approximate as closely as humanly possible to the various noises originating in man's natural surroundings. What painter and musician, then, create is an illusion of reality as perceived through the imagination. What the eye sees and the ear hears—the painting or the piece of music—is thus retranslated by the spectator and listener through a variety of sense impressions into the language of the mind. Frequently—and by a process which Pythagoras was the first to suggest—the illusion created by a painting evokes musical analogies while a piece of music is made "visible" through visual associations originating in the listener's memory. As long as the two arts keep within the framework of illusion the likelihood of their actual fusion into a compound work of art remains a distinct, if theoretical, possibility.

Throughout the nineteenth century, writers, both in poetry and prose, explored this likelihood as a matter of increasing practical application. As their medium was language they made use of discursive speech to rationalize the need for the fusion of the arts. The logic of their argument was indeed unassailable. What other medium but the word could establish a significant link between color and sound by a detailed analysis of the "complete," if illusory, work of art? Only human speech could supply, in terms of intellectual concepts, a new meaning to harmony in the arts considered as the most accomplished of all illusions.

One of the earliest and most curious attempts at describing such a fusion of the arts of painting and music occurs in a novel by Balzac, called after its protagonist, *Gambara*. Gambara is a failed musician who, provoked into telling the story of his life, expounds his theories of music in a remarkable mixture of Pythagorean and Bergsonian concepts. "Nature" is, indeed, the criterion applied to both arts. The human and the nonhuman, according to him, are interchangeable because "music is both a science and an art. Its roots plunge into physics and mathematics, and this makes it a science." Like Huxley a hundred years after Balzac he is also concerned with the vibrations of air columns which "find in us corresponding elements that answer, that vibrate sympathetically, and that are capable of enhanced significance by the application of thought." This explains, continues the musician, why the physical phenomena of sound "match ideas within us according to our capacities." Proust who will elaborate upon this in a somewhat subtler way and with greater psychological insight will add little to the musical theories of Balzac's frustrated musical hero.

But this is merely the beginning of the story. Warming up to his subject he provides a popularized version of the synesthetic effect of music on the visual imagination of composer and listener. For, he asserts, "in music the instruments play the role of colors used by the painter," because mathematical laws apply to both the arts alike. The ideal composer, says Gambara, would translate "the phenomenon of light, vegetation, and life itself" into harmonious sound. He repeatedly refers to the listener's "dormant memories," a very Bergsonian concept indeed, which would be awakened to a new life by the fusion of auditory and visual elements.[12] What this new life will be like is not spelt out in so many words. The reference here is evidently to the synesthetic effect of music, the evocation of a different kind of sense impression from that which one commonly associates with the experience of listening to a melody played on an instrument or sung by a human voice.

It is this evidence of fused sense impressions that De Quincey tried to provide in his *Dream-Fugue*, published as part of his *English Mail Coach* in 1849. Conceivably his addiction to opium had something to do with this remarkable dream-vision of man's mortality on earth. De Quincey's inspired piece of writing eliminates any distinction between what the ear hears or the eye sees, between actual and imaginative listening, between sight and insight. The dream which is the subject of this "fugue" releases the dreamer from the prison in which reason holds him captive. Thus he is enabled to experience sense impressions on a multiplicity of levels at a time. Music is at the very center of the experience. It evokes the response of all the senses simultaneously, as it were, and is equally assimilated by the sense of

sight, smell, taste, and touch. Music is all-pervading because it is
the stuff of which dreams are made. While reading the dream
fugue, the reader becomes aware of an uncanny sensation, that
of listening to a piece of music that has never been composed
and of seeing visions that have never been painted except in the
writer's overwrought imagination. This creation of a synesthetic
universe provides the most coherent illusion of an ideal work of
art. Such transcendental experiences had already, a few years
earlier, been defined by another opium addict, Edgar Allan Poe,
in terms of the poetry he wished to write. In a letter, probably
written to his publisher in 1831, Poe defines poetry as consisting
of "indefinite sensations, to which end music is an *essential*, since
the comprehension of sweet sound is our most indefinite conception. Music, when combined with pleasurable ideas, is poetry."[13]

No one could have agreed more readily than Baudelaire who
adapted and translated the work of De Quincey and Poe into
French. In his own poetry, perfumes, colors, and sounds establish confusing correspondences, sense impressions are no
longer what they seem to be, and the harmonies thus created are
of an esoteric nature.[14] In his various essays on Poe he praises
the American poet for having revealed new possibilities of self-
realization through his exploration of the kinship of poetry and
music. The following passage chosen at random reflects the
enthusiasm with which Baudelaire greeted this revelation of a
"paradis artificiel" where the poet and the musician would share
in equal measure an intimation of immortality. "It is at the same
time through poetry and beyond poetry, through and beyond
music, that the soul perceives the splendors that lie beyond the
grave."[15] When, some years later, Baudelaire discovers the music of Wagner he sees in the multiple associations of word and
sound as part of a stage-representation, the fulfillment of his
own dream of a synesthetic experience through art. While, on
the one hand, Wagner's operas remind him of medieval Mys-
tery-plays they also evoke the masterworks of painters, "those
great visions which the Middle-Ages spread across the walls of
its churches or wove into its magnificent tapestries."[16] This was
written in 1857. Some thirty years later Walter Pater in England,
without referring to Wagner and his synesthetic vision of a new
form of art and drama, made music the ultimate criterion by

which the excellence of art—be it poetry or painting—would be judged.

According to Pater not only does "all art constantly aspire towards the condition of music," music itself is assumed to be a principle of integration compelling the poet or painter to strive for that unity of matter and form which is most completely realized in a musical work. "In its consummate moment," continues Pater, "the end is not distinct from the means, the form from the matter, the subject from the expression; they inhere in and completely saturate each other, and to it, therefore, to the condition of its perfect moments, all the arts may be supposed to tend and aspire. In music, then, rather than in poetry, is to be found the true type or measure of perfected art."[17] We do not know, nor does Walter Pater tell us, what kind of music he had in mind when he wrote this. He certainly was influenced by the French *Parnassiens* and the esthetic theories advanced by Baudelaire a generation earlier. But taken out of its historical context Walter Pater's insistence on music as the ultimate criterion of beauty repeats in the language of late nineteenth-century estheticism what humanist writers on art had said centuries before: painting and music are a transmutation of nature in terms of proportion and measurement, while poetry is speech attuned to some transcendental universal harmony. All the arts alike express man's attempt at translating the discord prevailing in the quotidian experience of life into harmonious proportions.

Twenty years after Pater's essay on Giorgione where these lines occur, Mallarmé, in language visionary and obscure, dreams of an art "which shall complete the transposition into the book of the symphony," an art, he implies, which would encompass all that is most perfect in speech and in sound, "drawing to itself all the correspondences of the universe, the supreme Music."[18] This dream was shared by a whole generation of writers both on the continent and in England. John Synge who, in all likelihood had met Mallarmé during his stay in Paris imagined a new type of writer who would write of human life as "a symphony and the translation of this sequence into music, and from music again, for those who are not musicians, into literature."[19]

The temptation to find in music a universal criterion for *all* sense-impressions was particularly hard to resist whenever a writer's surrender to physical sensations became an end in itself. Baudelaire had pointed the way. Others followed, convinced that music had the power of transforming any sensation into sound. Thus one finds Huysmans in his notorious *A Rebours* (*Against Nature*) describing Des Esseintes' collection of liqueurs as a musical instrument "providing his palate with sensations analogous to those which music dispenses to the ear." To give but one example, "Dry curacao . . . was like the clarinet with its piercing, velvety note." The analogy is carried to absurd lengths. String quartets might be played by a subtle combination of various liqueurs. Major and minor keys were equally at his alcoholic disposal. And, to crown it all, "he even succeeded in transferring specific pieces of music to his palate, following the composer step by step, rendering his intentions, his effects, his shades of expression, by mixing or contrasting related liqueurs, by subtle approximations and cunning combinations."[20]

The symbolist movement in poetry and in prose used music as a catalyst. The least tangible of all the arts, it was therefore open to a larger variety of emotive associations than painting, sculpture, or architecture. It enabled the artist to fuse sound and color, melody and design, volume and shape, evoke more complex responses than any single art could ever produce, and, finally, directly appeal to sense impressions in such a way that the whole of the human personality was involved in the esthetic experience. Symbolism, as understood around the turn of the century, on the continent and in England, implied an intricate set of musical significances which neither poet nor novelist could do without. Speech itself had to be musically oriented. The poetic line as a melody, the novel as a sonata, became commonplaces of literary criticism. Literary and musical structures were found to originate in some common primordial principle of artistic creation. The "universal concert of things" underlying all symbolist doctrines on art was being trivialized until any analogy, however absurd, between music and the other arts was found to possess an innate validity no longer subject to rational argument. Huysmans' digression into the musical equivalents of the various liqueurs is as good an evidence as any for the symbolist claim of some ultimate harmony based on sense impressions rather than on Pythagorean mathematical insight.

3

W.B. Yeats who started his poetic career as a disciple of Walter Pater and an admirer of Mallarmé was the first to realize the pitfalls of a symbolist vision of art founded on the predominance of music over the other arts. Repeatedly he looked upon music as a threat to the poet's spoken word. He "would have no one write with a sonata in his memory," he wrote in 1906, for "music is the most impersonal of things and words the most personal, and that is why musicians do not like words."[21] In the same essay he asserts that there should be only so much music in poetry "as [the poet] can discover on the wings of words." Being himself tone-deaf he warns the reader against what he considers to be the illusory perfection of the musician's art. And when, still in the same essay, he compares the "spoken" music of Villon's verse when recited to the accompaniment of a guitar to a professional musician performing on a piano, "it is the piano, the mechanism, that is the important thing, and nothing of you means anything but your fingers and your intellect."

In earlier writings Yeats visualized a kind of poetry recital in which the meaning of the word would be stressed by the use of a musical instrument in the background. For though poetry and not music is the object of such experiments, as he calls them, he dreams of some primordial scene where the distinction between word and music had not yet become established in the minds of the listeners, a scene "of wild-eyed men speaking harmoniously to murmuring wires while audiences in many-colored robes listened, hushed and excited."[22] The "wires" are those of a "psaltery"—"a beautiful stringed instrument" producing what Yeats called "natural" music to which he had been introduced by Arnold Dolmetsch who at the turn of the century was one of the first to revive interest in old musical instruments and their music.

A few years before his death, Yeats was still convinced of the superiority of poetic speech over musical intonation. In October 1936, shortly before a BBC broadcast of some of his poems, he discussed the possibility of using a drum or other musical instrument between stanzas or between poems. The idea was "to heighten the intensity of the rhythm, but never behind the voice," for, he explained, "there must never be an accompaniment, and no words must be spoken through music." The musical notes "must never be loud enough to shift the attention of the ear."[23]

In spite of all misgivings Yeats's preoccupation with music and particularly the singing voice never ceased. Some of his most accomplished poems make use of musical metaphors in a context of significant human experience, not a mere accompaniment but the very stuff of which poetry itself is made. "Sailing to Byzantium" (1926) is, very largely, a poem about the life of the poet translated into musical terms. It begins with the "sensual music" of "generation," leading up to the poet's own attempt at "singing" and his conviction that there is no "singing school but studying/Monuments of its own magnificence." The poet, therefore, decides to sail to Byzantium to meet there his "singing masters" who will teach him how to translate his anguish and desires into an "artifice of eternity." Such an artifice is the golden nightingale singing of the passing of time to the lords and ladies of Byzantium. This appears to be the subtlest attempt made by a poet to realise Mallarmé's vision of an art that would draw to itself "all the correspondences of the universe, the supreme Music." For though Yeats certainly knew little enough of Byzantine music, his "Sailing to Byzantium" traces the transformation of poetry into music as part of his own experience of growing old, an expression of his awareness that in order to outlast time the sensuous music of youth must be replaced by the immutable, timeless singing of the golden bird.

When, at a still later stage, Pythagoras is introduced into Yeats's poetry, it is as a mathematician and philosopher rather than as the discoverer of the "music of the spheres." He appears in three of Yeats's major poems. In the first "Among School Children," he is rejected outright, together with Plato and Aristotle. Yeats contemptuously refers to their teaching as "Old clothes upon old sticks to scare a bird" and chooses "passion, piety, or affection" instead. Within the context of a poem written in praise of "the great rooted blossomer," this rejection of all philosophical systems has an inner consistency of its own. There is no place for "golden thighed Pythagoras" who "fingered upon a fiddle-stick or strings / What a star sang and careless Muses heard" among Yeats's images of "labour" which is both blossoming and dancing. Yet, the body of the dancer is "swayed to music." Conceivably, the reader of the poem may think there would have been no dance had there been no music. And if it is in music that all dance originates, would this not be true as well of all the other arts, of which dance is the most perfect physical embodiment?

Six years later Yeats writes one of his most humorous, but also one of his most disturbing poems, "News from the Delphic Oracle"(1934). Here Pythagoras is found in the company of Plotinus but also of Niamh and Oisin, transplanted without any more ado from Irish mythology to classical Greece. What these four have in common is that they are bored and in great need of love. "Tall Pythagoras", no better than the other "golden cadgers," "sighed amid his choir of love" (possibly an ironic reference to the music of the spheres), yawned and apparently fell asleep. It is against the background of this spectacle of sterile longing that Yeats resurrects the "dolphin-torn and gong-tormented sea" of an earlier poem ("Byzantium"), a paradise of sexual promiscuity ruled over by a different sort of music. For

> Down the mountain walls
> From where Pan's cavern is
> Intolerable music falls.

The implication of how "intolerable" this music is, is made fairly clear in the lines that follow. It is a music of the body rather than the spirit, no more measurable in terms of numbers. Pythagoras, defeated by the intensity of lust, is contrasted to the god Pan, mathematical contemplation to the laughter of the "ecstatic waters" where nymphs and satyrs "copulate in the foam."

A year before his death, in his poem "The Statues", Yeats returns once more to ancient Greece. Tormented by his vision of "The Second Coming", by the threat of "Asiatic vague immensities" overcoming all that Western Europe has created in art and literature, he writes a poem on the origin of the European sculptural tradition which, he now believes, must be preserved. The basis of that tradition is to be found in the Pythagorean theory of numbers which provided sculptors with a mathematical basis for their work.

> Pythagoras planned it. Why did the people stare?
> His numbers, though they moved or seemed to move
> In marble or in bronze, lacked character.

One remembers Yeats's dislike of "character" as part of the

vocabulary of psychological realism. It is in keeping with his worship of the body "swayed in music" that "passion" is now substituted for character. Pythagoras, in this remarkable poem, achieves a kind of paradoxical resurrection. He helped sculptors to model "with a mallet or a chisel . . . these Calculations that look but casual flesh" and thus created "live lips upon a plummet-measured face." By making the creation of these statues possible Pythagoras also "gave women dreams and dreams their looking-glass."

During the last year of his life Yeats expressed, this time in prose, his belief that only a reborn affirmation of harmony as the sole criterion of Western art can save Europe from final self-destruction. "There are moments when I am certain that art must once again accept those Greek proportions which carry into plastic art the Pythagorean number, those faces which are divine because all there is empty and measured. Europe was not born when Greek galleys defeated the Persian hordes at Salamis; but when Doric studios sent out those broad-backed marble statues against the multiform, vague, expressive Asiatic sea, they gave to the sexual instinct of Europe its goal, its fixed type."[24] "The Statues" of which this passage is an exact comment reflects Yeats's final return to mathematical proportion as the first step to be taken by the artist on his way towards perfection. What is being reaffirmed here is an archetypal vision of the oneness of all created life whether it be in painting, sculpture, or indeed in music. There is here that affirmation of stillness which pertains to music no less than to statuary, to poetry no less than to the visual arts. If Yeats does not mention music in this remarkable poem it is because his preoccupation with the human body as a criterion of perfect living proportion precluded all that is abstract and impersonal, and devoid, as he then thought, of powerful instinctual urges. By the time he wrote this poem he must have become aware of the perils to the human soul in Pan's "intolerable music." Like the waters which echoed this music it is "ecstatic," and like the dolphins on whose back the slim adolescents had come to play in the sea it is "brute."

T. S. Eliot's poetry is less visually oriented. In his poetry musical images and metaphors abound. The musical experience furnishes him with some of his most persuasive "objective correlatives". Thus human beings and their response to the environment in which they live come to life as if they were musical themes, counterpoints of thinking and feeling, harmonious chords or shrill dissonances in an orchestral piece of always surprising and, at times, bewildering variety. Thus Eliot's use of music in his poetry leads to a widening of the reader's range of response in terms of both formal and thematic significances.

Eliot's critical pronouncements reveal an equal preoccupation with musical patterns and content. Not altogether surprisingly, a survey of musical analogies in Eliot's critical work discloses his suspicion of inadequacy on the part of the man of letters who goes to music in order to find critical support in his attempt at perfection in art for which literary criticism has not yet developed a suitable vocabulary. Thus, in the winter of 1933, Eliot in an unpublished lecture delivered in New Haven, Connecticut, is supposed to have said that he had in his own poetry, attempted "to get beyond poetry as Beethoven, in his later work, strove to get beyond music." What Eliot meant by getting "beyond poetry" is unambiguously stated in the same lecture: it is an attempt to let poetry speak for itself "with nothing poetic about it", or poetry "so transparent that we should not see the poetry". Eliot does not tell the reader what Beethoven was doing when he "strove to get beyond music". But the analogy clearly refers to a criterion of absolute esthetic purity where poetry—as Eliot would like to write it—would "stand naked in its bones," combining within itself the ideal perfection of both poetry and music.[25]

Neither words nor ideas need be sacrificed to this perfection. Meanings may not only be preserved by may acquire additional levels of significance. In an early essay on "Ezra Pound, his Metric and Poetry"(1917) Eliot makes his position clear. Dismissing the merely emotional appeal of music in the poetry of Shelley or Swinburne as being nearer rhetoric "than to the instrument," he concludes, "For poetry to approach the condition of music (Pound quotes approvingly the dictum of Pater) it is not necessary that poetry should be destitute of meaning" as long as there is "a definite emotion behind it."[26] Frequently, when speaking of Shakespeare's plays Eliot implies the existence of a significant relation between musical pattern and poetic response, between a formal structure, musically conceived, and the moods, emotional disposition or frame of mind it evokes in those who witness a performance of the play.

Thus, in 1951, in a lecture entitled "Poetry and Drama" Eliot visualizes "a kind of mirage of perfection of verse drama, which would be a design of human action and of words, such as to present at once the two aspects of dramatic and of musical order." Referring, in particular, to the garden scene in *Romeo and Juliet* he discovers there "a musical pattern . . . as surprising in its kind as that in the early work of Beethoven." Though Eliot is concerned here with the poetry spoken on the stage rather than with plot or character, he finds a kind of musical perfection in the scene which is the result of Shakespeare having discarded "the stiffness, the artificiality, the poetic decoration, of his early verse," thus achieving "a simplification of the language of natural speech"[27] and a perfection of poetry brought about by the integration of the musical pattern into the poetry of this scene. Already in an earlier essay, "The Music of Poetry", Eliot had advised the poet to go to music in order to acquaint himself with musical techniques and, in particular, with the effect that such techniques may have on the reader of poetry. Eliot here stresses "possibilities for verse which bear some analogy to the development of a theme by different groups of instruments; there are possibilities of transitions in a poem comparable to the different movements of a symphony or a quartet; there are possibilities of contrapuntal arrangement of subject-matter."[28]

The poet whose only tool is the word may find it impossible to compete with the multiplicity of thematic variations inherent in the use of diverse instruments to express a large variety of musical ideas or emotions. Musical analogies which refer poet or reader to musical patterns, communicating no meaning beyond what the sounds themselves express, may ultimately convey a sense of the inadequacy of all speech when measured by musical criteria. For this sense of the completeness of revelation that great music transmits finally silences even the most articulate among literary critics. Nothing of any intellectual validity whatever can be said about such music. Words themselves appear irrelevant, and the most erudite commentary merely a trivial appendage to the wordless message of perfection conveyed through the musical experience. Northrop Frye, for instance, confesses to such "a feeling of definite revelation" after listening to a Palestrina motet or a Mozart Divertimento. "Here," he says, "is a simplicity which makes us realize that the simple is the opposite of the commonplace, a feeling that the boundaries of possible expression in art have been reached for all times."[29] And T.S. Eliot wrote, in answer to a letter by Stephen Spender who was reminded of Beethoven's posthumous music when reading "Ash Wednesday", "I have the A-minor Quartet on the gramophone and find it quite unexhaustible to study. There is a sort of heavenly or at least more than human gaiety about some of his later things which one imagines might come to oneself as the fruit of reconciliation and the relief after immense suffering; I should like to get something of that into verse before I die."[30]

4

The novelist's concern with the musical experience is necessarily and for similar reasons of an equivocal nature. As long as he could portray the thoughts, feelings, and sense impressions of his fictitious characters without recording the inwardness of this experience, the musician or the listener to music differed from other characters only in so far as they were "musically" oriented. The way they listened and responded to music could still be described "realistically" and in the language of everyday life. In this way the musical experience, just like any other esthetic experience, could be absorbed by the reader's imagination. There was no need to render it as pertaining to different levels of consciousness which partook of this experience.[31]

Increasingly the novelist, at the beginning of the twentieth century became aware of states of consciousness where sensory impressions and thought are inextricably intermingled, a pleasing twilight of indefinite sensations which pertains more to the realm of poetry than of prose. Language itself had to undergo a process of transformation in order to integrate this newly discovered reality. Realizing that all human speech, instead of communicating the true nature of experience, introduces an inevitable element of alienation, the novelist in the early decades of this century attempted the almost impossible: to capture the moment of emotional intensity (for example, when listening to music) at the very instant of sudden and inexplicable revelation. Time itself, the fleeting moment of experience, the instant of perception, had to be given verbal permanence.

The challenge the modern novelist had to face was to render the time-bound nature of music and thought into speech which (though itself part of the flow of time) would be "always present." Eliot's self-evident assertion, in *Burnt Norton*, that "Words move, music moves/Only in time" appears to establish a common denominator applicable to both writer and musician. For the patterns formed by words and the patterns formed by music originate in the same silence that existed before and will again be after the words and the music have reached the listener's consciousness. It is, says Eliot, the "stillness" out of which all art grows. He compares it to a Chinese jar which "still/Moves perpetually in its stillness". "Not," he adds, "the stillness of the violin, while the note lasts" but rather the "co-existence" of past, present and future in both music and poetry. The true predicament of the artist, then, is to render simultaneously "the moment in and out of time", that is the moment experienced first as time passing and then as a still point in time. In "The Dry Salvages," Eliot, attempting to formulate the predicament, refers to music "heard so deeply/That it is not heard at all, but you are the music/While the music lasts." There is, thus, no common criterion applicable to both musical time and the time it takes to "describe" it, and the time needed to read such a description. Different levels of consciousness are involved. The poet rightly assumes that sound actually heard and sounds echoing in the memory may evoke different responses. It is the novelist's rather than the poet's business to disentangle stillness from movement, silence from sound, memory from experience. Eliot is a dependable guide in this apparently contradictory welter of imcompatibilities. For when, at the end of *The Four Quartets*, he concludes that "Every phrase and every sentence is an end and a beginning", he may well mean the musical phrase and the sentence spoken by the poet, both equally and in the same proportion moving perpetually in their stillness, time-bound as well as timeless, existing in a present no longer measurable by the clock.

As far as the novelist is concerned this implies a re-assessment of visual reality in terms of sounds heard in time or remembered "out of time." Eyesight is replaced by daydream, the world of objects by the imaginative recreation of a universe in which material phenomena undergo a seachange and are tranformed into fantasy. Human beings, landscapes and the sensations they evoke are "seen" as through a mist, floating on the surface of

memory, no longer subject to the controlling authority of the
conscious mind. Finally, a sequence of sounds played or sung at
a certain pitch and rhythm or a change from major to minor key
are found to evoke a variety of associations and memories,
frequently, though not always, related to sense impressions received in the past. It is this complex interrelationship between
the musical experience and the mental process it initiates that
stimulates the novelist to investigate the twilight where the
encounter between music and human consciousness takes place.

Novelists, repeatedly and in growing numbers ventured into
that no man's land of the mind although they realized, sooner or
later, that what had been initially composed as a sequence of
sounds, for instance a melody which could be musically defined
by such simple concepts as key, pitch, or rhythm, did not lend
itself easily to transposition into even the most imaginative and
expressive of prose-fictions. Though words may be used "musically", in the sense in which symbolist poets attempted to supply
a musical equivalent for an experience without altogether
dispensing with language, they cannot transform time-bound
reality into a timeless continuum. Yet novelists in search of
linguistic correspondences for human experiences inaccessible
to logical analysis, were increasingly attracted to that borderland
of the mind where concepts, values, and attitudes, acquired, as it
were, musical features, where a sequence of thoughts was shown
to be related to some imaginary modality of sounds and an
emotion could be rendered through consonance or dissonance
or in a minor or major key. Underlying this search was the
assumption that the semantics of human speech correspond in
some intangible way to the semantics of musical composition,
that it might, after all, be possible to translate the meaning of a
melody into linguistic terms. As far as psychic processes were
concerned it seemed almost self-evident that especially through
music could significances be revealed which lay below the
threshold of consciousness.

Yet language is a singularly inept vehicle of expression when
it is called upon to say something adequate about the content of
a musical work. The modern novelist whose concern with music
grew out of his preoccupation with mental processes could
hardly have recourse to technical language and write a musicologist's novel. Any attempt at transposing musical content into a

prose freed of semantic rigidity and thus approaching the fluidity of musical progression, turned the musical experience into
an objective correlative used by the novelist to portray states of
mind or a particular emotional setting which everyday language
was unable to convey. The musical experience was thus used as
a mirror with the help of which a character could be viewed, a
relationship portrayed, an idea realized through the sounds that
were found to be most expressive of what this idea stood for
within the context of the novel. Musical content appeared to be
the obvious equivalent for the vague and amorphous psychic
states for which language had not evolved any adequate vocabulary. The novelist who aimed at unravelling the complexities of
the human soul discovered in music an esthetic equivalent for
the interior monologue, expressiveness uncontaminated by the
ambiguity of verbal communication.

This discovery led to a dilemma that no novelist could solve in
a satisfactory way: the writer of fiction had no other means of
communicating the pure expressiveness of music but through
linguistic equivocation. If music was indeed an objective correlative for experiences that could only be expressed in nonverbal
terms, the novelist became increasingly aware of the fact that—
as Susanne Langer puts it—though music is indeed the "logical
expression" (though not the cause or cure) of feelings, yet "it
has its special ways of functioning that make it incommensurable
with language."[32] The writer's experiments with musical content translated into the prose of his fiction were, thus, from the
outset, of a most problematic nature.

No one was more troubled by the absence of an objective
correlative which would denote musical meaning than Marcel
Proust. Throughout his monumental novel he makes it abun-
dantly clear that though various individuals may indeed associate a musical phrase with memories of experiences colored by
sense impressions of a nonmusical nature, these memories
need not in any way correspond to the musical statement made
by the composer but be mere approximations to the "meaning"
underlying the music. The reader may easily be misled by
Proust's concern with the effect of Vinteuil's "petite phrase" on
Swann and Marcel into assuming that Proust's impressionistic
technique of transcribing the musical phrase into a literary
image served as an end in itself. For the music that accompanies

the reader from volume to volume is generally interwoven in a stream of only partially controlled memories. The melody repeatedly appears as an indistinct floating image, wrapped in a mist of associations derived from the hearer's past. In Proust's imagination this melody is "ensevelie dans la brume" (entombed in fog) or "noyée dans.le brouillard" (drowned in mist). Already at the beginning of the novel after having heard Vinteuil's sonata only once "it remained almost wholly invisible to me, like a monument of which its distance or a haze in the atmosphere allows us to catch but a faint and fragmentary glimpse."[33]

Images of indistinctness that crowd in on Swann's mind when he remembers Vinteuil's music have no material equivalents in reality. Their frame of reference is and remains throughout the book the hearer's memory. Thus, he would like to remember the music as one recalls any other sense impression "of light, of sound, of perspective, of bodily desire."[34] Similarly, Marcel, long after the little phrase had been absorbed in his waking consciousness, remembers it as "the expression of certain states of the soul analogous to that which I had experienced when I tasted the madeleine that had been dipped in a cup of tea."[35] If we compare this passage with a much earlier one where the effect of the little phrase on Swann is described as being "closely akin . . . to the pleasure which he would have derived from experimenting with perfumes"[36] there is little to differentiate between Proust's various uses of the musical correlative in terms of either taste or smell or sight. Memories resurrected through musical associations, may differ in intensity of sensuous perception, one sense impression being replaced by another, the indistinctness of a monument perceived from far away in a haze may be substituted by the dreamlike vision of a woman, "this invisible creature whose language I did not know and whom I understand so well—the only stranger that it has ever been my good fortune to meet;"[37] it is with such impressions as these that the reader may place Vinteuil's little melody in a world of experiences which constitutes at best only an image, "a reflection, like water or glass" (these are Swann's words), the shadow of a shadow, and, more often than not, a memory remembered, a dream recaptured an infinite number of times.

An objective correlative, however, does not cease to carry

manifold significances because of its indistinctness. In memory,
as in dreams, relation between things and people assume
blurred and confused shapes. The memory of a melody may
indeed appear at one time as the scent of "roses in the evening,"
at another as "the cooing of a dove", and again as "an invitation to partake of intimate pleasures". What these memories
have in common constitutes the dimly perceived reality of the
melody in so far as remembered sense impressions may at all
correlate music with actually experienced events in one's life.
Proust is naturally inclined towards metaphorical speech—as if
in memory there is no place for any sort of explicit analogy—
enabling the reader to reexperience the event itself though in a
somewhat modified and distorted way. Thus while Vinteuil's
sonata is described with the help of such adjectives as "slender,
frail, tender, rustic, pale, candid, and timid", the first bars of the
septet by the same composer recall the image of "continuous,
level surfaces like those of the sea, in the midst of a stormy
morning beneath an already lurid sky . . . in eery silence, in an
infinite void . . ." The transition from adjectival writing to the
evocation of an objective correlative implies a greater maturity
of expression on the part of the composer and of receptivity on
the part of the hearer. The homeliness of the earlier work has
grown into the complexity of Vinteuil's old-age composition.
Obscurity and indistinctness have been transformed into a clar-
ity of vision which, as in a flash of lightning, illumines a world
"so harsh, so supernatural, so brief, setting athrob the still inert
crimson of the morning sky above the sea."[38]

Proust's observations on the musical experience and the way
it affects the central characters in his novel create a psychological universe of considerable complexity. Listening to music, and
especially to the kind of music represented by Vinteuil's little
melody, produces an intensely emotional response from which
the rationality of the thinking mind is excluded. The melody,
from this moment onward, is a haunting presence which takes
possession of the hearer's memory. All those events of his life
that are overshadowed by violent emotions such as jealousy or
physical desire, the fear of losing a beloved person or the
anguish caused by such a loss, become entangled in the web
woven by the melody. With the regularity of a conditioned
reflex the emotion may be provoked by the music just as the

emotion itself may arouse the memory of the corresponding musical phrase. Emotional and musical arousal are thus almost identical. In memory they become one and indivisible—so much so that when a particular piece of music ceases to exercise its fascination upon the hearer, the emotion usually associated with it is no longer found to be of any validity. The hearer, in effect, asks himself how it could have happened that at any one time this music represented the unbearable anguish of jealousy and cannot remember how the association between the musical phrase and his jealousy came into existence.

Considerations such as these are liable to interfere with the even flow of the narrative. The problem that Proust faced—and Joyce was going to solve in his own way—was how to transcribe not merely the melody but the memory of it and the meaning it acquired when being remembered in reasonably intelligible prose. If as Proust says at the beginning of the novel, all musical impressions are *"sine materia"* and speaks of the memory of these impressions as "the presence of one of those invisible realities,"[39] he thereby implies that the novelist has no way of translating this immaterial and invisible reality which is music into the language of fiction except in terms of subjectively experienced sense impressions.

This is what Proust repeatedly and insistently does. As the novel progresses these images, scents, and tastes become progressively more lucid. As Vinteuil's music grows more complex under the shadow of his approaching death, his melodies communicate a message which requires no material explanation as it provides what Proust calls "the profound equivalent . . . of how the composer heard the universe and projected it far beyond himself."[40] The novelist's attempt to render this profound yet invisible "equivalent" in words makes Proust speculate as to the possible relationship between the composer's musical and the novelist's literary projection of reality into the work of art.

The first of what might be called the major post-Wagnerian novelists, he was also the first to formulate what happens when the novelist adapts musical content to the writing of a work of fiction. Beginning and end of the novel no longer depend on the chronological development of plot and characters but on the introduction of themes, *le leitmotif* as Proust so characteristically calls it, which prepare the reader for what is to come. It is through the elaboration of a given theme that duration in the novel acquires depth and substance. The transposition of musical into literary themes involves the writer in a process of "musicalization". "It is impossible," writes Proust, "to foresee the total work by the first volume alone which makes sense only in terms of those that follow ... It's similar to those [musical] pieces which one does not realize to be leitmotifs when one listens to them in isolation at a concert in an overture."[41]

Proust unquestionably assumes that musical themes originate in the unconscious and that, therefore, the writer of fiction by introducing leitmotifs into his novel has to make them intellectually accessible to the reader. This may explain the following remark made by him in an interview: "If I presume thus to reason about my book, it is because the book is in no way a work of reason: it is because its most trifling details have been supplied to me through feeling; because I first of all noticed them deep down within myself, without understanding them, having as much trouble to change them into something intelligible as if they were foreign to the work of the intellect just as is—how shall I put it?—a theme of music."[42]

Marcel's desire to write a novel different from any work of fiction written previously is mentioned for the first time in the last volume of *A La Recherche* which, Proust tells a friend in a letter, "was written immediately after the first chapter of the first volume. All the 'inbetween' part was written subsequently."[43] The inspiration to write the novel came to him while listening to Vinteuil's music which, in effect, is first mentioned in the first volume (when Swann hears "la petite phrase") and occurs again in the last volume when Marcel listens to Vinteuil's septet in which the same musical phrase has acquired greater complexity and significance. The idea which progressively takes possession of Proust's mind was thus already there, at the very beginning of *A La Recherche*. The growth of that idea to its final realization, the writing of a work of fiction, is what this novel is all about. It is also a deliberate attempt on the part of the novelist to prove to himself and his prospective readers that music can aspire to the "condition of language", and this not necessarily by a contrapuntal modulation of themes or a set of variations, but rather by transposing the novelist's (in this case Marcel's) experience of reality—within the limitations imposed by time, place, social context and the writer's own temperamental predilections—into music.

By the time the reader finishes reading Proust's novel, he may well ask himself whether any dividing line can be drawn between music remembered and music heard, and between sense impressions evoked by music and a musical theme emerging from any one of these impressions. Such questions are themselves valid critical comments on the relationship between the art of the story-teller and that of the musician in an age where clear distinctions between the two are no longer called for. When, for example, Proust writes that "a prolonged smile is like a sustained G sharp"[44] he relates a psychological observation to the tonal quality of a particular sound or chord as if the two—his observation of the smile and his awareness of the singular effect produced by the playing of a chord in G sharp on an instrument—constituted one and the same kind of tonality. Such a correlation may be indefensible by either musicological or psychological criteria, yet it paves the way for further experiments with language when the G sharp will not "stand for" or be "like" a prolonged smile but *be* the smile itself. Proust indeed asks himself whether this is not what might have happened "if there had not come the invention of language, the formation of words, the analysis of ideas, the means of communication between one spirit and another." Remembering the precision with which music could express what lies below the threshold of consciousness, Proust describes his return to language "from the unanalyzed" as "so inebriating, that on emerging from that paradise [i.e. music], contact with people who were more or less intelligent seemed to me of an extraordinary insignificance."[45]

Once the novelist claims the validity of musical equivalents for words and thus transcribes the reality he perceives around him by way of tonality or atonality, there is nothing to stop him from rendering his observation of human nature in terms of sound symbols. Such a musical correlative will be—like sounds themselves—immaterial and invisible. No objective correspondences will help the reader in his search for a valid psychological frame of reference. The only significance that can be attributed to such sound symbols will emerge from the way "the composer [and now also the writer] heard the universe and projected it far beyond himself."

E.M. Forster, in an early novel, does precisely this. At a loss
for the right word when describing the effect of a musical composition, in this case Beethoven's last piano sonata, opus 111, on
performer and listener, he can only suggest with the help of
nonmusical allusions what this music meant to those "whom
breeding and intellect and culture have alike rejected," the
outsider, the misfit, and the rebel. He, first of all, admits his
inability to "translate [the composer's] visions into human
words, and his experiences into human action." He realizes that
there is passion, "but it could not be easily labelled." Yet,
having ventured so far, he makes Lucy, in *A Room With a View*
(1908), play the first movement of this extraordinary sonata
before a musically indifferent audience, remarking, however,
that while she was playing she divested herself of her everyday
identity and entered "a more solid world" where "she was then
no longer either deferential or patronizing; no longer either a
rebel or a slave." She became what Forster designates as "trag-
ical", in the sense that she extracted from the music she played a
conviction of ultimate victory. For, adds Forster, Beethoven's
sonatas "can triumph or despair as the player decides, and Lucy
had decided that they should triumph."[46] In its final analysis it is
not Lucy but Forster who decides that Beethoven's last piano
sonata should embody the "victory" with which this novel ends.
The reader who is assumed to be familiar with this piece of
music may, after some hesitation, approve of Forster's choice
and will ask no more questions. He is, however, left with a
literary statement of considerable ambiguity.

A Room With a View was written long before Forster became
acquainted with Proust's work. When, in 1927, his *Aspects of the
Novel* was published Proust's concern with music is given a very
prominent place. The "little phrase," according to Forster, creates "a homogeneous world" as it provides the reader with
"complete orientation"—"stitching Proust's book together from
the inside" as part of the protagonist's memory. When Forster
writes about novels and the part music plays in them he is more
concerned with "rhythm" than with the actual content of any
given musical piece. It is the relation between various "blocks of
sounds" that he calls rhythm. It enters the mind without being
actually audible. To recreate this rhythm in the writing of a
novel, "this common entity, this new thing . . . the symphony as

a whole" is Forster's ideal of fiction-writing. "Music," he continues, "though it does not employ human beings, though it is
governed by intricate laws, nevertheless does offer in its final
expression a type of beauty which fiction might achieve in its
own way."[47] Forster calls this new type of literary structure
"expansion", a new way of looking at people which will emphasize the inwardness of all conscious response to music. The
musical experience is the essence of this "expansion" which will
lead the novelist away from mere story-telling and characterization towards a deeper psychological truth which no novelist in
the past ever ventured to portray.

The more the writer realized the need for increasingly subtler
forms of evocation than the prose of everyday life was capable of
expressing, the more was he likely to look in music for an
objective equivalent for emotions that might have been more
adequately expressed through poetry as they were too complex
to be conveyed in conventional speech. Virginia Woolf, in an
early story, probably written in 1921, before she became acquainted with Proust's work, illustrates this search for a new
language when she describes the effect of a string quartet by
Mozart on a listener, evidently herself, tortured, as she then was,
by a sense of loss and inner division. Here, the writer intention-
ally dispenses with description of the music in such ambiguous
terms as "victory" or "despair", but evokes the texture of the
music through images relating to her own past. Thus the prose
she employs shifts from interior monologue—"How lovely
goodness is in those who, stepping lightly, go smiling through
the world"—to nature associations originating in the hearer's
memory—"Fountain jets; drops descend . . . washing shadows
over the silver fish . . . leaping, splashing, scraping sharp fins"—
to encounters in the past charged with intense emotion—"I see
your face, I hear your voice . . . What are you whispering?
Sorrow, sorrow. Joy, joy. Woven together, inextricably commin-
gled, bound in pain and strewn in sorrow."[48]

The experimental nature of this short, fragmentary sketch is
of considerable interest to anyone concerned with the gradual
dissolution of conventional thematic structure and its effect on
the portrayal of human thought in contemporary fiction. The
novelty of this approach to the hearer—the music being the
medium through which human consciousness is portrayed—

points backwards to Proust's impressionistic literary experiments with music as well as towards Joyce's more daring representation of the stream of consciousness still to come. In later novels Virginia Woolf frequently refers to the virtually unrestricted expressiveness of music as contrasted to the limiting syntactical speech patterns employed by writers attempting to render emotions which elude the dictionary meaning of words. How, indeed, she asks herself in *The Waves*, can "falling in love for the first time" be denoted by words? Admitting the novelist's inability to say anything worth saying about the emotions aroused by first love, she calls for music to help her in her task. "Here again there should be music ... a painful, guttural, visceral, also soaring, lark-like, pealing song to replace these flagging, foolish transcripts—how much too deliberate! which attempt to describe the flying moments of first love."[49]

More disillusioned than in 1921 Virginia Woolf now knew that this desire for a linguistic transformation of sounds into words must remain unfulfilled. Yet a few pages later she once more returns to a musical image, this time to evoke characters rather than emotions. Are not, she asks, characters as they appear to us in life open to musical definitions, each one standing for a different instrument, a melody or chord? How much simpler it would be, Virginia Woolf meditates, to render the complexity of human nature in terms of a musical composition, thereby preserving the immediacy of musical communication in the face of the corrupting effect of all human speech? Thus she desires nothing better than to "compose" her characters until the imprecision of their human qualities is transformed into the exact polyphonic pattern of a symphony. Again in *The Waves* Virginia Woolf lets a character (Bernard) deliberate upon this form of musical revelation claiming for music a wider imaginative scope than descriptive prose can provide. "How impossible to order them rightly, to detach one separately, or to give the effect of the whole—again like music. What a symphony with its concord and discord, and its tunes on top and its complicated bass beneath, then grew up! Each played his own tune, fiddle, flute, trumpet, drum or whatever the instrument might be."[50] This passage was written, Virginia Woolf notes in her *Diary*, after she had listened to a Beethoven quartet one night and had felt the need to "merge all the interjected passages into Bernard's final speech."⁵¹ Music, actual or imaginary, rounds up a novel the rhythmic quality of which very nearly approaches the pattern of a musical composition, the ebb and tide of the sea, the coming and going of the waves.

Proust's experiments in the use of musical material in the thematic structure of his fictitious universe became known to the English reading public while E. M. Forster and Virginia Woolf were writing their novels. There seems little, if any, actual influence on the part of the French writer on either of them. When they *did* read him they felt overawed by the gigantic dimensions of his work. They also discovered in *A La Recherche* a similar concern with musical form and content as had been tentatively expressed in their own novels. The one writer—hardly at all familiar with Proust at that time—who had become even more deeply aware of the need to turn the writing of fiction into something resembling musical composition—was Thomas Mann.⁵² Even before Proust had finished writing his novel Mann had already published a number of short stories dealing with the devastating effect of music on individuals of an artistic temperament.

As early as 1918, Thomas Mann who called himself a man of letters (*ein Literat*) characterized his work as that of a musician, comparing it to the writing of Schopenhauer and Nietzsche who were "men of letters as well as musicians, but the latter more than the former." As for his own writings, "they were good scores (*Partituren*), everyone of them." Not without pride Mann added that "musicians also loved them; Gustav Mahler, for example, loved them."⁵³ When, in 1938, Thomas Mann was asked to write an introduction to an American edition of his stories, he insisted on the need for a musical interpretation of his early work. He traced the development in his use of musical themes which, as a true Wagnerian, he calls *leitmotifs*, from being a mere structural device to a psychological concept underlying all his later prose fiction. In *Tonio Kröger*, he says, "I first learned to employ music as a shaping influence in my art. The conception of epic prose-composition as a weaving of themes, as a musical complex of associations, I later on largely employed in *The Magic Mountain*, only that there the verbal leitmotif is no longer as in *Buddenbrooks* employed in the representation of form alone, but has taken on a less mechanical, more musical character, and endeavours to mirror the emotion and the idea."[54] Once more, in 1953, Mann, writing an introduction to the American edition of *The Magic Mountain*, emphasizes the specifically musical enjoyment which the awareness "of the structural coherence of the thematic fabric" gives the reader. In order to derive the greatest benefit from the novel, Thomas Mann, in effect, suggests that the book should be read twice. For only the second time is the reader able to "really penetrate and enjoy its musical associations of ideas. The first time the reader learns the thematic material; he is then in a position to read the symbolic and allusive formulas both forwards and backwards."[55] Finally, in a letter to Theodore Adorno whose advice proved so helpful in the writing of *Doctor Faustus*, Mann returns to his first assertion made in 1918, that he has "always been adept at literary music-making, [has] felt myself to be half-and-half of a musician" and has "translated the technique of musical interweaving to the novel."[56]

The concern with musical form and content on the part of such different novelists as Proust, Forster, Virginia Woolf and Thomas Mann, in the first half of the twentieth century is no coincidence. Nor can it be attributed to such purely musical influences as Wagner's music and the impressionism of Debussy and his school. All of them alike turned to the musical experience as embodying a primordial vision of human life expressed through rhythm or melody, pitch or volume, concord or discord. In their search for a faithful representation of the inwardness of experience, be it through individual consciousness or through the awareness of social identity, they discovered in music a metaphor of harmonious coexistence. As in the modern novel the Pythagorean planets increasingly drift "in evil mixture to disorder," the wish to make sense of that disorder impelled the novelists to apply a musical perspective to the mind of man. Thus the musical experience in the modern novel is no longer a merely literary device to create a congenial background to events and characters, but has itself become an essential ingredient of contemporary fiction writing. The vibrating air column of the flute and the vibrating strings on the violin acquired an almost metaphysical significance. What was involved was not only the application of scientific theories to the esthetic laws governing the creation and performance of music, but a new vision of the way human consciousness functions, expressed in the novel through a fusion of sense impressions and thought, the texture of sounds and the texture of words, music and speech.

Notes to Chapter One

1. Aldous Huxley, *Point Counter Point*, p.31ff.
2. *Much Ado About Nothing*, II, 3, 61.
3. Montaigne, tr. Florio, ed. Morley, p. 42.
4. Quoted from Stanley, *History of Philosophy*, ed. 3, 1701, p.393, part IX, Sect. IV chapter III.
5. *Antony and Cleopatra*, V, 2, 83–84.
6. Quoted in E. H. Gombrich, *Symbolic Images, Studies in the Art of the Renaissance*. 1972, p. 174.
7. From *The Literary Works of Leonardo Da Vinci*, ed. by J. P. and I. A. Richter, 2 vols., Oxford Univ. Press, 1939. Quoted in *A Documentary History of Art*, selected and ed. by Elizabeth G. Hold, vol. I, A Doubleday Anchor Book, 1957, pp. 278–279.
8. Poussin's letter to Chantelou, dated Rome, Nov. 24, 1647, quoted in *Artists on Art*, compiled and edited by Robert Goldwater and Marco Treves, Pantheon Books, 1947, pp. 151–152.
9. James A. McNeill Whistler, from a letter, dated Cheyne Walk, London 1878, *ibid.*, p. 347.
10. Mondrian's painting is reproduced and analyzed in E. H. Gombrich, *Art and Illusion, A Study in the Psychology of Pictorial Representation*, Phaidon, London, pp. 311ff.
11. Le Corbusier, *The Modulator — A Harmonious Measure to the Human Scale Universally Applicable to Architecture and Mechanics*, Harvard Univ. Press, 1954, p. 129. Quoted in Rudolf Arnheim, *Towards a Psychology of Art, Collected Essays*, Faber and Faber, London, p. 105.
12. Honoré de Balzac, *Gambara* (1837-1839). Quoted in *Pleasures of Music. A Reader's Choice of Great Writing about Music from Cellini to Bernard Shaw*, ed. & with Introduction by Jacques Barzun, The Viking Press, 1951, pp. 109ff.
13. E. A. Poe, "A letter to B–", in *The Portable Poe*, selected and edited by Philip van Doren Stern, The Viking Press, 1957, p. 585 (italics in the original).
14. See his *Correspondances:*
    Comme de longs échos que de loin se confondent
    Dans une ténébreuse et profonde unité,
    Vaste comme la nuit et comme la clarté,
    Les parfums, les couleurs et les sons se répondent.
15. Charles Baudelaire, "Notes Nouvelles sur Edgar Poe". This is the preface written by Baudelaire to his own translation of *Nouvelles Histoires Extraordinaires*, published in March 1857; in Charles

Baudelaire, *Critique Littéraire et Musicale*, Librairie Armand Colin, Paris, 1961, p. 209 (my own translation).

16. "Richard Wagner et Tannhäuser à Paris", published, in *La Revue Européene*, 1 April 1861 (*ibid.*, p. 370) (my own translation).

17. Walter Pater, "The School of Giorgione"(1877) in: *The Renaissance*, The Modern Library, N.Y., n.d., pp.111ff.

18. Quoted in Arthur Symons, *The Symbolist Movement in Literature*, (1899), ed. 1958, p.73, published originally in French in *Vers et Prose*, "Divagations Premières (1893), Perrin, Paris, 1935. The following is an extract from a lecture delivered at Oxford on March 1st, 1884, entitled "La Musique et les Lettres": "Je pose, à mes risques, esthétiquement, cette conclusion . . . que la Musique et les Lettres sont la face alternative ici élargie vers l'obscur; scintillante là, avec certitude, d'un phénomène, le seul, je l'appelle, l'Idée. L'un des modes incline à l'autre et y disparaissant, ressort avec emprunts: deux foix, se parachève, oscillant, un genre entier." (*Oeuvres Complètes de Stéphane Mallarmé*, Bibliothèque de la Pléiade, 1945, p. 649).

19. From an unpublished play quoted in *The World of W.B. Yeats*, ed. Skelton & Ann Addlemyer, University of Washington Press, Seattle, 1955, p.207.

20. J.K. Huysmans, *Against Nature* (1884), Translated by Robert Baldick, Penguin Books, 1959, pp. 58–9.

21. W.B. Yeats, "Discoveries",1906, in: *Essays and Introductions*, Macmillan & Co., Ltd. London, 1961, p. 267–269.

22. W.B. Yeats, "Speaking of the Psaltery", 1907, *Ibid.*, pp. 13ff.

23. Quoted in Joseph Hone, *W.B. Yeats, 1865-1939*, Macmillan,1942, pp.453–4.

24. W.B. Yeats, "*On the Boiler*", in *Explorations*, selected by Mrs. W.B. Yeats, Macmillan, 1962, p. 451.

25. Quoted in F.O. Matthiessen, *The Achievement of T.S. Eliot*, p. 90.

26. *Ibid.*, p. 28

27. T.S. Eliot, *On Poetry and Poets*, "Poetry and Drama", pp. 93–94.

28. *Ibid.*, "The Music of Poetry", p. 32.

29. Northrop Frye, *The Anatomy of Criticism*, p. 344. Claude Lévi-Strauss makes this point even more explicitly though from a structuralist rather than literary point of view when he observes that "only in music is there a complete congruence of abstraction and expressive embodiment", for music "filters and organises the life-experience, substitutes itself for it." And finally, he adds, the joy derived from music is "that the soul is invited for once to recognize itself in the body." (*L'Homme Nu, Mythologiques IV*, Paris, Plon, 1972).

30. Stephen Spender, *Eliot*, ed. Frank Kermode, Fontana, 1975, pp. 128–129.

31. A characteristic instance of a musical experience measured by social standards and commented upon ironically occurs in Jane Austen's *Persuasion*. Marianne is invited to sing before a group of guests who consider music to be at best a pleasant and not too au-

dible background noise to small talk. These are the thoughts that pass through her mind while she is observing the audience: "Colonel Brandon alone, of all the party, heard her without being in raptures. He paid her only the compliment of attention; and she felt a respect for him on the occasion, which the others had reasonably forfeited by their shameless want of taste. His pleasure in music, though it amounted not to that extatic delight which could sympathize with her own, was estimable when contrasted against the horrible insensibility of the others, and she was reasonable enough to allow that a man of five and thirty might well have outlived all acuteness of feeling and every exquisite power of enjoyment. She was perfectly disposed to make every allowance for the colonel's advanced state of life which humanity required." (World's Classics, Oxford University Press, 1944, pp. 32–33).

32. Susanne K. Langer, *Philosophy in a New Key*, p. 242.
33. Marcel Proust, *Remembrance of Things Past*, vol. III, pp. 134–148.
34. *Ibid.*, vol. II, pp. 180–185.
35. *Ibid.*, vol. X, part II(*The Captive*), p. 242.
36. *Ibid.*, vol. I, pp. 301–302.
37. *Ibid.*, p. 73.
38. *Ibid.*, vol. X, part II, p.60.
39. *Ibid.*, vol. I, pp. 289–292.
40. *Ibid.*, vol. X, part II, p. 234.
41. In a letter to Lucien Daudet, in: *Autour Soixante Lettres de Marcel Proust*, Gallimard, 1929, p. 76 (my own translation).
42. Quoted in Milton Hindus, *The Proustian Vision*, p. 40.
43. Letter to Paul Souday, *Correspondances*, III, pp. 69–70, English translation in *Letters of Proust*, edited by Mina Curtiss, New York, 1949, p. 338.
44. *Du Côté des Guermantes*, III, p. 56, quoted in Victor E. Graham, *The Imagery of Proust*, p. 187.
45. *Remembrance of Things Past*, vol. X, part II, p. 71.
46. E.M. Forster, *A Room with a View*, 1908, p. 34.
47. E.M. Forster, *Aspects of the Novel*, pp. 236 ff. Something very similar must have been in André Gide's mind when, in his *The Counterfeiters* (1925), he makes Edouard, who is himself a novelist and keeps a diary, write: "What I should like to do is something like the art of fugue writing. And I can't see why what was possible in music should be impossible in literature."(Part II, chapter III) Another fictitious novelist, in Huxley's *Point Counter Point*, wishes to "translate Beethoven's Diabelli Variations into a novel: "The whole range of thought and feeling, yet all in organic relation to a ridiculous waltz tune ... get this into a novel ... All you need is a sufficiency of characters and parallel, contrapuntal plot." (p.408).
48. Virginia Woolf, "The String Quartet", in *A Haunted House and Other Stories*, 1944, pp. 24–28.
49. Virginia Woolf, *The Waves*, p. 177.
50. *Ibid.*, p. 188.

51. Virginia Woolf, *A Writer's Diary*, p. 162 (Monday, December 22nd, 1930).
52. In a letter to R. Tieberger (1938) Mann says he "did not make the acquaintance of Proust until long after finishing *The Magic Mountain*." Quoted in Gunilla Bergsten, *Thomas Mann's "Doctor Faustus"*, p. 107.
53. Thomas Mann, *Betrachtungen eines Unpolitischen*, p. 311 (my own translation).
54. Thomas Mann in his Introduction to *Stories of Three Decades*.
55. Thomas Mann, "The Making of *The Magic Mountain*", p. 725.
56. *Letters of Thomas Mann, 1889–1955*, p. 362. This letter is addressed to Theodor W. Adorno, dated Pacific Palisades, California, 30 December 1945.

II
The Musical Unconscious

1

A novelist's musical preferences are reflected in the kind of music he introduces into his novels. It is, for example, of considerable interest that so many of the novelists discussed in this study preferred high-brow classical music to experiments with more contemporary musical idioms. At a time when twentieth-century composers looked for ways of self-expression through syncopation and chromaticism, dissonance and atonality, the novelist remained immersed in the music of Bach, Mozart and Beethoven. His preoccupation with states of consciousness deriving from tensions and conflicts characteristic of our age should have been expected to stimulate his interest in contemporary music. Where but in the nontonal works and the serial composition of Schönberg, Alban Berg and Webern could musical equivalents for the modern novelist's concern with complex and recondite states of mind be found?

Yet among novelists already mentioned Thomas Mann alone drew the only logical conclusion—to which a chapter will be devoted in this study—when, in his old age, he wrote the story of his fictitious composer Adrian Leverkühn whose musical theories and practice reflect those of Schönberg in an unmistakable way. But Thomas Mann's heart was heavy with misgivings when he started on this most tragic of all his novels. The spectre of Wagner's music and the music of those that had come before him continued to haunt him. It is no coincidence that in the description of his life in California while writing *Doctor Faustus* he refers to the many chamber-concerts at his home where the music of Mozart, Beethoven, and Schubert was being played by eminent performers who were his friends and neighbors at that time. Proust though less knowledgeable than Mann in musical matters was also a "Wagnerian." His "little phrase" consists of remembered musical impressions ranging from Schubert, Wagner's overture to Lohengrin, to César Franck. E.M. Forster and Virginia Woolf remained faithful adherents of Beethoven's music, his symphonies and his chamber music. Huxley's main musical interest lay in baroque music, Bach and his predecessors and, of course, in Beethoven's later quartets to which, and not without reason, Thomas Mann also returned again and again.

The only one among the eminent novelists of the first half of this century whose musical taste was unquestionably, obstinately, and ostentatiously low-brow was James Joyce. This is the more remarkable as he was the most "musical" of them all, had inherited a tenor voice of considerable range from his father, and in early manhood had played with the idea of becoming a singer. Among his favorite operas were Bellini's *Norma*, Berlioz' *La Damnation de Faust*, and Rossini's *Guillaume Tell*. Famous tenor-arias from these operas exercised a powerful, almost obsessive, influence on him. His solicitude for John Sullivan, an Irish tenor whose career he followed with much enthusiasm all over Europe, is a case in point. Wagner meant little to him. He strongly objected to the sensual nature of much of his music and is reported to have told one of his pupils in Trieste that "Wagner puzza di sesso" ("Wagner stinks of sex").[1] He never missed an opportunity of deflating what he considered to be Wagner's pompous and hollow musical eloquence.

A number of episodes mentioned in Richard Ellmann's biography of Joyce, however, illustrate his readiness to respond to musical experiments. He was fascinated by some of the contemporary composers he met in Paris, among them Antheil, Satie, and Darius Milhaud. When he attended a performance of the *Ballet Suedois* on October 4, 1923, Antheil himself played his *Sonata Sauvage*, *Airplane Sonata*, and *Mechanisms*. The music intrigued Joyce. He must have become aware of resemblances—however hard to define—between Antheil's unconventional use of musical patterns and his own work in progress. When Antheil suggested the plan for an "electric opera", based on the *Cyclops* episode in *Ulysses*, Joyce found the idea stimulating and worth pursuing. According to Antheil, "the opera was to have for orchestra twelve electric pianos hooked to a thirteenth which played the master roll; on this would be recorded drums, steel xylophones, and various blare instruments. The score was to be run off at top speed, with crescendos and diminuendos achieved by switching pianos on and off. The singers, seated below the stage and out of sight, would sing into microphones attached to loud speakers on the stage, and a *corps de ballet* would present the action in pantomime."[2] Though nothing came of all this it is hard to imagine any other novelist at that time committing himself to an idea which must have seemed to most of them a preposterous and frivolous pseudomusical experiment.

One of the reasons why Joyce felt attracted to Antheil's avant-garde compositions may have been the discovery that his music was being rejected by the average concert goer in very similar circumstances and for the same reasons as a wide section of the reading public rejected his own literary output as eccentric and incomprehensible. It is certainly no coincidence that in a recent musicological study of modern music in the first half of this century "the linguistic possibilities" in the new methods developed simultaneously by cubist painters and serial composers should have been stressed.[3] It is in this discovery of a common artistic vocabulary developed by contemporary painters and musicians, frequently independent of one another, that Joyce's experiments with words must find their place.

Though Joyce's encounter with Antheil had little actual influence on his writing, his growing familiarity with contemporary musical idioms is of some significance. It creates a sense of cultural continuity in the mind of the twentieth-century reader. Various art forms began to adapt themselves to what the age expected of them. For this reason any discussion of Joyce's "musical" technique in fiction writing need not concern itself with references to actual music, heard or performed in his novels, but with the musical experience as a metaphor for life and for the novelist's attempt to translate this metaphor into words.

At a time when tonality was being abandoned by the composer and the illusion of visual perspective was being discarded by the painter, the novelist, concerned as he then was with what appeared to him the timeless pattern of human consciousness, could at last abandon chronological time by which, in the past, the progress of a story could be measured. Joyce's frequent use of popular folk-ballads and well-known arias from nineteenth-century operas are an intrinsic part of the metaphor. Nowhere but in memory does the novelist's consciousness create that intermingling of mental and musical processes, the fusion of visual and auditory sense impressions, experienced in the past but never altogether forgotten. In this sense Joyce is a true contempoarary of Proust.

It is no mere coincidence that Joyce, in *A Portrait of the Artist as a Young Man*, written at a time when he had not even heard the name of Proust, should have related the very act of speech to musical composition. "He drew forth a phrase from his treasure and spoke it softly to himself: A day of dappled seaborne clouds. The phrase and the day and the scene harmonized in a chord."[4] Or, "His own consciousness of language was ebbing from his brain and trickling into the very words themselves which set to band and disband themselves in wayward rhythms."[5]

From the impressionistic estheticism of his earlier work to his later experiments with the fusion of musical and linguistic semantics through the medium of a dismembered syntax and an emphasis on verbal tonalities, his allegiance to words never faltered. But even in his earliest stories the meaning of a word did not necessarily depend on the object it denoted but on the sonority and intonation of the speaker's voice; for even then Joyce addressed the listener rather than the reader; frequently and, at times, out of his concern with the sound of words, he appears to be writing for public recital rather than for the secluded study of the scholar.

His mind has on more than one occasion been called "symphonic"[6] in view of the many-leveled nature of his writings. In effect, the emphasis shifts as we follow Joyce from novel to novel, from linear writing to composition in depth: sight and sound associations are inextricably intermingled and the resulting texture provides the frame for auditory marvels which can never be fully understood but in terms of a musical dimension. As music penetrates to the very roots of words, the scope of Joyce's language widens to encompass meanings never before suspected, a deepening of significances which derives as much from musical as from linguistic origins. As layers of meanings are progressively uncovered, the origin of the word is revealed in the dark and backward abysm of its primordial sound. Thus, the narrator at times returns to archaic word formations ranging from the meaningless to the transmutations of subtle thought processes into a highly organized musical design. The articulation of a word within a tonal sequence which, in more conventional language is called a sentence or a paragraph, causes an infinite number of echoes to vibrate in the reader's mind. It is these echoes that form a texture of meanings woven into a web of associations which the writer invests with musical and linguistic significance.

Joyce begins his investigations into the equivocal relationship between music and language where Proust ends his.[7] Like Proust at the end of his life the young Joyce is obsessed with music recalled from the past rather than with music heard in the present, some melody remote in time and space which serves as a misty background to the fluctuating emotions of love. Frequently it is music that comes to the hearer out of some obscure recess of remembered time arousing associations of other similar sound modulations. It is in the very nature of these modulations that real and imaginary melodies interweave, both being enveloped by the same kind of hazy mistiness. For in the early Joyce all music is fused with night or sleep or dream. The awakening takes place when the music is over, the memory shattered, the dream dissolved. What remains is the non musical reality of thought, of analytical introspection and, more often than not, of self-deprecating irony.

In the last and most moving of the stories in Joyce's *Dubliners*, husband and wife, at a moment of emotional unrest, stop for a moment in the dark of a staircase to listen to a voice singing above them. Looking at her he becomes nostalgically aware of the "grace and mystery in her attitude" as of something long lost and long forgotten, but which at the present instant of surrender to the singing voice seems to him to correspond to something indefinable in the music. As his mind wanders from the distant melody to the vision perceived in semi-darkness, and back again to the music, he imagines how he would reproduce this scene if he were a painter and resolves to call the painting "Distant Music" if indeed he could preserve the strange fascination of her physical presence in the dark through an interplay of colors and sounds. When, a few pages later, he remembers words of happiness that he had written years before, his memory transforms them once more into "distant music". Towards the end of the story, "after the kindling again of so many memories, the first touch of her body, musical and strange and perfumed, sent through him a keen pang of lust."[8]

Though the lyricism is characteristic of Joyce's early manner, the reader of Proust will find himself in familiar musical territory. The scene, charged with violent but suppressed emotions, acquires its specific coloring of remoteness and mystery from the music vaguely heard or remembered. Sense impressions when absorbed by consciousness can no longer be clearly separated—sounds, colors and words form the ingredients of an elusive kind of beauty which exists in the imagination alone. The body of the beloved woman is itself turned into a symbol of all that is strange and submerged in the musical phrase. Just as Swann, in Proust's novel, related Vinteuil's melody in his memory to a variety of perfumes, so the remote strangeness of the woman's body in Joyce's story is enhanced by the perfume that seems to emanate from the distant music heard by the two on the dark staircase.

All this is in the tradition established by Proust though Joyce when he wrote this story was, in all likelihood, quite unaware of Proust's single-minded struggle to adapt the musical experience to the writing for fiction. What Joyce adds is an undercurrent of irony such as when the husband, rather self-consciously and as if defending himself against his own sense of emotional insecurity, asks himself what a woman may possibly symbolize when she is seen standing on the stairs in the shadow listening to distant music. This element of deflation and self-mockery—in painful contrast to the seemingly unselfconscious lyricism of the passage—characterizes much of Joyce's early writing when it concerns music and its impact on the hearer. In a later sketch, probably written in 1914 but only recently published, this clash between the spontaneous enjoyment of music, however distant in time and place, and the listener's awkwardly self-conscious comment on the experience, is even more evident. As this is an autobiographical fragment, written in the form of a diary, it constitutes valuable evidence for Joyce's own attitude towards that "distant music" which haunts him throughout his early years in exile. Once more it is a love situation and a moment of unresolved and undeclared passion. It is, again, in memory that the music is heard: "Ian Pieters Sweelink. The quaint name of the old Dutch musician makes all beauty seem quaint and far. I hear his variations for the clavichord on an old air: Youth has an end. In the vague mist of old sounds a faint point of light appears: the speech of the soul is about to be heard. Youth has an end: the end is here. It will never be. You know that well. What then? Write it, damn you. Write it! What else are you good for?"[9]

Listening to distant music, even if in memory, and then writing about it, represent two contradictory states of the mind. The former implies a surrender to the ancient melody which tells a story of beauty, youth, and love doomed to end and man's nostalgic yearning for a return of the past. The rude awakening that follows is an intrinsic part of the experience: it speaks the language of the present and reminds the listener of his own inability to transform the present intensity of his love emotion into a piece of perfect music. Language is indeed an inadequate tool of communication. It addresses the reader here and now, in the implacable present. Inflexible and unbending it can say only one thing at a time. Even in his most sublime flights of imagination the writer remains tied to the ground, aware of the limitations of his craft and conscious of his inherent inability to give a literary shape to "the vague mist of old sounds". Turning the quaint remoteness with which the ancient song transformed "the speech of the soul" into words is a form of self-immolation and self-denial. "What else are you good for?" is the sarcastic comment of one whose sense of inadequacy and incongruity was deeply rooted in the awareness that while music conveys the essence of man's inner life, words can only be its imperfect paraphrase.

In *A Portrait* there occurs a passage implying the same self-doubt turning into anguish. Once again Joyce is concerned with music remembered, with a love relationship that remains unfulfilled, and with the dichotomy between the simple spontaneity of ancient songs and the self-conscious return to the reality of the one who listens. Stephen Dedalus remembers how one day in the past he was sitting at the piano, "striking chords softly from its speckled keys and singing, amid the talk which had risen again in the room, to her who leaned beside the mantlepiece a dainty song of the Elizabethans, a sad and sweet loth to depart, the victory chant of Agincourt, the happy air of Greensleeves.

While he sang and she listened, or feigned to listen his heart was
at rest, but when the quaint old songs had ended and he heard
again the voices in the room he remembered his own sarcasm."[10]

Memory and music are the main spiritual ingredients of
Joyce's portrait of the young man turning his back on religion. It
is mostly music heard in the mind, chords or melodies which
elude the uncertain grasp of words, recalling experiences which
Stephen Dedalus has been only vaguely aware of but which had
haunted him in the past and which the music resurrects in the
present: "He heard a confused music within him of memories
and names which he was almost conscious of but could not
capture even for an instant; then the music seemed to recede, to
recede; and from each receding trail of nebulous music there fell
away one long-drawn calling note, piercing like a star the dusk
of silence."[11] This is characteristic of the musical mode in which
Joyce's first novel is written. Whether in weariness or unrest, it
accompanies the young hero throughout the book. No single
passage will do justice to the intensity with which Stephen
Dedalus listens to music, be it from within or from without.
Frequently it is the sound of people singing in the dark that
helps him to realize the meaning of his own emotions. Listening
to a children's choir "with pain of spirit," he becomes aware of
"the overtone of weariness behind their frail, fresh, innocent
voices,"[12] a sense of unfulfilled longing that he projects into the
children's singing. On another occasion, listening to music at
night, "the sentiment of the opening bars, their langour and
supple movement, evoked the incommunicable emotion which
had been the cause of all his days' unrest. . . . His unrest issued
from him like a wave of sound."[13] When the promise of a
renewed present recalls him, it is once more in musical images
that "the new adventure" presents itself to his mind. "It seemed
to him that he heard notes of fitful music leaping upward a note
and downward a diminished fourth, upward a tone and downward a major third, like triple-branching flames leaping fitfully,
flame after flame, out of a midnight wood. It was an elfin
prelude, endless and formless; and, as it grew wilder and faster,
the flames leaping out of time, he seeemed to hear from under
the boughs and grasses wild creatures racing, their feet
pattering like rain upon leaves."[14]

As the young man grows into the artist he builds around him a defensive moat of words to prevent reality from invading the territory that his soul had chosen for itself. Reality is whatever is healthy and crude and therefore insensitive to sounds. Man in his struggle to be himself, is constantly engaged in beating off the onslaught of the analytical mind, the restlessness which results from it, the weariness which follows. Transforming the real into the imaginary corresponds to the composer adding sound to silence or resolving the discordant note before the last into some final numinous harmony. It is a process of growth, observed and noted down by the intensely introspective young man in terms of words, heard as a sequence or congruence of sounds, a melody or a chord, seen—if seen at all—as bright or dark colors. Words require no tangible shape that might be evoked through syntactic language; the pattern which they create resembles that of a melody, "the poise and balance of the period itself,"[15] expressed through the rhythmic rise and fall of sounds, very much like waters "lapping and flowing back and ever shaking the white bells of their waves in mute chimes and mute peal and soft low swooning cry."[16] Lines of poetry assume colors which, in their turn, are made audible through the singing voice. The process is equally reversible: for the "colors" of the poetry spoken in his mind may evoke a musical design, so that the line from Thomas Nashe he—wrongly—remembers, "Darkness falls from the air", is turned into an amalgam of colors and sounds which do not require any associations derived from the thinking mind. The young man listening to "the verse with its black vowels and its opening sound, rich and lute-like,"[17] is aware of a confused musical impression radiating forth its colors in insidious rhythmic cadences according to which the white flows into the black as the foam of a wave is absorbed in the impenetrable depths of the sea. The texture of the young man's experience of inner music is indefinite and fluid as is the density of water, but at all times translucent and pure, indeed a mirror of his own liquid, dew-like soul.

Sea images accompany the reader throughout Joyce's writing like a musical leitmotif, reminding Stephen of the fluidity of his own existence: the dissolution of his defiled mind into immaculate nothingness after death, the distillation of imprecise speech into pure sound when thinking is no longer possible or even desirable; the immersion of individual aspirations into a vast, amorphous yearning for fulfillment common to all men when they cease to carry the burden of their illusory identity and return to the impermeable, indivisible darkness of the sea. When Stephen Dedalus, in the "Proteus" espisode in *Ulysses* listens to the sound of the waves, it is no longer in the conventional language of intelligible speech that Joyce conveys to the reader what Stephen thinks he hears but in the primordial language of sounds reaching the mind through musical associations only, dispensing with the visual evocation of colors and designs. The following passage, from one of Stephen's early soliloquies in *Ulysses*, is a stepping-stone to Joyce's coming experiments with words and convincingly sums up the young man's preoccupation with the sound of things, so characteristic a feature of the earlier book: "Listen: a four-worded wavespeech: seesoo, hrss, rsseeiss, ooos. Vehement breath of waters amid sea-snakes, rearing horses, rocks. In cups of rocks it slops: flop, slop, slap: bounded in barrels. And spent, its speech ceases. It flows purling, widely flowing, floating foampool, flower unfurling."[18]

Reading the passage backward does not diminish but merely modifies the impressions of acoustic liquidity, the melting away of all syntactic verbal distinctions in a medley of sounds,—the sense also of a world immersed in some primeval tonal imprecision which confronts man and his mind with its dark monstrous universe of sounds.

2

Stephen Dedalus and Leopold Bloom articulate their thoughts in an unceasing flow of words. Frequently their consciousness adapts itself to the rhythm and the modulation of the sounds they hear. It may be a man's singing voice or the roar of waves rising and falling, the din of traffic passing in the street or the tinkling of a piano in an adjoining room. Stephen introspectively recreates the sounds that nature and poets create into the private language of his thoughts, formless and disjointed, yet a faithful mirror of his mind's unending search for correspondences between the meaning and the sounds of words. Leopold Bloom, wandering among men, listens to the resonance of people's voices when they speak or sing and when they fall silent. What he hears enters his mind to become part of a stream of consciousness which absorbs all human articulation, speech as well as song, snatches of conversation overheard in the street as well as the sentimental outpourings of a tenor voice in a bar-room, without drawing any fine auditory distinctions by imposing abstract intellectual arguments on what he hears.

Stephen's "fourworded wavespeech" comes to him as a form of musical revelation when he stands facing the sea, the mother of all things, giving and taking life with equal indifference, rhythmically repeating the same message over and over again of how sound grows out of the caverns of the deep to be absorbed in the unfathomable process of birth, decay, and death. It is a music that has no beginning or end. As one wave dissolves into the next, so the sounds merge into one another, a theme without counterpoint and few, if any, variations. Thus, Stephen's response to the music of the sea is timeless. It may evoke memories of the past or anticipate a future still to come. It moves in a circle, its tonality unchanged, its rhythm dictated by the interval of silence that separates one note from another.

Leopold Bloom's ear is attuned to the everyday sounds heard in the present moment of listening. Instead of the timeless "fourworded wavespeech" of the sea, the melodies he hears are sung by men in a bar-room while he is eating his lunch. Whenever his mind wanders, the songs bring him back to the present. In his imagination he can hear the same songs sung in the past by others, evoking similar emotions and images. The music he hears not only takes place in time but recreates a vision of time resurrected in memory. The songs are real and so are the voices of those that sing them. Leopold Bloom's mind, not being endowed with the gift of imaginative empathy, is a self-contained instrument of response. It echoes the melodies with non-musical notions derived from the life of the grosser senses. For the perfume that the music reminds him of is not that of the rose but of the chamber-pot. When his erotic imagination is aroused it does not create an idealized vision of a beloved woman listening to "distant music" but the act of copulation being committed at that very moment by his adulterous wife and her lover.

Now whether we identify Leopold Bloom with Ulysses tied to the mast and compelled to listen to the Sirens' song representing, in Joyce's own words, "The motif of the artist, who will lay down his life rather than renounce his interest,"[19] or whether, according to Joyce's so-called Linati scheme of *Ulysses* which he sent to Carlo Linati in September 1920, Leopold Bloom "in this episode is Orpheus . . . trying to win his Eurydice back from the Lethean shadows of forgetting him,"[20] or whether, lastly, Leopold Bloom listening to bar-room music is symbolized by the tuning fork, "the conscience of the episode . . . the norm of humanity,"[21] his response to music is evidently open to a variety of interpretations. Conscious listening is intermingled with unconscious associations, the sounds he hears and the memory they evoke form one inseparable whole, and the language in which all this is being reported freely moves from one extreme of "musical speech" to the other extreme of pseudo-scientific explanation of various acoustic phenomena. Far from being unintelligible this constant shift from the sentimental to the naively credulous makes the reader insistently aware of the bar-room situation in which the latterday Ulysses is placed with its none-too-pleasant associations connected with the hearer's digestive tract, his vegetative nervous system and the functioning of the sex hormones in a man's body at a moment of suppressed jealousy, when listening to music. The multiple layers of this musical experience thus constitute a testing-stone for the reader's readiness to respond to music with the whole of his personality involving the highest flight of fancy to the relation between musical afflatus and constipation. Somewhere between the myth of Orpheus, the epic dimensions of Ulysses, and Leopold Bloom's diffuse stream of consciousness, the musical reality of Bloomsday will have to be found.

Joyce's own comments on the Sirens episode are scarce and somewhat misleading. Apart from those already quoted and his general remark that "each adventure (that is, every hour, every organ, every art being interconnected and interrelated in the structural scheme of the whole) should not only condition but even create its own technique,"[22] there is little to go by beyond certain generalizations regarding the musical devices employed by Joyce in the writing of this episode. Thus, he appears to have told his friend Borach on June 18, 1919, after having finished writing the Sirens chapter, that he wrote it "with the technical resources of music. It is a fugue with all musical notations:

piano, forte, rallentando, and so on. A quintet occurs in it, too, as in the *Meistersingers*, my favourite Wagnerian opera." He, however, not altogether surprisingly, adds that since finishing this episode, "I haven't cared for music any more ... I see through all the tricks and can't enjoy it any more...."[23] In a letter to Harriet Weaver of July 10, 1919, he tells her that it took him five months to write this episode and that various people, among them Ezra Pound, disapprove of the musical technique employed by him, while others have written to him requesting him to explain to them "the method (or methods) of this madness". A month later he once again refers to the writing of this chapter in a letter as "the eight regular parts of a *fuga per canonem*," and adds an explanatory note why this seemed to him the only possible technical device suitable for the writing of this episode, "I did not know in what other way to describe the seductions of music beyond which Ulysses travels."[24]

The overture which precedes the episode has provoked much bewilderment among uninitiated readers. As a kind of condensed prelude to what is to follow it actually requires little explanation, least of all in literary terms. It states the themes one by one, the leitmotifs which will accompany the reader throughout this section of the novel. As a verbal introduction to the musical episode that follows, it fulfills its function within the limits of what language can express "musically" without ceasing to be language. The words used are those that will recur at frequent intervals in the episode itself. Read in isolation as part of this "overture," they are, largely, unintelligible—just as a Wagnerian leitmotif before the whole opera is heard a number of times, remains unrelated to the rest of the musical material, and is therefore only of secondary interest. The question that has frequently been asked in this connection—whether musical phrases are translatable into words, except by crude onomatopoeia—is of little relevance here: Joyce "composed" these two pages as if they were a musical score, yet constantly aware of the fact that his "musical" equipment consisted of words and that his loyalty to language has never been in doubt. He did not "translate" musical themes into speech but adapted words to a musical technique which introduced in a more eloquent way an episode in which both ideas and language are conditioned by the musical context. This section of the novel, thus deviates in no way from other episodes in *Ulysses*. Plot, characterization, time and place, as well as the physical circumstances of the episode, are conveyed in a stylistic tour de force that tends towards a complete fusion with the musical content of the narrative. In this sense the overture is no eccentric technical device. It grows out of the musical situation in which Leopold Bloom is placed. James Joyce did not really "compose" the overture. It composed itself.

Leopold Bloom is no profound thinker; nor do his occasional remarks about music and its impact on the hearer indulge in profound philosophical or psychological generalizations. An amateur in his scientific deliberations, he is also an amateur musicologist: "Words? Music?," he reflects, "No: it's what's behind." Explaining himself more fully a few pages later, his somewhat uncertain grasp of the relationship between music and mathematics successfully prevents all escape into sentiment. His sense of humor combined with a smattering of popular science, an uninhibited acceptance of the pitfalls that the flesh is heir to, a disillusioned understanding of the comedy of all human endeavors to control man's fate, all of these together produce a realization of the absurdity of surrender to music which Joyce, in all likelihood, identified with the average listener's attitude to the musical experience—especially when it threatens his emotional equilibrium: "Numbers it is. All music when you come to think. Two multiplied by two divided by half is twice one. Vibrations: chords those are. . . . Symmetry under a cemetery wall. . . . Musemathematics. And you think you are listening to the ethereal. But supposing you said it like: Martha, seven times nine minus x is thirty-five thousand. Falls quite flat. It's on account of the sounds it all is."[25]

Throughout the episode Bloom's thoughts dwell on women, their attitude to music ("What do they think when they hear music?") and the singularly erotic symbolism embodied in the musical act itself. ("We are their harps. I. He. Old. Young.") He also becomes unpleasantly aware of the sexual arousal that inevitably follows from too submissive an attitude to music. If—as has been pointed out—the Sirens episode "is set in the ear world, the ear being female, receptive, a cave for sirens to sing in,"[26] much of the erotic symbolism in Leopold Bloom's thought derives from his realization of perils inherent in the seductiveness of all music which enters the mind through the ear rather than through the intellect. The temptation that has to be resisted at all cost is the transformation from detached listener to mere instrument, from actively engaged intelligence to passive surrender. Thus, Bloom's musical memory shifts from masculine conquest to scenes of feminine submission. At one moment it is, "Tenors get women by the score. Increase their flow. Throb, a throb, a pulsing proud erect . . . Bloom. Flood of warm jimjam lickitup secretness flowed to flow in music out, in desire, dark to lick flow, invading. Tipping her tepping her tapping her topping her. Tup."[27] This is followed soon after by what for lack of a better term might be designated as an instance of musical orgasm, "It soared, a bird, it held its flight, a swift pure cry, soar silver orb it leaped serene, speeding, sustained, to come, don't spin it out too long long breath he breath long life, soaring high, high resplendent, aflame, crowned, high vast irradiation everywhere all soaring all around about the all, the endlessnessnessness . . . Consumed."[28] Bloom's response to the songs heard in the bar-room serves the purpose of a safety valve. It can be opened at will whenever sentiment threatens to overflow the boundaries imposed by language and commonsense upon the mind. This is the way Bloom muses on the associations aroused by chamber music, a musical genre dear to Joyce's own heart, "Could make a kind of pun on that. It is a kind of music I often thought when she. Acoustics that is. Tinkling. Empty vessel make most noise. Because the acoustics, the resonance changes according as the weight of the water is equal to the flow of falling water. Like those rhapsodies of Liszt's Hungarian gipsyeyed. Pearls. Drop. Rain. Diddle iddle addle oodle oodle. Hiss."[29] Sexuality and popular physics have never before been so closely and ludicrously fused in the musical experience as here.

The ineluctable modality of the audible is identified with the senses, and, in this episode, with their surrender to the Sirens' song. Bloom's thought reveals a more than common level of understanding of the threat this music embodies. With the precision of a tuning fork the reign of reason must be re-established against any possible deviation from the emotional norm. Seeing through the tricks that music plays on his mind he must now go beyond it and rediscover his lost freedom. "Freer

in air. Music. Gets on your nerves ..." is his farewell to a
temptation which threatens to deprive him of the use of reason
and from which he must now rescue himself. In Richard
Ellmann's analysis of the end of this episode, "Words, turned to
notes, take back their own again and become words once more.
Music is like a shell, which, according to Bloom, gives back the
sound of the listener's ear. Ulysses recovers his verbal universe."[30] This is as complex an experience as any portrayed in
Ulysses. It, first of all, involves the hero in musical memories
vividly resurrecting a past which throws light on the present. It,
in addition, arouses his jealousy because the adultery committed
by his wife coincides in time with the music he is compelled to
listen to. Furthermore his own sense of guilt troubles him as he
is writing a letter to Martha Clifford, the typist, hinting at the
possibility of a future assignation with her. Lastly he is also
plagued by memories of his dead son. He is in a confessing
mood and longs for redemption. The music he hears is thus
both a blessing and a curse. What it reminds him of should
better be forgotten. It acts like a threat to his masculine inde-
pendence. He would like to submit to the music most willingly
were it not for the need to resist the blandishment of sounds
and travel beyond their mindless seduction. What has, ultimately, to be rescued is his consciousness which—enthralled by
the sensuous impact of the melody—has almost ceased to play
its part as a standard and common norm of civilised rationality.

3

James Joyce's preoccupation with the stream of consciousness
embodies this concern with time and its varying dimensions. In
this the writing of *Ulysses*—and in particular the Sirens episode—
once more resembles the composition of a musical score: the
stream of thought, no less than the melody, once it is given
shape and articulated, is no longer bound to chronological
duration. Though both may be measured by clock-time they
elude conventional time dimensions when heard within the
mind. Thought and music progress, as it were, in a linear way,
achieving a living continuity free of arbitrary time divisions.
Other, no less revealing correspondences, are involved: if the
stream of consciousness, or, for that matter, a melody cannot be

measured by chronological time, how is one to define in rational terms what is evidently a form of psychological duration without taking into account the sense of time passing as experienced by reader or listener?

The question how long a symphony or any part of it "lasts" results in endless and fruitless ambiguities. All musical measurement is arbitrary: though it serves a necessary structural purpose, neither musical memory nor musical associations are divisible into bars. Meter, either regular or irregular, merely establishes a horizontal standard of division. Its emotional impact on the hearer eludes any kind of objective time evaluation: there is no metronome that could be used in measuring the depths of affective involvement, no time dimension that could be applied to the echoes vibrating in the hearer's mind.

What, then, the thinking process and the musical experience have in common is their aloofness from chronologically measurable time. Though one may say: Leopold Bloom sat in the restaurant for half an hour, eating, listening to music from an adjoining bar-room and thinking, the actual verbalization of the thinking process itself—though it might have taken Joyce five months to put it on paper and the reader only 45 minutes to read through it—eludes all chronological assessment. Similarly, while the writing of a symphony might have taken the composer a number of years, the performance, however, lasting scarcely an hour, the hearer's consciousness responds to the music in a continuous present which comprehends all his past and, in all likelihood, projects a vision of the future into the music, producing a sense of timelessness which itself becomes an integral part of the musical experience.

Bergson calls the time required by a sequence of changing sounds to form a melody "real duration". It matters little, he says, whether it is the composer or the hearer who experiences it, for "whether it is a question of the internal or the external of ourselves or of things, reality [that is the melody] is mobility itself . . . What we have is a present which endures."[31] The natural corollary to this "real" or pure duration is that it "forms both the past and the present states into an organic whole, as happens when we recall the notes of a tune, melting, so to speak, into one another, even if these notes succeed one another, yet we perceive them in one another . . . their totality may be compared to a living being, whose parts, though distinct, permeate one another."[32] This corresponds, almost literally, to what James Joyce was doing when, instead of plot and character, he lets the stream of consciousness speak for itself: "There is no past, no future; everything flows in an eternal present," he is reported to have said,[33] thereby, knowingly or unknowingly, establishing a common denominator relating the thought process and the way music is experienced in terms of human consciousness.

Thomas Mann, with characteristic German thoroughness, investigated, in *The Magic Mountain*, what he thought was the true relationship between the time it takes to play or listen to a piece of music and what he calls the "mortal time" of a narrative. He distinguishes between actual duration which is that of the time-bound story told by the novelist and "relative" duration which he also designates as "musical" time—of the greatest concern to the modern novelist those interest resides in those undefinable dimensions of the timeless where "the events of five minutes, might, by extraordinary consciousness (sic!) in the telling, take up a thousand times five minutes, and even seem short, though long in its relation to its imaginary time."[34] This, in effect, is James Joyce's way of expanding or contracting duration according to the rhythm in which thought moves forward either at great speed or slows down. In this he once again seems to follow Bergson who, in a particularly revealing passage, visualises some future novelist who "tearing aside the cleverly woven curtain of our conventional ego, shows us under this appearance of logic a fundamental absurdity, under this juxtaposition of simple states an infinite permeation of a thousand different impressions which have already ceased to exist the instant they are named."[35] This description corresponds, in all relevant details, to what other writers felt when they first discovered the new and superdimensional ego in *Ulysses* and praised James Joyce for having had the courage to record what Virginia Woolf called "the myriad impressions . . . the atoms as they fall upon the mind in the order in which they fall . . . however disconnected and incoherent in appearance, which each sight or incident scores upon the consciousness." Recommending James Joyce to the "common reader", she adds, "If we want life itself, here surely we have it."[36]

A portrayal of life in a fictitious narrative as James Joyce conceived of it at the time he wrote *Ulysses* increasingly appealed to the reader's sense of musical continuity: like a melody the stream of consciousness moves forward, most frequently on the surface of the narrative, at times, however, as a mere *continuo* or bass accompaniment. An interesting instance of this interplay of two voices singing in counterpoint, as it were, occurs in Virginia Woolf's *To the Lighthouse* when Mrs. Ramsay reading a story to her little son and thinking of something else at the same time, discovers that the two, the narrative and her own thought, complement each other, "for the story of the Fisherman and his Wife was like a bass gently accompanying a tune, which now and then ran up unexpectedly into the melody."[37]

The intermingling of conscious thought and the vague stirrings of unconscious responses to what is seen and heard, to people and things, constitutes what literary criticism has misnamed the stream of consciousness. For obvious reasons James Joyce did not attempt in *Ulysses* to draw any dividing line between egocentric "thinking" and those visions arising from some collective unconscious which are beyond and above discursive thought and no longer determined by individual memories and associations. If Leopold Bloom has been called an archetypal figure it is because his consciousness stands for the mythical residues in the mind of modern man and because he acts his part in a modernized version of an archetypal situation the relevance of which can be found in the primordial depth of nonhistorical time. Simultaneously he represents a common type of twentieth-century man, the outcome of an increasingly democratic way of life, largely undistinguishable—in spite of personal idiosyncracies—from his contemporaries in time and place. Yet the "stream of consciousness" which Joyce represents in terms of a continuous interior monologue shifts from the personal to the impersonal, from memories of Leopold Bloom's past to what might be called "racial" or "collective" memories without his being aware of it. The reader who is confronted by a soliloquy moving simultaneously on several levels, the conscious and the unconscious, is equally unaware of these shifts in perspective. Once again, Thomas Mann, with remarkable insight, employs a musical image to render this movement from the surface of consciousness to the deepest layers of "collective" memory in a novelist's portrayal of interior monologue. In his *The Young Joseph* there occurs a passage that can well be used as a generalised formula for what Joyce attempted to do in *Ulysses*. It is the most convincing evidence provided by a contemporary novelist that words when used to represent a stream of thought, may be employed contrapuntally, not on one but on several planes of meaning at once. "His actual thoughts were not with these mechanical and superficial prayers and lamentations but far below them, while lower down again were others yet more real, like their undertone and ground basses, so that the whole was like a moving music, perpendicularly composed, which his spirit was occupied in conducting on all three levels."[38]

The analogy between thinker and conductor introduces a nonliterary concept into this study. Yet this applies to Leopold Bloom's "thought" throughout the hours of his waking day. It may be a moot question whether it is he, the hero of the book, or Joyce, its author, who is the real "conductor" formulating, organizing, and disciplining a "stream" which threatens at times to turn consciousness into chaos and thought into nightmare. In the Sirens episode the fusion of thought and music through the medium of words provides convincing proof of Joyce's consummate skill at "conducting" an exceedingly difficult score. And though he kept clear of such composers as Bach, Mozart, or Beethoven, who attracted the high-brow novelists of the time, he, more consistent than any of them, transformed the language of music into speech and the memories evoked by sounds into verbalized expression of the thinking process. He could do this only by a magic transformation of the various and frequently contradictory data in man's consciousness into a continuous "stream" in which are reflected ingredients of the unconscious of which the one who "thinks" might himself be unaware. For where else but in "the musical correspondence between the phenomena of the psyche and the phenomena of music" could the perfect continuity of thought be found? In the last analysis, "we must search in music for the symbols that permit us to comprehend the connection of physical phenomena."[39] This, in the words of a musicologist, is the most comprehensive formula that can be applied to Leopold Bloom, the listener to music, and to James Joyce who reported what the music conveyed to his hero in the language of his thought.

4

Stephen Dedalus listens to a multiplicity of sounds duly re-corded in his interior monologue. Voices of children in the dark, the memory of some quaint Elizabethan song, the "fourworded" speech of the waves, the sound of the vowels in Thomas Nashe's poems—all of them alike evoke a musical response unencum-bered by any theoretical knowledge of music, exhibiting no musical erudition of any kind. His affinities lie with folk-songs and popular melodies, his musical taste is conservative, in all likelihood inherited from his father who—like Joyce himself—also had a fine tenor voice. His response is thus free of any preconceived ideas as to what is meant by "good" music. His preferences are with the simple and authentic, the melodious and polyphonic, anything that might help him to escape from the involutions of his introspective mind. In this sense his own singing or playing the piano are unconscious compensations for his Hamlet-like burden of thought. Yet music never establishes a true communion between him and others. Whether as listener or performer he remains a solitary figure. And just as the labyrinth of his thoughts cuts him off from other men, so also music helps to remind him of his unredeemable isolation.

Leopold Bloom is sociable and communicative. Also his musi-cal taste conforms to what the average listener to music at the beginning of this century considered socially acceptable, snatches of popular songs, arias from the better-known Italian operas, melodies that have taken root in his unconscious but of which the words have either been forgotten or adapted to the present moment. Such musical reminiscences play no small part in his interior monologue. They rise to the surface of conscious-ness either because some sound or voice in the street recalls a melody or because some obscure association in mind—whether due to visual or auditory causes—evokes a musical response which is incorporated in his "stream of consciousness." That such a process takes place on a deeper layer of thought than could be subjected to rational analysis is in itself significant. When he wanders in the streets of Dublin or when the Sirens' song tempts him away from his true self, the level of response is far from always being accessible to conscious judgment. When he listens to the tenor voice from the adjoining room, the threat implied in this musical temptation is dimly perceived by him as a threat to his integrity as a thinking human being. Though he attempts to rationalize this growing sense of alienation from those who thoughtlessly make music without being troubled by such disturbing reminiscences, he is less articulate in his resistance to melodious sound than in his response to it. For his response to music occurs at a moment of somnolence, at that hour of the day when the mind hovers between sleep and waking, more than ever exposed to the hypnotic effect of sounds upon that twilight region where daydream replaces the sense of living reality.

It is not by chance that, on more than one occasion, Stephen Dedalus dreams the music he believes he hears into existence. For there is no music "in reality" though his response to imaginary melodies is as intense as if they had been real. The same—though in a less introspective way—is true of Leopold Bloom. Much of the music he hears in the Sirens episode is of his own making, the creation of his unconscious responding to the singing voice from the bar-room. What Stephen and Leopold Bloom, finally, respond to is not any "meaning" communicated to them through melodies or musical counterpoints, but an illusion, a fabrication of their own unconscious. In this sense Stravinsky's assertion that "music is, by its very nature, powerless to *express* anything at all, whether a feeling, an attitude of mind, a psychological mood, a phenomenon of nature"[40] fits the musical response of Joyce's two protagonists insofar as it is at all relevant to their characterization. If, on the other hand, one considers the intensity with which they react to sounds, the vehemence of the musical illusion is seen to be an integral part of their inner being. Much of their psychic organization reflects this preoccupation with various musical manifestations: the more violent the impact, the deeper the layer of the unconscious that appears to be affected.

Another contemporary composer formulated such a rationally inexplicable response to music in a way that might shock many lovers of music but which applies to Joyce's treatment of the musical experience in his novels. According to Aaron Copland, "we respond to music from a primal and almost brutish level—dumbly as it were, for on that level we are firmly grounded."[41] What is so remarkable about the two statements made by Stravinsky and Copland is that they reduce the appeal of music to the nonprofessional listener to an amorphous stirring of unconscious urges and memories over which the hearer has little or no control. In the last analysis there is little difference between their assertion and Darwin's description of the origin of all musical creations as a highly developed form of the sexual call of animals.[42]

In view of the criteria established by depth psychology all creation of music and the listener's response to it originates in the very deepest layers of the unconscious eluding all logical analysis and thus inaccessible to rationalizations. In a recent evaluation of the meaning of the musical experience, published in the *Times Literary Supplement*, both the creation of and the response to music are described in terms of the definition of surrealism given by André Breton in his *First Manifesto* of 1924, "dictated by the mind in the absence of any control exercised by the reason and alien to any aesthetic or moral consideration."[43] The unconscious is the more readily invoked as no systematic psychological investigation into what constitutes the "musical unconscious" has ever been made.[44] Stravinsky himself has repeatedly been described as "exploring ... the unconscious" when composing *Le Sacre*, while Schönberg's serial music has been interpreted as a "historic plunge into the Unconscious."[45] The most provocative of these claims assume that composer and hearer share a common source of unconscious memories which, finally, determine the meaning of a specific musical work and the kind of response this music will inevitably evoke. The attitude underlying such an assertion presumes the existence of a basically nonmusical framework of references that can be made to interpret in depth the response of a nonprofessional listener to music.

The reader of James Joyce's *Ulysses* with its multiple layers of musical response will find such assumptions not always borne out by the evidence of the text. According to one musicologist, for instance, "in the unconscious of the musical listener, professional or layman, a state of affairs exists, musically speaking, similar to that which exists in the unconscious of the composer. In other words, there will be similar groups of memories of the expressive uses of the various tonal tensions, attached to nonmusical experiences of a similar nature . . ."[46] This is the kind of statement which—whether applied to Stephen Dedalus or Leopold Bloom or to any other listener to music—would require a great deal of additional exploration to be proved valid. The same musicologist draws an ominous and menacing picture of the kind of revelation the study of the unconscious, as expressed in musical composition, may communicate. For if ever, he declares, the "fundamental content" of a musical work were revealed to the listener in all its implications, and if, he continues, "the language of music is finally deciphered, some terrible secrets may be revealed, not only about the particular composer, but about humanity at large."[47]

Now, neither Stephen Dedalus in *A Portrait of the Artist as a Young Man* nor Leopold Bloom in *Ulysses*—whenever they listen to music—are concerned with the inner life of the composer who created it, even assuming that they knew his name and the circumstances in which the music was composed. What they respond to is a texture of sounds which finds them in a responsive mood. Their unconscious, in so far as Joyce succeeded in translating it into words, throws upon the screen of their imagination visions of past experience, at times of an explicitly sexual nature, but always a true mirror of their own idiosyncratic selves. Would their interior monologue have been different, one wonders, if they had listened to a symphony by Tchaikovsky, who is known to have had homosexual inclinations, to a song by Hugo Wolf, the germs of whose schizophrenia can be discerned in his music, or to a quartet by Schubert who is presumed to have died of syphilis? No "terrible secrets" are necessarily revealed to the reader in Joyce's handling of the stream of consciousness when echoes of a musical experience are absorbed into it. What, on the other hand, should be of particular interest to the student of Joyce is the specific literary conditioning which makes Stephen Dedalus respond to music in the language of late nineteenth-century impressionism while the prose style of Leopold Bloom's musical meditation—in spite or because of all the sexual innuendos—is, in the words of Wyndham Lewis, "the very nightmare of the naturalist method . . . the sardonic catafalque of the Victorian world . . . the last stagnant pumpings of Victorian anglo-irish life."[48] The musical unconscious is, as far as the contemporary novelist is concerned, more often than not, a matter of language, of literary style, and, thus, of semantics rather than of psychology.

Thus, when *Finnegans Wake* was originally published, a number of critics suggested in all seriousness that to grasp the meaning of this book one had "to listen to its paragraphs as if they were music."[49] This implies a shift in emphasis from literary to musical analysis. Joyce could now be legitimately be called a composer of scores, as indeed he appeared to be, rather than a writer of prose fiction. For, says another interpreter of *Finnegans Wake*, he brought over into literature "not only music's structural form . . . but the harmonic modulations, the suspensions and solutions of music: effects in words which parallel a composer's effects of working with relative and non-relative keys."[50] All distinctions between writing prose-fiction and composing music appeared to have been abolished in the printed text of *Finnegans Wake*. Joyce, in another reader's estimate, wrote his book "in every sense . . . like a composer who essays many forms. He must write chamber music, overtures, piano compositions, and songs, but he must try his hand also at the symphony."[51] Perhaps the most perceptive of them all made what appears to be a fairly legitimate complaint—that while musical rather than literary appreciation seems to be called for to understand *Finnegans Wake*, "the notation is unfamiliar, the scales alien."[52]

Notes to Chapter Two

1. Richard Ellmann, *James Joyce*, p. 393.
2. *Ibid.*, p. 569. At another concert in the Salle Pleyel in Paris in 1926 at which Antheil's *Ballet mécanique* was performed, the orchestration consisted again of eight grand pianos, percussion, electric bells, and two airplane motors with their propellers. Antheil also had helped edit and orchestrate Ezra Pound's opera *Le Testament* based on the poem by François Villon. It was first performed in Paris in 1926. In the audience were Joyce, Hemingway, Eliot and others while Pound participated in the performance by himself playing on drums. It is not recorded what Joyce thought of this avant garde opera. As for Pound he is reported to have heard in Antheil's music "a world of steel bars, not of old stone and ivy." (See review of *Ezra Pound and Music*, ed. by R. Murray Schafer, in *The New Statesman*, 17/3/78, p. 368, and *The Times Literary Supplement*, 14/4/78, p. 415).
3. Donald Mitchell, *The Language of Modern Music*, p. 82.
4. James Joyce, *A Portrait of the Artist as a Young Man*, p. 193.

5. *Ibid.*, p. 208.
6. A good example may be found in Edmund Wilson's *Axel's Castle*: "Like Proust, [James Joyce] is symphonic rather than narrative. His fiction has its progressions, its developments, but they are musical rather than dramatic." (p. 209).
7. According to Richard Ellmann, Joyce had read hardly any Proust at all by 1921 and "insisted that Proust's work bore no resemblance to his own." (pp. 523–524).
8. James Joyce, *Dubliners*, "The Dead", p. 270; pp. 275–6.
9. James Joyce, *Giacomo Joyce*, p. 16.
10. James Joyce, *A Portrait of the Artist as a Young Man*, p. 257.
11. *Ibid.*, p. 194.
12. *Ibid.*, p. 190.
13. *Ibid.*, pp. 82–3.
14. *Ibid.*, p. 191.
15. *Ibid.*, p. 193.
16. *Ibid.*, p. 265.
17. *Ibid.*, p. 274.
18. James Joyce, *Ulysses*, p. 51.
19. This is what Joyce told George Borach on July 31, 1917, as reported in "Conversations with Joyce", translated by Joseph Prescott, *College English*, XV (March 1954), 325-7, quoted in Ellmann, *James Joyce*, p. 430.
20. As reported by Richard Ellmann, *Ulysses on the Liffey*, p. 107.
21. The image of the tuning fork can be found in Richard Ellmann, *op. cit.* p. 103 and in Stuart Gilbert, *James Joyce's "Ulysses"*, p. 249n.
22. Quoted from Gilbert, *Letters*, I, pp. 146–7, in Robert H. Deming, *James Joyce, The Critical Heritage*, vol. I, p. 19.
23. Quoted in Richard Ellmann, *James Joyce*, p. 47.
24. See his letters to Harriet Shaw Weaver, dated Zurich, 20/7/1919 and 6/8/1919 in *Selected Letters of James Joyce* ed. Richard Ellmann, 1975, pp. 240–242. Some relevant critical comments, all of them emphasizing the inadequacies of Joyce's "fugal" technique, are given below:
   a. "When the program notes of Joyce's commentators classify the form as *fuga per canonem* they do not make clear whether it is the language or the situation that is being treated fugally. Should we then accept each syllable as an interval in a melodic phrase? Or should we assume that the characters work out their own counterpoint, with Bloom as subject and Boylan as counterpoint. . . . Polyphonic prose . . . is rarely more than a loose metaphor." (Harry Levin, *James Joyce*, p. 98).
   b. "The literary technic (sic) here employed is an exact transposition of the musical treatment of the *leitmotif*, the Wagnerian method. But there is this difference, that the musical *motif*, is complete in itself and aesthetically satisfying. . . . But the *word-motif*, unintelligible in itself, acquires a meaning only when I relate it to its context. . . . Joyce has deliberately ignored this essential difference between sounds and words, and, for this rea-

son, his experiment is of questionable value." (Ernst Robert Curtius, "Technique and Thematic Development of James Joyce", *Neue Schweizer Rundschau*, XXII (January 1929), translated by Eugene Jolas, *transition*, No. 16-17 (June 1929), 310–325).

c. "The musical analogy is rather a sham. For in music it is possible to present different notes in an instant of time, to have a chord each of which is heard precisely the same moment, or to have two melodies going together, progressing with perfect contemporaneity. But this cannot be done with the written word. Nor is there any literary equivalent of the counterpointing of two independent melodies—there is a literary equivalent of orchestration, in the sense of harmonizing a melody, but not of counterpoint. . . . No amount of other musical allusions and devices . . . can hide from us the failure of this major technical device." (David Daiches, *The Novel and the Modern World*, p. 133).

25. Jame Joyce, *Ulysses*, p. 273.
26. See Richard Ellmann, *Ulysses on the Liffey*, p. 101.
27. James Joyce, *Ulysses*, p. 270.
28. *Ibid.*, p. 271.
29. *Ibid.*, p. 278.
30. Richard Ellmann, *Ulysses on the Liffey*, p. 109.
31. Henri Bergson, *The Creative Mind*, p. 174.
32. Henri Bergson, *Time and Free Will*, p. 100.
33. Joyce to Jacques Mercantor, in "The Hours of James Joyce" Part I, *The Kenyan Review*, XXIV (1962), 702.
34. Thomas Mann, *The Magic Mountain*, pp. 683–684 (The translator probably meant "conscientiousness".).
35. Henri Bergson, *Time and Free Will*, pp. 132–134.
36. Virginia Woolf, *The Common Reader*, First Series, "Modern Fiction", pp. 189–190.
37. Virginia Woolf, *To the Lighthouse*, p. 65.
38. Thomas Mann, *The Young Joseph*, p. 21, as quoted in A.A. Mendilov, *Time and the Novel*, pp. 147–148.
39. Victor Zukerkandl, *Sound and Symbol. Music and the External World*, p. 144, p. 263.
40. Igor Stravinsky, *Chronicles of my Life*, pp. 91–92, quoted in Deryck Cooke, *The Language of Music*, p. 11.
41. Aaron Copland, *Music and Imagination*, p. 23.
42. Stravinsky's own description of how his *Le Sacre* was composed is a commentary relevant to this theme; according to him *Le Sacre* first appeared to him in a dream. The work was composed "in a state of exaltation and exhaustion." Stravinsky then describes how he tapped "some unconscious 'folk' memory". He also writes, "I heard and I wrote what I heard. I am the vessel through which *Le Sacre* passed." (Quoted from Richard Middleton's "*Stravinsky's Development: A Jungian Approach*" in: *Music and Letters*, vol. 54, No. 3 (July 1973) Oxford University Press, London.)
43. Alejo Carpentier, "A Feeling for Music", in *The Times Literary Sup-*

plement (22 September 1971), 1097f. The apparent affinity of
Joyce's prose style with states of mental disequilibrium may have
inspired some of the following reviews:

a. "Like the lunatic whose speech degrades into a set of arbitrary
   sounds more and more remotely connected with his interior
   preoccupations. . . . There is a remarkable similarity between
   Mr. Joyce's compositions and the prose style of certain luna-
   tics." (Unsigned review of *Finnegans Wake*, *The Times Literary
   Supplement*, January 23, 1937).

b. "One might imagine that Mr. Joyce had used his great powers
   deliberately to show the language of a schizophrenic mind." (B.
   Ifor Evans, review of *Finnegans Wake*, *Manchester Guardian*, May
   12, 1939).

c. "Idiocy has its charm, the distracted utterances of a dislocated
   mind seem to bear some relation to one another, to suggest a
   dim coherence like a faded picture." (Malcolm Muggeridge, review of *Finnegans Wake* in *Time and Tide*, May 20, 1939,
   654–655).

44. Here are some examples of attempts made to define the musical
    experience and the response following it in psychological terms;
    according to one writer, "some essence, as it were, of the life of
    feeling is objectified in the aural image and freed from the de-
    mands of the immediate. It becomes then an object of contempla-
    tion; it is meaningful to the psyche: it has relevance, in a formal and
    concentrated way, to life in its generality." (Gordon Epperson, *The
    Musical Symbol, A Study of the Philosophic Theory of Music*, p. 169). An-
    other writer, speaking of the Prelude to Wagner's *Tristan*, suggests
    that his "conception of the work . . . must have stimulated certain
    of the most expressive tonal tensions to materialize from the D mi-
    nor/A minor key-area of his unconscious." (Deryck Cooke, *The
    Language of Music*, p. 189). A third mentions Proust's "little phrase"
    as an example of "the affinities of certain melodies to some uncon-
    scious or preconscious emotions." (Theodor Reik, *The Haunting
    Melody*, p. 27).

45. See Donald Mitchell, *The Language of Modern Music*, p. 44 and p. 50.

46. Deryck Cooke, *op. cit.* p. 206 and p. 216.

47. *Ibid.*, p. 273.

48. Wyndham Lewis, "An Analysis of the Mind of James Joyce", *Time
    and the Western Man*, 1927, pp. 75–113.

49. L.A.G. Strong, Review of *Finnegans Wake* in *John O'London Weekly*,
    (5 May 1939), XLI, No. 1,047, 168.

50. Louis Bogan, Review of *Finnegans Wake*, in *Nation* (6 May 1939)
    CXLVIII, 533–535.

51. Leon Edel, "James Joyce and his New Work", *University of Toronto
    Quarterly*, IX (October 1939), 68–81.

52. Unsigned review of *Finnegans Wake* in *The Times Literary Supplement*
    (6 May 1939), 265–266.

III
The Fictitious Listener

1

The novelist as composer, a modulator of themes, opting for one key rather than another, showing distinct preferences for chamber music, symphonic writing or inclined towards polyphonic or homophonic composition, opens up stimulating vistas for further exploration. How do structural and thematic musical devices as applied to the writing of a novel cohere? Can a valid relation be established between a given musical structure and techniques of characterization in a novel? Can contrapuntal writing be taken as an equivalent for plot construction?

Throughout the first half of this century the sonata form whether employed in compositions for solo instruments, for chamber music, or large orchestral works, was taken as a significant parallel for fiction writing. It is doubtful whether novelists were themselves always fully aware of such a correspondence. Literary critics were almost unanimous in their appraisal of some of the outstanding novels of the age as "sonatas in words". Thus, at one time or another, the structural and thematic coherence of Virginia Woolf's *Mrs. Dalloway*[1] and *To the Lighthouse*[2] has been compared to the sonata form. E.M. Forster's *The Longest Journey* and *A Passage to India* are supposed to have been planned "like symphonies."[3] Ezra Pound insisted in 1922 that the sonata is a clearer model for James Joyce's *Ulysses* than the epic. "Its introductory theme would be Stephen, its main theme Bloom; each, after a preliminary exposition, undergoes his own development, then a treatment in combination, and at last a recapitulation."[4] The structure of Thomas Mann's early story *Tonio Kröger*, the reader is told, "is clearly the sonata form, including respectively the exposition, development, recapitulation, etc."[5] Hermann Hesse repeatedly refers to his

Steppenwolf as having been written "as strictly and tautly . . . as a sonata." He also distinguishes between an introductory piece (Harry's journal), the first movement (the "tractate" of the Steppenwolf, with its tonic and dominant), a development and recapitulation, and adds, "perhaps the 'wolf' is the tonic, the 'bourgeois' the dominant."[6]

It is this emphasis on the dualism inherent in human nature that makes the sonata form so eminently suitable a model for the contemporary novelist. James Joyce's *Ulysses*, Virginia Woolf's *Mrs. Dalloway*, E.M. Forster's *A Passage to India*, Thomas Mann's *Tonio Kröger*, and Hermann Hesse's *Steppenwolf*, are each one of them in its own way, studies in human polarity employing a traditional musical form in order to illustrate opposing layers of consciousness which eluded the writers of fiction in less introspective periods of literary history. Each of these novels has, in effect, its "tonic" and its "dominant". In *Ulysses* they are represented by the intellectual preoccupations of Stephen Dedalus and Leopold Bloom's trivial mental peregrinations; in *Mrs. Dalloway* it is the memory of the past impinging upon the realization of the present; in *A Passage to India* the dualism inherent in the clash between Eastern and Western ways of thinking and feeling, in *Tonio Kröger* the inner conflict arising from the encounter between bourgeois self-regard and the artist's unceasing search for acceptance, and, finally, in *Steppenwolf* the desperate struggle for dominance between the outsider and the philistine. Each of these works of fiction displays its own characteristic "coda", its resolution in a final "chord" which brings together what has been sundered before and unites all the conflicting strands that make up the novel's spiritual or psychological universe in the undivided consciousness of one central figure. At times this resolution is merely hinted at as a remote though wished for possibility, such as when instead of the concluding chord, the echo of a dissonance persists or when a chromatic ascent remains without a final harmonious close.

The more introspective these novels become the greater the temptation to draw such musical analogies. If, repeatedly, it is the thematic structure of the sonata one encounters rather than the more unified compositions of earlier centuries, with their naive admiration for the one and indivisible, such as the motet or the madrigal, the reason for this must be looked for in social history rather than in the history of music. The novelist's increasing awareness of polarity in the life of the individual and the social antagonism with which he is faced appeared most forcefully reflected in the sonata form with its play upon contradictory emotional pressures and tensions, its tendency towards introspective self-analysis and its striving for resolution. Both the twentieth-century novel and the sonata are founded on a dialectical structure: the greater the emphasis on individual alienation, the more evident will be the social antagonism out of which such inner division grows. This explains why contrasting musical elements constitute the tonal universe of the sonata and why the contemporary novelist was so greatly attracted to this, above all other, musical forms. Thus, the roots of psychological stress were inherent in the sonata form itself. For while, in the words of an eminent musicologist, "fugal polyphony ... is the basic musical equation for Oneness or the state of Being ... the later sonata principle ... is the musical equation for dualism, growth through conflict, Becoming."[7]

Dualism, then, lies at the core of the archetypal character in twentieth-century fiction. While listening to a piece of music, whether it is actually a sonata or not, contrasting possibilities of being are revealed to him of which he had previously been unaware. A world of contradictory thoughts and emotions is made audible and calls for response. That is why the manner in which a character in fiction is portrayed when engaged in a musical experience constitutes a relevant comment on certain facets of his personality. Committed as he inevitably must be to a diversity of social and professional activities and human relationships, the esthetic experience, and in particular the response to a work of music, may at first sight appear to be of mere marginal interest. The reader of fiction who may himself be an adept in musical theory or practice will soon enough discover that most of the characters who are shown to respond to music in the course of a fictitious narrative are rarely qualified—when judged by professional standards—to apply criteria of structural or thematic analysis to what they have heard. All that can safely be asserted is that their commitment to the musical experience at a particularly sensitive point in the narrative provides the novelist with an insight into thought processes and behavior patterns deriving from affective causes of considerable psychological and cultural significance.

Thus, the impact of a melody on the fictitious hearer may be said to reveal, on the one hand, musical associations uncontrolled by the mind, yet integrated by consciousness and thus capable of being articulated through the medium of words; on the other hand, the response to the same melody may be an indication of the manner in which cultural adaptation and social conditioning give shape and substance to a character's inner life. This is why an analysis of musical response in terms of unconscious images and memories such as the one that has been described in the two previous chapters does not tell us all one might like to know about one character's preference for a popular ballad rather than a fugue by Bach or another character's choice of an Elizabethan song sung to the accompaniment of a lute rather than of a Beethoven quartet. The contemporary novelist who places the musical experience, if and when it occurs, within a socially valid framework makes this aspect of the novel, no less than any other, available to social and cultural interpretation.

The work of fiction considered as a product of social tensions and pressures thus creates its own cultural frame of reference within which composer, performer, and hearer assume their place. To those three must be added the reader, himself a member of a social group which determines his attitude to music in general as well as to the experience in the novel which evokes the musical response, in particular. Ideally, novelist, fictitious character, and reader should be similarly conditioned so that no discrepancy need arise between the musical response of the one who creates the character and the one in whose imagination the character comes to life again. This ideal state of affairs is rarely, if ever, achieved. The musical expectations of the novelist may differ in many significant ways from those of the reader. Elizabethan music which evidently meant a great deal to Stephen Dedalus might leave the reader brought up on classical musical structures of nineteenth-century German music unaffected. Similarly, the culturally conditioned preference for works of considerable musical sophistication in certain novels by Virginia Woolf or E.M. Forster may bewilder the musically sensitive reader whose allegiance may lie with polyphonic music rooted in the tradition of early Baroque madrigals. Last but not least, the reader may be hard put to respond to music which has never been actually composed but had its origin in the novelist's own imagination, music which no one has ever heard and yet which becomes an audible presence in a fictitious setting such as the various musical compositions of Vinteuil in Marcel Proust's remembered vision of the past or Adrian Leverkühn's imaginary musical creations which fill the pages of Thomas Mann's *Doctor Faustus*.

The fictitious listener is as difficult a character to fit into any traditional social classification as is the fictitious composer. He may indeed conform to what society or that part of it which constitutes the reading public expects his musical taste to be like. His response to music may, in effect, be identical with that of the majority of the readers of the novel. He may, however, for reasons the novelist will not leave unexplained, be nonconformist in his musical preferences. He may resist social pressures and their effect on musical response on the assumption that such pressures are founded on premises that have nothing to do with the appreciation of music or any other art, but are based on the complex system of economic and social organization that characterizes contemporary life. Moreover, ambivalent responses to music may frequently be the result of a sense of cultural alienation. The assertive listener, on the other hand, whose preferences and dislikes can be clearly articulated may merely express his intellectual pretensions without any true understanding of the music he hears. This is no less true of the fictitious listener than of the reader of the novel. In varying degrees musical responses may be said to result from either social adaptation or maladaptation which, in turn, may lead to the integration or rejection of musical tradition as a creative force in the life of the community.

The concept of musical tradition is itself open to a variety of interpretations especially when considered in terms of the concert-going public whose parochialism in musical taste at times constitutes the only available evidence for the existence of such a tradition. To Mozart's contemporaries, for instance, his most mature works seemed excessively dissonant, "an outburst of violent passion" and an expression "of hard bitter, and biting pains."[8] The relation between consonance and dissonance has been viewed differently by listeners according to the readiness of the age in which they lived to accept musical innovation. At times the painful associations evoked by dissonance, for instance, were found to be a necessary ingredient in compositions aiming at greater expressiveness. For, as one Renaissance writer puts it, if compositions were "made up entirely of consonances, although beautiful sounds and good effects would issue from them, they would still be somehow imperfect, both as sound and composition, seeing that . . . they would lack the great elegance that dissonance affords."[9] Modern attitudes towards consonance and dissonance as well as towards chromaticism again differ in their emphasis on the pain or pleasure evoked by them. One musicologist stresses the ambiguity found in any chromatic progression which creates suspense and uncertainty and may, finally, produce a sense of profound and, at times, unbearable anguish in the hearer,[10] while another views the emergence of dissonance within the cultural context of humanism and thus equates chromaticism with what "was most creative about the humanist belief in the personal consciousness."[11] The same writer speaks of Dowland's "In Darkness let me dwell" as "a complement to the introspective melancholy of Hamlet and to the self-analytical love-poetry of Donne" and concludes his analysis of this song by calling it "an achievement of civilization" while in the same sentence *Tristan* is made to stand for the end of a civilization "and of a phase of European consciousness."[12] The use of dissonance in a musical composition may thus stand for what is either affirmative or self-denying in the human psyche. It may be the musical expression given to a reawakened interest in the dramatic possibilities inherent in conflict situations as can be found on the Elizabethan and Jacobean stage or it may stand for the growth of cultural alienation expressed most vividly in the dissonanace employed by twentieth-century composers. Moreover if dichotomy is of the very essence of dissonance and chromaticism it may also be interpreted in terms of conflicting class interests which, in turn, are reflected in the individual consciousness of composer and listener alike.[13]

For similar reasons, the growing interest of psychotherapists in the use of music as a cure to mental illness—frequently brought about by the alienation of the individual from contemporary civilization—is of considerable interest to the student of twentieth-century fiction. In the opinion of one psychologist, "it is relatively easy to find music with tempos and rhythms to fit the needs of each patient."[14] Another, more specifically, recommends Romantic music because it "favors a release of emotion, while modern impressionistic music affords an escape into fantasy."[15] A third, more manifestly opposed to chromaticism, is of the opinion that "habitual preoccupation with music of a specific type, e.g. Debussy, may end by creating a permanent state of psychological instability, so that in a sense music may sometimes really be a cause of melancholia."[16] To the student of the function of the musical experience in a work of modern fiction with its inevitable emphasis on the alienated individual in a hostile environment, the opinion expressed by one more psychotherapist that music aids the return to reality by dispelling delusions and hallucinations will come as a surprise.[17] For while music may, in effect, release emotions and encourage fantasy formations, it rarely persuades the listener—and in particular the mentally unstable—to adjust himself to a reality from which he had initially escaped to find solace in an imaginary world of sounds.

This digression into a study of dissonance as a cultural phenomenon and the presentday psychotherapeutic uses of music in the treatment of the emotionally insecure and the culturally alienated provides ample evidence for the need to study the personality of the listener to music in a work of fiction from a sociologically relevant angle. His response to music will inevitably take place within a social frame of reference represented by the "establishment" which dictates the esthetic criteria according to which musical response is being regulated. Thus, various musical theories may be in fashion at one time, out of fashion a generation later. Dissonance and chromatic progression, for instance, may be adopted by the concert-going public as a matter of cultural expedience rather than for any musical considerations. The listener as a cultural consumer follows a pattern of ritualistic behavior according to which the enjoyment of music is a kind of fetish-worship to be indulged in either in private or in public. At the same time he makes use of music as an outlet for those affects that have to be either regulated or repressed; the musical experience thus facilitates escape from the increasing pragmatism in the ordering of the life of the individual which dictates prevailing survival patterns. In many such cases listening to music provides the sole opportunity to indulge in "free-floating" associations which the hearer either pours into the music or extracts from it. The anguish caused by growing alienation may in this way be first projected and then "sublimated" into music. The most desirable by-product of what might be called musical consumption is, in effect, a sense of liberation from the restrictive affect-regulations which society and civilized conduct impose upon the hearer.[18] The very concept of reality to which both psychotherapists and literary critics so frequently pay homage acquires ambiguous overtones: musical response, whether in life or in a work of fiction, does not necessarily foster a "return to reality"—especially when conflict situations arising from cultural insecurity threaten the individual's sense of identity. For while listening to music the fictitious hearer constructs out of a world of contradictory experiences an imaginary ego, a sense of individual integrity largely unrelated to the life of his contemporaries among whom he is condemned to live. The only "reality" which he may be aware of outside the musical experience is that of cultural "dissonance" and the chromatic regression of the individual from stability to instability, from sheltered adaptation to the breakdown of a traditional system of values.

2

In the novels under discussion the social setting is invariably underemphasized. Yet it supplies a standard of conformity against which the protagonist's thoughts, emotions, and actions, may be measured. Almost without exception these novels portray a divided world where the central figure and the social setting which provides the framework for inner growth are shown to be two contradictory and mutually exclusive ways of looking at life. The fictitious hero embodies no vision of communal effort and achievement but is portrayed as a stranger, an outsider, or misfit who by circumstance of origin, character or upbringing is compelled to live among those who have chosen a life of acquiescent and complacent affirmation of things as they are.

Such a figure, placed in a middle-class setting of moral smugness and indifference, feels himself rejected by his contemporaries. As he is being judged by standards of conduct foreign to his way of thinking and feeling, he escapes into the protective shell of his private visions which are the intro-spective's natural spiritual home. Out of these visions he builds for himself a world of wish-fulfillments which reflect his growing estrangement from the life of the average man. The philistine acceptance of the principle of conformity becomes an object of satire and contempt. As he withdraws from his contemporaries in order to find the meaning of his life within the context of his own nonconformist attitudes and beliefs, his self-imposed isola-tion transforms all experience into a mirror-image of the self though blurred by excessive introspection and distorted by his vision of a private self-contained universe.

This is especially true of his musical behavior. The most personal of all the arts, the hearer is at all times free to supply his own measure of significance to the music he hears. The outsider's response is characterized by a sense of aloofness mixed with contempt for those whose involvement with music is colored by sentiment and self-dramatization. The novelist is thus throughout the portrayal of the experience aware of an underlying dichotomy which concerns the hero's attitude to music: for by comparing the philistine's response to a musical work to his own and contrasting the former's hollow pretense with what he feels to be its true meaning, he integrates the music in his own particular kind of wish-fulfillment and makes it part of his vision of unreality which denies the existence of all social compulsions. As in these novels all musical response is placed within such an unresolved dichotomy there is reason to believe that this reflects the novelist's own gradual alienation from a reality principle that has ceased to embody any viable convic-tions. The fictitious listener, at times indeed a self-portrait of the novelist himself, withdraws into a universe where his per-sonal visions provide the only valid frame of reference to which he may—and indeed does—apply a variety of names, Love or God or Being, all of them synonymous with a sense of harmony which is not to be found outside the shell where these musical experiences take place.

No other writer in the twentieth century was as much con-cerned with the element of social compulsion in portraying aspects of the musical experience among upper-class listeners to music as Proust. Repeatedly he refers to musical fads, instances of musical snobbery, such as "le Wagnerisme" of Mme Verdurin or Mme de Cambremer's fashionable enthusiasm for the music of Chopin. The complete ignorance of all things musical among those same upper-class concert-goers is satirized and contrasted to Marcel's own commitment to music. When, in 1895, at a concert where Beethoven's Fifth was being performed, Proust observed the audience, he was struck by the appearance of the people who seemed "sunk in a state close to that of hypnosis, hashish smokers who had become intoxicated together, whose faces breathed, in different instances, a languid voluptuousness" or "an almost aggressive animation." Not without sarcasm he describes the listeners as people who "gradually allowed themselves to be seduced by the promise of a consolation that soon will soothe them."[19]

At about the same time, Proust described Swann's musical experience after having repeatedly listened to Vinteuil's "petite phrase" as a communication of "actual ideas, of another world, of another order, ideas veiled in shadows, unknown, impenetrable by the human mind . . ." and who in attempting to describe the purely personal nature of this experience speaks of music and the response it evokes as "that great impenetrable night of our soul."[20] Thus, in volume after volume, first Swann and later Marcel, find revealed in Vinteuil's music what social reality most deprived them of—an awareness of the truth of their own inner being.

The reader of Proust will be confronted at every stage of this gigantic novel by a contradiction inherent in the writer's vision of the individual's attempt at social integration. While, on the one hand, the aristocratic way of life seems eminently desirable, its hollowness and hypocrisy are never denied. Aristocratic standards of conduct may be worthy of imitation, but individuals who pride themselves on their upper-class origin are revealed as intellectual nonentities or emotional cripples. Shorn of its pretensions the aristocracy portrayed in Proust's novel inhabits a self-contained world of utter fatuousness, indeed a fictitious universe peopled by noble eccentrics, sexual deviants, and their somewhat promiscuous followers. Towards the end of the novel Proust, in effect, admits that in this world of make-believe music alone "might be real" because it "gives us an emotion which we feel to be more exalted, more pure, more true" than the superficiality of the salons where it is being performed, so that, in its final analysis, the musical experience alone corresponds "to some definite spiritual reality."[21]

But long before this final recognition Proust is at pains to relate music—as seen from the point of view of composer, performer, or listener—to some inner truth. This is the "counterpoint" that, structurally and thematically determines the form and content of his novel. Thus, when Marcel attends a symphony concert at the beginning of the novel, and is not yet under the influence of Vinteuil's violin sonata, he is conscious of an intensity of experience which social reality deprives him of, so that "in order to understand [the musical works played at the concert] I drew out from myself and put into them all that was then best and deepest in me."[22]

Again and again the amorphous nature of the society into which Proust tries so hard to be integrated is recognized for what it is and treated in the spirit of satire. Similarly Marcel's love for Albertine is revealed as a delusion from which music alone can save him. For it "helped me to descend into myself, to make there a fresh discovery: that of the difference that I sought in vain in life." The "difference" to which he refers here is that between the social world of make-believe which attracted him so powerfully and the vision of individual integrity attainable through music. For whenever he speaks of the "completeness" of music as opposed to the fragmentary nature of all social life he realizes that every musical work "is indeed filled with so many different musics, each of which is a person."[23] Once again when he compares the unexplored country where artistic creation originates to the stereotyped and predictable sources of upper-class conduct Proust discovers in art, and in particular in music, "man himself" or, as he puts it, "the intimate composition of those worlds which we call individual persons."[24] Proust's discovery of Vinteuil's "petite phrase" coincided with the growth of his awareness that the only salvation from inner division lay in complete surrender to the musical experience. When, at the end of the novel, Marcel decides to write a book which would transcribe this process of self-recognition in the form of a work of fiction, he resolves to trace this magic metamorphosis from unreality to reality as if it had indeed taken place at the very instant that he, for the first time, heard Vinteuil's never-to-be-forgotten melody.

3

Huxley's attempt at portraying the intellectual pretensions of upper middle-class life, shortly after the First World War, in *Point Counter Point*, reads, in some respects, like a parody of Proust's large-scale portrayal of a decaying French aristocracy before and during the war. It is a society that had lost a fixed code of values and had become prey to conflicting political ambitions. It lacked any principle of creativity to sustain it from within and was devoid of any sense of communion with either God or man. It is in this moral and social void that a number of musical experiences take place. In each the personal response to music on the part of the outsider is contrasted with the conformist musical attitudes of the concert-going public. Thus, John Bidlake, observing the invited guests at Lord Edward's house listening to Bach's Suite in B minor for flute and strings, whispers to Lady Edward, "There's only an intellectual hypocrisy now. The tribute philistinism pays to art, what? Just look at them all paying it—in pious grimaces and religious silence."[25] Though a number of people are present at this musical soirée who are shown to meditate on the effect of the music on their rather shallow emotional life, no one among them experiences the music as a form of personal revelation. The obtuseness of a consistently personal response is, however, made manifest, and with a probably intentional emphasis on the eccentricity of such a response when Spandrell, at the end of the novel, listens to Beethoven's quartet, opus 132, in A minor, and in particular to his "Hymn of Thanksgiving to a Deity" on recovering from a serious illness. Now, Spandrell, throughout the novel, has been portrayed as the archetypal outsider who enjoys "stewing in [his] disgusting suppurating juices," who is too busy "thinking about death and God" to be able to live, and who, finally, liked "to play the part of the anchorite of diabolism." The social context in which this extraordinary musical experience takes place is reflected in Spandrell's growing inability to come to terms with his contemporaries. As he looks upon them as so much vermin, he is inevitably forced to conclude that this earth on which men are compelled to live may well be "some other planet's hell."

The sense of recovery from the evil of alienation Spandrell experiences when listening to Beethoven's solemn music is the result of a spiritual revelation of sublime transcendence. Yet this recovery serves no spiritual end, for at the very height of musical surrender Spandrell is shot when he opens the door to the assassins he had himself invited. It is a deliberate *mise-en-scène* providing an absurd musical setting for the dramatic exit of one who no longer shared any viable beliefs or attitudes with his contemporaries. Thus, Spandrell, knowing that his murderers are already climbing the stairs leading to his apartment, can say about the music, "It proves all kinds of things—God, the soul, goodness, unescapably. It's the only real proof that God exists; the only one because Beethoven was the only man who got his knowledge over into expression."[26]

Huxley, in later years, tried to justify this debasement of the musical experience into unmitigated physical terror by referring to the effect of the A-minor quartet being played on the stage in a dramatized version of *Point Counter Point* which, according to him, created "an extraordinary atmosphere of mystical tranquillity in the midst of the prevailing horror."[27] Yet, it is Spandrell, the misfit, the nonconformist, the self-indulgent despiser of other men, through whose inner ear we are made to listen to Beethoven's most mature music. The solution to his personal problems—which results from the "prevailing horror" of collective and individual alienation—merely contributes a greater sense of fragmentariness of the human condition in the world of post-war Europe. For Spandrell's unnecessary death has solved no problems, no horror has been overcome by his declaration that he has found the proof of God's existence in Beethoven's music. As the sounds of Beethoven's *Hymn* penetrate the shell in which he has isolated himself, he becomes intolerably aware of his own inadequacy as a human being. The dichotomy upon which this musical experience is founded is the only reality the reader is finally conscious of.

E.M. Forster, more subtly than Huxley, introduces the same discrepancy between individual musical response and that of the philistine when, at the beginning of *Howards End*, the two heroines of the novel, Helen and Margaret, attend a concert in the company of some of their friends at which Beethoven's Fifth is being played. Forster's sympathy is all with Helen who, in the course of the novel, develops into an outsider and rebel. She alone responds to the music of the *Scherzo* in terms of her search for her own true identity. At the start of this movement she hears "a goblin walking quietly over the universe, from end to end," reminding her "in passing that there was no such thing as splendour or heroism in the world" and that she was alone in her realization of "panic and emptiness". It is this awareness that distinguishes her from others and turns her response to the symphony into a shattering spiritual experience. For she knows now—"the notes meant this or that to her, and they could have no other meaning, and life could have no other meaning."[28]

It matters very little to Helen that her sister blames her for "muddling things." Forster, throughout his literary work, shows an attractive weakness for people who muddle things by getting themselves involved in situations over which they have only partial control. When Margaret ironically refers to her sister's irritating habit of confusing music with life, and life with music, attributing a musical content to nonmusical experiences and profoundly symbolic meanings to perfectly innocuous musical themes, it only strengthens one's impression of Helen as a musical eccentric and one of life's outsiders. What Forster satirizes here is not so much Helen confusing music with life as a general tendency of the age to substitute one art form for another by eliminating all dividing lines between the various arts and between art and life. In Margaret's own words, Helen would like "the course of the Oder . . . to be like music. It's obliged to remind her of a symphonic poem. The part of the landing stage is in B minor. There is a slodgy theme in several keys at once, meaning mudbanks, and another for the navigable canal, and the exit in the Baltic is in C sharp major, pianissimo."[29]

It is by "muddling things" that Helen becomes aware of the threat posed to her integrity as a human being she first discovered in the music of the *Scherzo* in Beethoven's Fifth. By transposing this sense of horror from the musical theme to the life of the people around her, she is the only one in the novel who achieves freedom from social compulsion. It is in social and economic pressures to which she and her sister are exposed that this horror of spiritual emptiness is embodied. Music provides a kind of ironic counterpoint. For while Helen faces the revelation of the goblin "walking quietly over the universe" in her self-chosen solitude, the other members of the concert-party indulge in their own favorite wish-fulfillment while listening to Beethoven's music. Thus, Margaret "can only see the music", while their brother Tibby "is profoundly versed in counterpoint". A Fräulein Mosebach "remembers all the time that Beethoven is 'echt deutsch'." Her boyfriend, moreover, "can remember nothing but Fräulein Mosebach" during the concert.[30] Proust's description of the fatuous expression on the faces of a concert audience, quoted above, applies to the English setting just as well. In his emphasis on the authentic listener to music as a character endowed with a singular insight into the folly and insensitivity of the socially conditioned concert-goer, Forster reveals himself a faithful disciple of a tradition first established by the French writer in his great novel.

4

Hans Castorp, in Thomas Mann's *The Magic Mountain*, represents at the beginning of the novel the archetypal *petit bourgeois* with a very German inclination to ask metaphysical questions concerning the meaning and purpose of life. By placing him within "the hermetic, feverish atmosphere of the enchanted mountain", Thomas Mann makes him undergo a kind of intellectual and emotional education which reaches its climax in a musical experience of manifestly metaphysical dimensions. Growing up in an age "that affords no satisfying answer to the eternal question of 'Why?', 'To what end?' ", Hans Castorp lacks those qualities of "moral remoteness and single-mindedness"[31] that could justify survival in terms of the average and the mediocre. His "simple soul", in its quest for truth, "received no answer save a hollow silence[32]". Had he remained in the "flat-lands" of Northern Germany he would never have become aware of the "panic and emptiness" that characterized the life of the middle classes in Western Europe before, during, and after the First World War. Quite literally confined within the walls of the T.B. sanatorium in Davos without really being sick in mind or body, he shares the various preoccupations of its inmates without being one of them, an outsider against his own will, a detached observer of the foredoomed struggle between health and disease, affirmation and denial of moral values, life and death. The ordinary stuff of which he is made, his "simplicity" bordering on mediocrity "undergoes a heightened process which makes him capable of adventures in sensual, moral, intellectual spheres, he would never have dreamed of in the 'flatland'."[33] For like the Quester in the Grail legends he has to pass through ordeals and rites of initiation before he is permitted "to approach the esoteric mystery" which leads to self-knowledge. One of the most striking revelations occurs during a musical experience. It portrays his voluntary submission to a power beyond rational analysis, his adventures into the invisible and the inexplicable, a reaching out towards a wisdom which, Thomas Mann says, "is always bound up with the 'other world', with night and death."[34] This confrontation between the "guileless fool" on his enchanted mountain and this newly acquired wisdom takes place in the seclusion of the music room at the Sanatorium where Hans Castorp holds his nightly musical séances in front of a gramophone which plays out to him his favorite records one by one. That he is alone with his music qualifies his response to it. The solitude in which the fictitious listener confronts the musical works is indeed the most characteristic feature of the musical experience in the contemporary novel.

A close analysis of the musical content of Hans Cantorp's favorite records reveals a great deal about the listener himself—not so much about his musical taste, for he has little, but his metaphysical preferences. The questions which life had left unanswered assume a musical form, they transform themselves into melodies whose rise and fall reflect the interplay of dissonance and consonance in the life of the listener, and leads by way of suspense to final resolution. To the solitary and contemplative Hans Castorp these melodies are indeed metaphors of spiritual transcendence and of man's search for some ultimate harmony. Three of these melodies are arias from late nineteenth-century operas, one a piece of orchestral music, Debussy's L'Après-midi d'un Faune, and one more is a Schubert Lied. Every evening, for weeks on end, Hans Castorp shuts himself up in the music room and listens to these records long after all the other patients have gone to sleep. The deliberately melodramatic nature of the operatic arias, at times bordering on the cloyingly sentimental, does not disturb him. In so far as they appear to him to be metaphors of life and death, they penetrate the deepest layers of his consciousness and open up vistas of self-recognition that the teaching of his two mentors, the Italian Settembrini, with his belief in the possibilities inherent in enlightened human progress, and the Jesuit Naphta, with his insistence on the need for revolutionary action, had never revealed to him.

The first of these opera records, the closing duet of Radames and Aida, sung in the underground vaults of the palace, seems to the solitary listener an expression of the blending of anguish and ecstatic harmony he had never before imagined possible. The contrast between the reality of slow suffocation, hunger, and, finally, death—and the musical vision which Thomas Mann describes in quasi-technical terms ("that simple, rapturous ascent, playing from tonic to dominant, as it mounts from the fundamental to the sustained note a half-tone before the octave, then turning back again to the fifth") appears to the listener an instance of indescribable poignancy. The young man in the dimly lit room, realizing the desperate situation of the two lovers in their dungeon, wonders at "the triumphant idealism of the music, of art, of the human spirit; the high and irrefragable power they had of shrouding with a veil of beauty the vulgar horror of actual fact."[35] Hans Castorp's interpretation of this musical passage may not be altogether in the spirit of Verdi's opera, but it conforms to his own state of mind still wavering between an acceptance of the *status quo* of conformist moral standards and the unanswered questions as to the "meaning and purpose" of life, and his own life in particular. It is, in effect, during his seven years' stay at the Sanatorium that he has become aware of the frail vulnerability of human desires. Now the "triumphal idealism" of Radames' ecstatic renunciation of life for the sake of the woman he loves proves the ultimate incorruptibility of the human spirit. The musical metaphor seems to have conquered what conformist moral attitudes consider the irreversible limitations of human existence.

Hans Castorp's repertory consists of two more operatic arias. First, Don José's pleading for mercy before Carmen who scorns him for preferring military honor to her love. Once again it is a melody of farewell, sung by a man in his anguish at having to make a choice between two kinds of desperate action, Thomas Mann, faithfully and somewhat ironically, providing a running commentary ("rising two tones from the tonic and thence returning ardently to the fifth"). This record is followed by another military figure, Valentine in Gounod's *Faust* whose song consists of a prayer to God to protect his beloved sister, if and when it should please heaven "to call him to Himself." Once again the choice is between two kinds of despair, embodied in the world of action and the world of love. The issue remains undecided: the listener, however, knows how to interpret the meaning of the musical metaphor in the light of his own choice in favor of the life of the spirit. Hans Castorp's sympathy with such values as derive from submission to harmonious sound are even more vividly manifest in his response to Debussy's setting of Mallarmé's poem. His solitude and that of the flute-playing faun is immersed in one and the same kind of oblivion. Here, at last, he finds the final rejection of the "vulgar horror" which "actual fact" exposes in all its hideousness. For once you separate yourself from the world of action, all dichotomies are abolished, contradictions and conflicts eliminated, forgetfulness alone holds sway, "a blessed hush, the innocence of those places where time is not." For in this music Hans Castorp discovers "the very apotheosis of rebuff to the Western world and that world's insensate ardour for the 'deed.'"[36]

The key-passage in this section of *The Magic Mountain*, entitled "Fullness of Harmony" occurs while Hans Castorp is listening to Schubert's *Der Lindenbaum*, one more melody of farewell addressed to a receding past and sung by a wanderer whose voyage will take him to remote countries, an alien in an indifferent universe, suffering the "bitter blasts" of fortune, and nostalgically remembering the rest and peace under the fair branches of the tree beside the fountain at the entrance to the village which is his true home. It is this nostalgia—already apparent in the four previous records—which finally qualifies Hans Castorp's response to his favorite music. For it is colored by the enchanted inaction of his life on the magic mountain, his striving for harmony in a world dominated by the dissonance of conflicting forces, his yearning for the "solemnity" of death which like "the sustained note a half-tone before the octave.

thus turning back again to the fifth," holds a promise of final fulfillment which life does not offer. Schubert's enchanting *Lied*, the very embodiment of simplicity of soul quite alien to a life of action, thus becomes a confirmation of the young man's metaphysical longing for extinction. As an answer to his many simple-minded questions it speaks the language of solitude, alienation, and death. In its final analysis, this most lovely of Schubert's songs, in effect, "was the fruit of life, conceived of death, pregnant of dissolution; it was a miracle of the soul."[37]

Thomas Mann, at the end of this "musical" chapter, implies that the power of music may lead the listener to an unresisting acceptance of the impulse towards death which all these compositions, so dear to Hans Castorp's heart, have fostered. Yet, the music may equally well have the opposite effect, that of making the listener aware of the ultimate triumph of love over death. In the last lines of the novel, written under the impact of the war which Hans Castorp had joined as a volunteer, he, the most singular of German soldiers that ever appeared in the pages of a novel, is seen stumbling across the shell-holed battlefield, humming, without his being aware of it, Schubert's song while "the product of a perverted science, laden with death . . . raises up a fountain as high as a house, of mud, fire, iron, molten metal, scattered fragments of humanity."[38]

The final challenge, then, is not merely the result of a personal confrontation between the solitary listener and the message of dissolution the *Lied* so powerfully communicates to him. Hans Castorp and his guileless soul are raised to a level of spiritual awareness when musical response acquires archetypal significance. Thomas Mann, making full use of the ambiguity inherent in the musical experience itself relates his simple hero's disappearance in battle to Schubert's death-inspired song. For "it was worth dying for, the enchanted lied! But he who died for it, died indeed no longer for it; was a hero only because he died for the new, the new word of love and the future that whispered in his heart."[39]

It was a magical musical metaphor that led the hero of this novel back to life from which he had been absent for so long only in order to let him perish in the dissonance of human conflict, the melody on his lips and a glimmer of hope in his eyes for the future when Schubert's melody would fulfil itself through love and compassion. Having cut himself off from common humanity in the hushed music-room of the T.B. sanatorium (itself a metaphor of a decaying civilization) in order to listen to the music of his own choice, his foredoomed death, in music and horror, is turned into a metaphor of a brighter future still to come. This, at least, is what Thomas Mann appears to have believed in 1924 when the novel was published.

5

The alienated individual as the prototype of the artist in search of his art—this is Antoine Roquentin in Sartre's first novel *La Nausée*. Separated from other men by an act of his will, despising their absurd and obsessive striving for wealth or pleasure, nauseated by their vegetative and aimless existence, he notes down the symptoms of his "nausea" in his diary: he is incapable of passion, for a great vacuity has taken its place; he lives in solitude and speaks to no one; he neither receives nor gives; language has become redundant, for there is nothing to tell; he has no secrets and therefore he has no confessions to make. All around him, in the streets of the small provincial town in which he lives, in the coffeehouse he frequents, in the library which he visits to do research on M. de Rollebon, a somewhat eccentric eighteenth-century nobleman and political opportunist, Roquentin is aware of life's grotesque fecundity, its amorphous, cancerlike growth, the vague, flabby, nightmarish quality of its proliferation. It is this awareness that distinguishes him from others. But it is a sterile form of realization, a point of observation without any morally valid frame of reference, the more absurd as it is mainly conscious of its own absurdity. Thirty years later Sartre described Roquentin—who appears to be a portrait of himself at the time the novel was written—in his twofold capacity as "the elect, the chronicler of hells" as well as "a photomicroscope of glass and steel bent over my own protoplasmic juices."[40]

It is into this hell of self-consuming introspection that a "petite phrase" is introduced, a tiny piece of musical triviality, which acts like a tonic upon his melancholic meditations and restores his will to live and to create. As if Sartre were parodying Proust, this insignificant rag-tune, first heard during the war whistled by American soldiers in the streets of Paris, then on a worn-out record played over and over again in the coffeehouse he visits, opens up vistas of "extra-terrestrial" bliss, potentialities of being which lift Roquentin out of his seclusion. After listens to the tune, just as Marcel knew (because the music could completely frozen after a trek through the snow and who suddenly comes into a warm room."[41] Yet those who composed and sing the little tune on the record are no musical virtuosos but an impecunious Jew on the top of a New York skyscraper who invented the tune because he was in need of money and a Negress, no less impecunious, whose velvety voice, accompanied by the bleating of saxophones, was found to be adequately seductive in an undisguised erotically titillating way. All this Roquentin knows because his imagination is at work while he listens to the tune, just as Marcel knew (because the music could not conceal it) all about Vinteuil's secret sorrow and the outrageous goings-on between his daughter and her lesbian friend.

By surrendering to that quality in music which, in Proust's words, is *sine materia*, Roquentin achieves a kind of knowledge which outgrows the limitations imposed by the process of birth, decay, and death, an awareness of nonhuman duration when the music "filled the room with its metallic transparency, crushing our miserable time against the walls." Nothing can stand in the way of the melody "nothing which comes from this time in which the world has fallen."[42] Its time is the eternal present when each note dies so that a new note may be born; there are no visions seen as in a mist, no vague memories of a past to be recaptured, for "the melody stays the same, young and firm, like a pitiless witness."[43] Nothing exists beyond or above or behind the melody. It alone *is*. This is the final knowledge which replaces the nausea and estrangement by a will to live and to transform the raw material of this life into a work of art. Sartre's parody of Proust's response to Vinteuil's *petite phrase* concludes with the desire of the artist to eternalize the present through magical metamorphosis, to transform the complacency, self-pity and "drab intimacy of the world" into "a glorious little suffering," a melody without compassion, shamelessly exhibiting an "arid purity," "this little jewelled pain which spins around above the record and dazzles me." Roquentin now feels free to comment on those who—like his aunt Bigeois—look for consolation in music. Thus, he describes the concert halls overflowing with "humiliated, outraged people who close their eyes and try to turn their pale faces into receiving antennae" so that the sounds should flow into them and "their suffering become music, like Werther; they think that beauty is compassionate to them. Mugs."[44]

The desire "to drive existence out," to wash himself "of the sin of existing," qualifies Roquentin's response to music throughout the novel. It is a response colored by Sartre's own philosophical preoccupations at the time he wrote the book. For what he is concerned with is not so much the anguish of the listener, his existential suffering in the individual context of his own time and place, but the metamorphosis of his anguish into pure being which takes place when the artist applies his craft to what his imagination bodies forth within the context of his all-too-human existence. The basic difference between a cry of anguish "in reality" and a song of anguish expressed through music is that though you can "describe" the former, nothing at all, of any relevance whatever, can be said about the latter. In later years, Sartre formulates this search of the artist for artistic validity in abstract terms. "Beauty is a value," he declares, "which is only applicable to the imaginary and which requires the negation of the world in its essential structure. That is why it is stupid to confuse the moral with the aesthetic."[45] Yet this confusion is the very stuff of which the musical response in the twentieth-century novel is made. For whenever music stimulates the imagination of the alienated, the spiritually disoriented or the emotionally insecure, he confronts his moral existence and all its inadequacies with a resurrected sense of his own true being. The fusion of the moral and the esthetic may, in effect, lead to the dizzying experience of having to live on two contrasting levels of awareness simultaneously. For moral equivocation is inherent in all musical experience and the seemingly transcendent nature of the listener's response to music may, finally, be the most faithful mirror of the ambiguity which resides in the listener's own contradictory self.

When, at the beginning of this chapter, the sonata form was repeatedly invoked as a valid equivalent for contemporary fiction in the first half of this century, the "fictitious listener" is indeed the focus providing a unifying principle where the various strands that constitute the fictitious universe created by the novelist meet. He alone reflects the contradictions inherent in his search for personal fulfillment in an indifferent or hostile environment. It is within the discords created by social conflict situations that the hero strives to achieve a sense of inner harmony through the musical experience. Yet much nineteenth-century music is founded upon the assumption of a discordant universe—whether audible as dissonance or inaudible but experienced as the result of unresolved conflicts in the musical work itself. It may, in effect, produce in the hearer a sense of emotional insecurity and social vulnerability threatening the integrity of his whole moral being.

Notes to Chapter Three

1. See Robert Humphrey, *Stream of Consciousness in the Modern Novel*, p. 99 on *Mrs. Dalloway* as a sonata: "It is easy to identify a first theme, a bridge passage, a second theme, development and recapitulation."
2. E.M. Forster in his Rede Lecture on Virginia Woolf: "*To the Lighthouse* is in three movements. It has been called a novel in sonata form." Quoted in E.K. Brown, *Rhythm in the Novel*, p. 64.
3. Peter Burra, Introduction to the Everyman edition of *A Passage to India*, 1942, quoted in *A Passage to India, A Casebook* edited by Malcolm Bradbury, Macmillan, 1970, p. 63.
4. This is a summary given by Harry Levin, *James Joyce, A Critical Introduction*, 1941, p. 79, of Ezra Pound's view as expressed in his essay "James Joyce et *Pecuchet*," *Polite Essays*, 1937, originally published in *Mercure de France*, (June 1922), CLVL.
5. Calvin S. Brown, *Music and Literature*, p. 214–215. See also: H.A. Basilius, "Thomas Mann's use of musical structure and techniques in Tonio Kröger," *Germanic Review*, XIX (December 1944) 248–308.
6. Hermann Hesse as quoted in Mark Boulby, *Hermann Hesse, His Mind and Art*, p. 162. See: T.J. Ziolkowski, "Hermann Hesse's *Steppenwolf*: a sonata in prose," *Modern Language Quarterly* XIX (1958), 115–133, and a letter by Hesse addressed to Mrs. M.W., dated 13 November 1930 (*Briefe*, pp. 36–37) as well as his letter to Felix Braun, 8 July 1927, quoted in *Materialien zum Steppenwolf*, p. 121.
7. Wilfred Mellers, *Harmonious Meeting*, p. 68. See also his *Man and his Music, The Story of Musical Experience in the West*, Part III: "The Sonata Principle."
8. Quoted from Hanslick's *Vom Musikalisch Schönen*, p. 16, in Martin Foss, op. cit., p. 160.

9. Jioseffe Zarlino, *Institutione armoniche*, book III, quoted in Oliver Strunk, *Some Readings in Musical History*, p. 232.
10. Leonard B. Meyer, *Emotion and Meaning in Music*, p. 220.
11. Wilfrid Mellers, *Harmonious Meeting*, p. 19.
12. *Ibid.*, p. 92.
13. See Ernst Bloch, *Das Prinzip Hoffnung*, volume 3, p. 1249.
14. Paul R. Farnsworth, *The Social Psychology of Music*, p. 220.
15. S. D. Mitchell and A. Zanker, "The Use of Music in Group Therapy," *J. Ment. Sci.* (1948) *94*, 737–748.
16. Charles M. Diserens, *A Psychology of Music*, p. 196.
17. M. G. Ruegnitz, "Applied Music on Disturbed Wards," *Occup. Therapy and Rehabilitation*, *25* (1946), 203–206.
18. A detailed sociological analysis of the listener to music in contemporary Europe will be found in Theodor W. Adorno's *Einleitung in die Musiksoziologie*, 1968 (*Introduction to the Sociology of Music*).
19. Quoted in Alejo Carpentier, "A Feeling for Music," 1971.
20. Marcel Proust, *Remembrance of Things Past*, vol. II, pp. 180–185.
21. *Ibid.*, *The Captive*, Part II, vol. X, p. 233.
22. *Ibid.*, vol. III, p. 388.
23. *Ibid.*, *The Captive*, Part I, vol. IX, p. 210.
24. *Ibid.*, Part II, vol. X, pp. 69–70.
25. Aldous Huxley, *Point Counter Point*, p. 33.
26. *Ibid.*, p. 591.
27. Letter to D. H. Lawrence, in *Letters*, 11 February 1930, p. 328.
28. E. M. Forster, *Howards End*, pp. 34–35.
29. *Ibid.*, p. 79. This may be compared with Forster's own admission: "When music reminded me of something which was not music, I supposed it was getting me somewhere. 'How like Monet!' I thought when listening to Debussy and 'how like Debussy!' when looking at Monet. I translated sounds into colours, saw the piccolo as apple green and trumpet as scarlet." (Quoted in E. K. Brown, *Rhythm in the Novel*, p. 70).
30. *Ibid.*, p. 32.
31. Thomas Mann, *The Magic Mountain*, p. 32.
32. *Ibid.*, p. 144.
33. Thomas Mann, *The Making of "The Magic Mountain,"* pp. 725–726.
34. *Ibid.*, p. 728.
35. *The Magic Mountain*, p. 645.
36. *Ibid.*, p. 646.
37. *Ibid.*, p. 651. The same formula is used by Thomas Mann as applied to romantic music in general in "Nietzsche and Music", *Past Masters*, quoted in Brennan, *op. cit.*, pp. 76–77, and also in "*Vorspruch zu einer musikalischen Nietzsche-Feier*" (1924) ("Preface to a musical celebration in honour of Nietzsche"), in *Altes und Neues, Kleine Prosa aus Fünf Jahrzehnten*, p. 278.
38. *Ibid.*, p. 715.
39. *Ibid.*, p. 653.
40. Jean-Paul Sartre, *Words*, p. 171.

41. Jean-Paul Sartre, *Nausea*, p. 177. A somewhat watered-down version of Sartre's Roquentin may be found in Saul Bellow's protagonist in his *Dangling Man* (first published in 1944). Listening to a Haydn divertimento for the cello, played by Piatigorsky, alone and in great distress, he thinks: "It was the first movement, the adagio that I cared most about. Its sober opening notes, preliminaries to a thoughtful confession, showed me that I was still an apprentice in shuddering and humiliation. I had not even begun. I had, furthermore, no right to expect to avoid them. So much was immediately clear. Surely no one would plead for exception; that is not a human privilege. What I should do with them, how to meet them, was answered in the second declaration: with grace, without meanness. And though I could not as yet apply that answer to myself, I recognized its rightness and was vehemently moved by it. Not until I was a whole man could it be my answer, too . . ." (p. 45).

42. *Ibid.*, p. 22.

43. *Ibid.*, p. 176.

44. *Ibid.*, p. 174.

45. Jean-Paul Sartre, *The Psychology of Imagination* (first published in 1940) p. 252. A few pages earlier Sartre, discussing what happens to the listener at a concert where Beethoven's Seventh Symphony is being performed, applies the same argument to Beethoven's music as he did to the rag-tune in *La Nausée*: "[The musical work] is completely beyond the real. It has its own time, that is, it possesses an inner time, which runs from the first tone of the allegro to the last tone of the finale, but this time is not a succession of a preceding time which it continues and which happened 'before' the beginning of the allegro; nor is it followed by a time which will come 'after' the finale. The Seventh Symphony is in no way *in time*. It is therefore in no way real. It occurs *by itself*, but as absent, as being out of reach. I cannot act upon it, change a single note of it, or slow down its movement. But it depends on the real for its appearance . . . It therefore occurs as a perpetual elsewhere, a perpetual absence . . . It is not only outside of time and space—as are essences, for instance—it is outside of the real, outside of existence . . . the passing into the real is an actual waking up . . . Nothing more is needed to arouse the nauseating disgust that characterizes the consciousness of reality." (pp. 251–252) (author's italics).

IV
Musical Equivocation

1

The process of withdrawal from reality, so intimately connected with the musical experience, involves a growing awareness of isolation, the result of a sense of moral inadequacy and social alienation, in a universe which appears to the listener increasingly hostile and incomprehensible. Thus, the fictitious character in a novel who projects his own identity into the music, discovers in it a meaning determined by the personal complexities of his own life, presumably only loosely related to the experience that provided the composer with the raw material for his composition.

If one considers the musical experience in terms of the musical encounter between the personality of the composer and that of the listener, the latter's escape into the sheltered seclusion of his own inner being prevents rather than fosters possibilities of spiritual communion between the two. For whether the experience takes place in a concert hall, as in Forster's novel, in a drawing room, as in Proust, in a barroom, as in Sartre, or in front of a gramophone, as in Mann, the spiritual meeting-place where the musical encounter between listener and composer takes place, may indeed be considered outside any historically determined moral framework. Yet, at the very instant of response, social and moral correspondences come into being which contradict the seemingly timeless nature of the musical experience. It is for this reason that the transcendental quality of all great music is liable to convey to the listener a sense of subtle moral ambiguity.

In the opinion of one contemporary composer music is "an image of moral order attained by the listener through his active collaboration in the act of musical creation,"[1] while another calls the composer "a creator of values."[2] Both assume that music expresses emotions in an ordered pattern affirming or negating those values that either provide or deny a moral significance to human life. Though it may indeed be said that "a composer can express an unambiguous moral attitude towards life,"[3] the pattern into which his emotions are made to fit may itself be an esthetically seductive metaphor of the irrational and the morally questionable. It may then be difficult, if not impossible, to adapt such a musical pattern to any sort of positive moral order. It is this kind of ambiguity that we are concerned with here.

Beethoven is frequently mentioned as providing the listener with affirmative emotions of resolution and fortitude in the face of suffering and distress, the one composer above all who, by translating his own faith in man into music, has been assumed to guide the listener back from his spiritual exile to the morally exalted values of human progress embodied in so many of his compositions. Yet his music led some of the most creative minds of the last century to question the moral assumptions out of which they had grown. Wagner could write in 1880 that Beethoven's symphonies set the hearer "free from the sense of guilt" because this music "preaches repentance and atonement in the deepest sense of divine revelation."[4] Tolstoy who always looked upon Beethoven not as the climax of the greatest period of music in Europe but as the representative of its decline spoke, at about the same time, of "the obscure, almost unhealthy excitement" that emanates from Beethoven's last compositions, blaming him, in particular, for the "nervous irritation evoked by this exclusive, artificial, and complex music."[5]

Any discussion of music as embodying an order of values must take into account the growth of the composer's own consciousness, his realization that his music or any music, would be of little value if it did not stand for some ethical principle of conduct. Simultaneously the listener's own capacity to absorb the message of the music may be considered as a yardstick by which to measure its effect on his moral nature. A strong character may resist the morally questionable implications of the music, a weak one may surrender to them. Thus Helen, in Forster's novel, discovers in the Scherzo in Beethoven's Fifth a revelation of "panic and emptiness," as if it were the musical pattern itself that insistently conveys the futility of all human endeavor. By resisting the appeal of what she feels to be Beethoven's life-denying music (and after having listened to the fourth movement of this same symphony, a glorious manifestation of man's strength to overcome all panic and emptiness), Helen builds her new life according to criteria originating in her fortified consciousness and her restored will to live. In contrast to this, we find Spandrell, wallowing in his own alienation and discovering in Beethoven's A-minor quartet the only evidence for God's existence available to man. This revelation, however, does not help him to live. It rather makes him face his own death as a matter of ultimate esthetic surrender: he chooses to die because the music has enabled him to transcend the time-bound scale of things. It seems as if Beethoven's quartet, by providing him with the final evidence of divine transcendence, had supplied him with the equally incontrovertible proof of man's self-deception, vanity, and folly.

If such different responses to the music of the same composer are possible, what is one to think of the following declaration supposedly made by Beethoven himself as reported in a letter, dated 1810, written by Bettina Brentano to Goethe: "Like all the arts, music is founded upon the exalted symbols of moral sense: all true invention is a moral progress. To submit to its inscrutable laws, and by means of these laws to tame and guide one's own mind, so that the manifestations of art may pour out: this is the isolating principle of art."[6] Even though neither style nor vocabulary are Beethoven's, one could easily imagine Beethoven thinking, if not actually putting on paper, ideas of this kind. That this constitutes an obvious simplification of a very complex problem is in keeping with the "heroic" mould of Beethoven's mind. Considered from the point of view of the listener, however, the ambiguity is inescapable: the composer as a "creator of values" stands between two irreconcilable worlds, that which his imagination creates and transmutes into music and that of the listener's conscious mind bringing with him his own ideas as to what constitutes a universe of moral order. It is an ambiguity which questions the ethical validity of the creative act itself. Thus, the encounter between composer and listener—just because of the intense moral identification of the latter with the former—may lead to considerable moral equivocation.

While the composer may, predictably, be unaware of it, the novelist makes use of this ambiguity to add a significant dimension of doubt and questioning to his universe of fiction.

The deeper the novelist's insight into the kind of moral turmoil music may cause, the greater his realization of the perils that attend the soul, once it surrenders to what Kant had called "the irresponsible delights" of music. Tolstoy who quotes Kant in his diary was singularly susceptible to emotional arousal through musical experience. His son reports that he had never seen anyone "who felt music so strongly and deeply as my father. It upset him, moved him, excited him, made him sob and weep. Sometimes it was against his will, for it caused him pain and he said: 'Que me veut cette musique?'. "[7] It was on such an occasion when, in 1899, two years after having begun his story of "sexual love," he listened to the violinist Yulu Lyasotta accompanied by his son Sergei on the piano perform Beethoven's "Kreutzer Sonata" that Tolstoy, who was powerfully moved by this performance of a piece he had heard many times before, decided to add the element of music to his as yet unfinished tale. A number of obsessions then took hold of him which turned this story into Pozdnischev's compulsive narrative of his wife's adultery with a musician and the murder of the musician by the enraged husband. One of Tolstoy's basic concerns during the last years of his life was that sex, except for the purpose of procreation, should be eliminated from human existence so that "the tragedy of the bedroom" as he called it, should be avoided in future. Equally obsessive was his suspicion that the musical experience as it affected composer, performer, and listener alike was to blame for the many forms of aberration that the flesh is heir to. Adultery appeared to him the most common effect of a surrender to music: while writing his "Kreutzer Sonata" he established the final link between adulterous conduct and the subtly evocative music of Beethoven's violin sonata. Thus, in the course of the story Pozdnischev makes the following astonishing remark: "Yet anybody knows that it is by means of those very pursuits, especially of music, that the greater part of the adulteries in our society occur."[8] When the narrator comes to describe the effect produced by Beethoven's music on him, Tolstoy makes him speak of the mixture of delight and horror, producing a kind of hypnotic

condition in the listener, and compelling him to identify with the
composer's state of mind when he wrote the music; for this
music, says the narrator, "transports me to some other position
not my own", and continues, "Take that Kreutzer Sonata, for
instance, how can that first presto be played in a drawing-room
among ladies in low-neck dresses? . . . At any rate that piece had
a terrible effect on me; it was as if quite new feelings, new
possibilities, of which I had till then been unaware had been
revealed."[9]

The real touchstone for the novelist's ambiguous attitude to
music was Wagner's music rather than Beethoven's. The creator
of psychological fiction could not help realising the close affinity
between the use of the leitmotif in music and the new vistas it
opened for the building of plot and development of character in
the novel. While a novelist like Proust tried to adapt the content
of his work to the ideational content of Wagner's music and
thereby succeeded in writing what may be called the first truly
Wagnerian novel of the century, others were much less ready to
submit to what they considered to be a deviation from long-
established tradition. Doubts were expressed in many quarters
both in Germany and elsewhere as to the possible degenerating
effect of such music on the minds of the listeners; for any
attempt at resisting the violent impact of Wagner's musical
message must fail in the face of the emotional intoxication it
provokes and the sensuality it preaches. Bernard Shaw, a lone
admirer of Wagner at that time in England, quotes Max Nordau's virulent attack against Wagner as an instance of the philistinism of the man of letters who refuses to understand the
freedom from prejudice embodied in Wagner's music: "How
unperverted must wives and readers be," wrote Nordau, "when
they are in a state of mind to witness these pieces without
blushing crimson and sinking into the earth for shame . . . The
lovers in these pieces behave like tom cats gone mad, rolling in
contortions and convulsions over a root of valerian."[10] Possibly
these lines were written with Tolstoy's equally violent attack
against Wagner in mind. For Tolstoy also speaks of the hypno-
tizing effect of Wagner's music and compares it to "maniacal
ravings pronounced with great oratorical power for several con-
secutive hours."[11]

It is with considerable difficulty that one can disentangle

musical from psychological motivation in the discussion that raged around Wagner's music during the last decades of the nineteenth century. Thus, Nietzsche when he finally came to reject Wagner in 1888 could describe this rejection as a kind of recovery from a fatal illness and contemptuously refer to Wagner as "having forgotten all sense of shame." For "he makes sick whatever he touches—he has made music sick." Finally he pronounces what proved to be the most explicit definition of art and the artist in an age which Nietzsche considered to be one of moral and spiritual degeneracy: "Wagner increases exhaustion: that is why he attracts the weak and exhausted . . . Wagner is *the modern artist par excellence* . . . The three great *stimulantia* of the exhausted—the *brutal*, the *artificial*, and the *innocent* (idiotic)."[12] Yet some twenty-five years earlier Baudelaire after having listened to Wagner's operas, and in particular to *Tristan*, wrote in a letter to the composer that this had been the most sublime musical experience he had ever undergone and, referring to *Tristan* in particular as "the supreme cry of the soul raised to its paroxysm", he declares the essence of this music to be "une extase faite de volupté et de connaissance,"[13] hinting thereby at the equivocal and yet intensely seductive nature of Wagner's most controversial opera, indeed a mixture of luminous sensuousness and dark recognition, something that Thomas Mann in his essay on the "Torment and Greatness of Richard Wagner" will call "Wollust der Hölle" (voluptuousness of hell). This singular combination of lust and damnation, this descent into the personal hell of the artist ruled over by his disordered senses and transmuted into a music where darkness and light, evil and good, the lust of the body and the transcendence of the spirit, are inextricably interwoven, constituted a moral challenge to more than one novelist. It is not by chance that Baudelaire spoke in his letter to Wagner of a "satanic religion," indeed a "counter-religion" his music had revealed to him. Among the many voices raised in the West attacking or defending Wagner in the second half of the nineteenth century, that of the opium-smoking French poet was the most prophetic. Yet he welcomes Wagner's music for precisely the same reasons that made Tolstoy and Nietzsche reject it: the unbridled freedom granted to music to sing of the depths of the human soul that no work of fiction had as yet dared to explore, the music's ecstatic portrayal of the damnation of the senses which the philistine's belief in the enlightenment of the human mind through progress utterly repudiated.

Very few novelists could altogether elude the fascination of this music. Here, for the first time, was an art form which, very much in advance of its time, dared to portray what had till then been unmentionable in literature. It was a music of desire unfulfilled, of longing so intense that it could be embodied only in figures taken from legend and myth, a chromaticism of passion that seemed not of this earth and yet was a faithful mirror of man's striving for wholeness through the transformation of his bodily essence into the perfect communion of two souls. This was not a music of pleasant tunes and melodies that could be hummed in a moment of passing musical reminiscences. Wagner's music contains no "petite phrase" to be associated in the listener's mind with the nostalgic memory of a past incident in one's life such as the taste of a madeleine dipped into a cup of tea, the perfume of flowers, or love gained or lost. It demands a total involvement on the part of the listener which allows no respite from anguish. It is the tormented cry of a soul that knows no fulfillment except in the long drawn-out agony of death. The leitmotifs of love's longing with which *Tristan* begins and that of love's death with which it ends are daring musical metaphors transcribing the ecstasies of the soul that finds fulfillment in the act of love only at the moment of dying.

2

In England, among the great novelists of the age, D. H. Lawrence alone recognized the perils that faced the listener who submitted too wholeheartedly to the equivocal fascination of such music. In 1912 Wagner makes a somewhat unexpected appearance in one of Lawrence's early novels, *The Trespasser*, when the main character, a professional musician, is heard whistling the bird music out of *Siegfried*, pieces of *Tristan*, and the Spring Song from the *Valkyrie*. The unbroken stroke of a train speeding through the night makes him "think of the well-known movement from the Valkyrie Ride." Helen, in self-conscious abandon, "for ever hummed fragments of the *Tristan*. As she stood on the rock she sang, in her little half-articulate way, bits of Isolde's love, bits of Tristan's anguish, to Sigmund."[14]

Many years later Lawrence described the music of *Tristan* as an escape from man's awareness of his physical being, a substitute of doubtful validity for what he considered to be the freedom of the body to fulfill itself in the sexual act. Listening to the music of *Tristan* is represented by him as a sort of musical self-abuse which, though it might titillate the imagination, leaves the desires of the body unfulfilled. When he compares works of literature such as Boccaccio's *Tales* where sex is treated without the inhibiting compulsions of guilt and shame to Wagner's music, he thinks of *Tristan and Isolde* as being "very near to pornography", for, says he, Wagner himself when he composed his music must have been "in the state where the strongest instincts have collapsed, and sex has become something slightly obscene, to be wallowed in, but despised."[15] Lawrence's approach to literature, the arts and music never deviates from the criterion of instinctual fulfillment as opposed to psychological evasiveness. His concern with music, as his novel *Aaron's Rod* amply illustrates, is identical with his concern with the liberation of the body from the suffocating embraces of the soul.

Though himself a master of the word and at home in the language of literature, he makes the central figure of the novel a musician whose flute is indeed the "rod" that represents his own independent way of life and his self-sufficiency as a human being, but is equally symbolical of fulfillment through the act of sex. The rod may either blossom or break according to the victory or defeat that issue from human contact. But when the rod assumes its original function of being a flute, it produces music of a distinctly non-Wagnerian kind. The tune it plays is "pure, mindless, exquisite" with a fluidity which fills the hearer "with strange exasperation ... to the point of intolerable anger."[16] It is a music that speaks of man alone, obstinately clinging to his "intrinsic and central aloneness [which] was the very center of his being."[17] When Aaron wishes to express ideas through his music they cannot be translated into words and concepts but are "dark and invisible, as electric vibrations are invisible no matter how many words they may purport." Lawrence, now speaking in his own voice, apologizes for having to use words in order to translate "the inaudible music of [Aaron's] conscious soul" which, Lawrence adds, "conveyed his meaning in him quite as clearly as I convey it in words: probably much more clearly."[18] Aaron is fascinated by the power of his rod to "make music" as if its magic could transform the inert into the quick, the somnolence of passive living into intense and yet always playful activity. At one point in the narrative Aaron tells the Marquesa that music makes him feel diabolical. He evidently refers here to the absence of any emotional surfeit, any clogging sensuality, and thus the tune he is playing suffers a metamorphosis into something nonhuman, almost indeed animal-like. Lawrence describes Aaron's playing of the tune before the Marchesa in the following way: "It was a clear, sharp, lilted run-and-fall of notes, not a tune in any sense of the word, and yet a melody: a bright, quick, sound of pure animation: a bright, quick, animate noise, running and pausing. It was like a bird's singing, in that it had no human emotion or passion or intention or meaning—a ripple and poise of animate sound."[19] This is Aaron's breakthrough "beyond this dank and beastly dungeon of feelings and moral necessity", his musical reaching out towards "a bit of true, limpid freedom". With it comes desire, "the powerful male passion, arrogant, royal, Jove's thunderbolt."[20]

Lawrence's identification of Aaron's "rod" with the phallus, not as a metaphor of procreation but of the indomitable, unconquerable power of instinct over intellect, of moral freedom over moral compulsion, will scarcely shock the reader of today. In 1922 when the novel first appeared in print it was hailed by the few as "the most important thing that has happened to English literature since the war."[21] Even fewer seem to have realized the musical—as distinguished from the literary—significance of this book. At a time when Wagner was all the rage among the concert-going public, Lawrence's was a lone voice in a musical wilderness. Unfashionable as he then was, condemned for being a social and intellectual upstart, despised for his uninhibited exposure of sexual hypocrisy among the upper middle-classes, the purity of his motives constantly put into doubt, he gave England an anti-Wagnerian novel, probably without himself being fully aware of the musical implications created by his flute-playing hero. For *Aaron's Rod* is not meant to be a battle-cry for or against any kind of musical tradition. Now, some half-century after its publication, it rather appears to be an unintentional contribution to the dispute (of which Lawrence in all likelihood was unaware) between the Wagnerians and the anti-Wagnerians in literature.

3

The most articulate among the novelists who took up a stand with regard to the new music of moral ambiguity was Thomas Mann. Having adapted Wagner's complex syntax of leitmotifs to the structure of the novel, he found himself compelled to formulate an attitude towards the psychology underlying the formal conception of fiction musicalized. The irrational itself had to be tamed by being verbalized. As his relation to Wagner's music was at all times divided between intense admiration and no less intense suspicion of, if not actually hostility to, those very same elements that could not but shock the philistine, his early stories and novels reflect his split attitude towards the effects of this music on his fictitious characters. When, in 1918, he sums up in an essay what he had previously portrayed in his creative writings, namely that a prolonged preoccupation with Wagner's music may become a kind of mania, a surrender, he calls it, to what is morally "corrupting and self-consuming" (verzehrend),[22] he merely provides a theoretical framework for what his fiction had so eloquently expressed before.

There are various layers of meaning which contribute to the complexity of Mann's use of the thematic material derived from Wagner's music. Within the context of his fictitious universe ironic significances abound, especially in musical episodes. At times the highest praise for Wagner's *Tristan* is put into the mouth of characters who are, by temperament, upbringing, or the circumstances of their life, least qualified to give expression to it. Similarly, *Tristan* may be condemned by people whose cultural prejudices and preconceptions disqualify them from making any relevant critical judgment about this or any other music. Thus, both admiration and contempt being placed within a context of satire, frequently imply the very opposite of what the speaker intends. It is a subtle and highly sophisticated procedure. For apart from revealing the various motives upon which musical discrimination may be based, it also serves the purpose of illustrating the equivocal nature of most pronouncements about music.

The first and most complex of the speakers is Tonio Kröger. This Hamlet-like figure of a modern intellectual finds himself condemned to the life of an outsider and therefore feels himself cast out from the simple and healthy experience of living, as others do, unreflectingly and without the inhibiting restraints of his over-alert consciousness. In his letter to Lisaweta he bitterly complains (as Wagner himself had once complained in a letter to Mathilde von Wesendonck and Nietzsche never tired of reminding his friends) of the status of the artist who instead of participating in life has to portray the life of others in works of fiction, be it in literature or in music. What, finally, he is concerned with is not merely the unsatisfactory situation of the artist in society but the artist's necessarily ambiguous, if not actually amoral, influence on the average bourgeois sensibility. And yet, while Tonio Kröger writes the following lines, the reader is aware of a singular fusion of contradictory emotions. For, at the end of the letter, he calls his attitude towards the bourgeois "a gentle envy, a touch of contempt and no little innocent bliss." As an artist he cannot help envying the simple-minded, the unsophisticated, the uncorruptible.

But what, he asks, would be the effect of Wagner's *Tristan* on them? "Take the most miraculous case of all," he writes in his letter, "take the most typical and therefore the most powerful of artists, take such a morbid and profoundly equivocal work as *Tristan and Isolde*, and look at the effect it has on a healthy young man of thoroughly normal feelings."[23] As a comic counterpart to this cry of anguish there is Hanno's music teacher in *Buddenbrooks*, Old Pfühl, who when asked for his opinion about Wagner's music exclaims, "This is demagogy, blasphemy, insanity, madness! It is perfumed fog, shot through with lightning! It is the end of honesty in art."

This mixture of the serious and the comic characterizes all references to Wagner's music in Mann's early fiction. He knew, of course, of Wagner's own doubts as to the validity of his art when measured by the standards of bourgeois normality. What, therefore, amazed and frightened Thomas Mann most was Wagner's own timidity, almost amounting to self-torment, when he expressed his fear as to the possible effect his art might have on the "healthy" mind of the uninitiated. Did he not, in a letter, express his hope, after finishing the third act of *Tristan*, for "mediocre performances" only? For "completely good performances would drive the people crazy [muessen die Leute verrückt machen]—I cannot imagine otherwise."[24]

Two of Mann's early stories deal with the effect of Wagner's music on emotionally vulnerable characters. In the first which he named *Tristan*, a poet of minor literary gifts becomes infatuated with the wife of a prosperous businessman. Both are patients in a T. B. Sanatorium. At one time she used to be a pianist of some distinction. When he asks her, one evening, to play something for him on the piano, she plays extracts from *Tristan*, a twilight performance with disastrous consequences. For Frau Klöterjahn—Thomas Mann always had a remarkable gift for inventing the most comically extravagant, in this particular case the most unmusical, names for his characters—dies that same night of a ruptured blood-vessel. This twentieth-century Tristan brought up-to-date, though somewhat damaged, decides on the spur of the moment and under the impact of his personal tragedy, to write a letter to the distressed husband. It is not a letter of condolence but of contempt for the bourgeois who had never listened to *Tristan* because he was incapable of transcending his philistine normality. The writer of the letter despises not only the uncomprehending husband but his healthy baby-son and the future in store for him. Thus, he puts on paper these remarkable lines: "But your son . . . is living and flourishing. Perhaps he will continue in the way of his father, become a well-fed, trading, tax-paying citizen; a capable, philistine pillar of society; in any case, a tone-deaf, normally functioning individual, responsible, sturdy, and stupid, troubled by no doubts."[25] The myth has been deflated, the legendary figures brought down to earth, the musical ecstasis, finally, identified with disease and ultimate physical disintegration.

What is being satirized here is not merely Frau Klöterjahn's playing *Tristan* to her infatuated friend, but the equivocal fascination with Tristan's musical yearning and Isolde's *Liebestod* which Thomas Mann so often described as the orgiastic and profoundly questionable fulfillment of all that occidental music had ever stood for. The transmutation of this music into sickness and death as exemplified in this story is pathetic to the extent of being grotesque. The narrative instead of leading to a tragic conclusion, ends with the farcical letter and the husband's scandalized, but still perfectly articulate oral reply. For though he hears no music, he is still a loyal representative of all those values that uphold a code of decency in human relationships and he thus finds it quite natural to resist the onslaught of an art that has no right to speak for the feelings of the common man. By deflating the myth Thomas Mann conveys the sense of inadequacy that overcomes the "well-fed, trading, tax-paying" hearer when he is compelled to come to terms with the music. By placing the story in a sanatorium and translating the legendary hero and heroine into T. B. patients, he—in the most "civilized" manner possible—reduces the music of *Tristan* to human proportions. The term "human" acquires ironic connotations when used thus, though this may, finally, depend on the reader's own prejudices and expectations as to the effects of musical equivocation on his spiritual well-being.

The second story, *The Blood of the Walsung*, is more explicitly still a tale of moral disintegration. Here it is not the adultery committed by Tristan and Isolde that concerns Mann, but the incest between brother and sister, the story of Siegmund and Sieglinde as transposed into music in Wagner's *Valkyrie*. The social setting of Thomas Mann's story is indeed conducive to the growth of emotional deviation. Brother and sister (who are twins) belong to a vaguely outlined upper-class family in postwar Germany and are used to a life of leisure and comfort, accepting the context of spiritual decay into which they were born as a kind of aristocratic privilege. They are children of surfeit, excessively pampered by material well-being and thus flourish best of all in the perfumed hothouse atmosphere of self-indulgence. They are naturally fond of each other, a fondness which still gropes in the darkness of unawakened sensuality, innocent of any erotic undertones, unaware of any possible perils to their fragile, vulnerable selves.

A visit to the opera proves to be a traumatic experience. Wagner's *Valkyrie* is being performed, the first act representing the meeting between Siegmund and Sieglinde, their mutual recognition, their incestuous embrace. When Sieglinde falls into her brother's arms "the music swelled into a roaring, foaming whirlpool of passion—swirled and swirled, and with one mighty throb stood still."[26] This entrancing music casts a spell on the nineteen year old twins. Not only do they surrender to the excess of unrestrained passion which the music expresses, they, on their return home, reenact in the privacy of her bedroom the scene they had just now witnessed on the stage. She welcomes her brother's advances not because of some inherent moral corruption. The impact of the music was such that whatever inhibitions might have existed before were swept away. The end of Thomas Mann's story shows us the two helpless adolescents surrendering to the disease the germs of which had lain dormant in them long before they heard the music. Not flowers of evil but rather a pair of lovers who in their despair, as in Shakespeare's sonnet, are consumed by that which they were nourished by. Thomas Mann in describing this final submission to the sickness of the soul uses similar language as in his description of the music at the end of the first act of Wagner's opera, only, once more, translated, if not actually deflated, into human terms: "She did not blush at his half-spoken, turbid, wild imaginings; his words enveloped her senses like a mist, they drew her down whence they had come, to the borders of the kingdom she had never entered ... They breathed it in, this fragrance, with languid and voluptuous abandon, like self-centered invalids, consoling themselves for the loss of hope. They forgot themselves in caresses, which took the upper hand, passing over into a tumult of passion, dying away into a sobbing."[27]

Terms such as "emotional deviation" are themselves equivocal within the context of a musical experience of such intensity. Would it not then be true to say that it is the vulnerable in particular who are attracted to the violence of such music, uprooting their already weakened convictions and beliefs as to the existence of a moral framework within which their emotional life must take place or else break to pieces, unresistingly surrendering to disintegration as the sweetest of all the poisons that makes life bearable? Thomas Mann, in his stories, does not ask such questions. His concern, as so often in his longer fiction, is not so much with man as with a metaphysical problem of which the human being is merely a frail symbol of imperfection. The musical experience as an invitation to submit to the darkness of the irrational, the wordless, the undefinable, raises questions of a philosophical no less than psychological nature. If this surrender is complete, little remains of man's spiritual essence, his power to think, to analyse, and to use language so as to put order into chaos. Thomas Mann when he does answer these questions, will have to be content with more equivocations: for, after all the metaphysical questions that fill his books have been asked, he returns to the "self-centered invalid" as he calls man

in all his pitiable vulnerability, and finds him to be more equivocal still than Wagner's music had made him out to be.

Already at the end of his *Buddenbrooks*, he had turned young
Hanno, the last scion of a family which at one time had been
pillars of society into a music-maker on a small scale, an impro-
vising daydreamer on the piano. As decay sets in and the family
disintegrates, and with it all those forces that made for material
prosperity and moral leadership, Hanno escaping to his piano
from a reality he has not the strength to face, becomes an
emblematic figure symbolizing the decline not merely of a family but of middle-class society in general. Dissonance and
chromaticism are the musical symptoms of the darkness and
disorder into which western civilization is going to plunge. Little
Hanno's improvisations invite comparison with *Tristan*: yet it is
only an aimless musical meandering from one chromatic modulation to the next, but always centering on one "short-winded,
pitiful invention". For Hanno's imagination is limited by his
ignorance of musical structure and by the immaturity of his
visions. All he knows is the anguish that is within him and that
calls for expression. But his anguish undergoes no variation,
always returning where it started from, directionless and self-
consuming, "questionless, complaining, protesting, demanding,
dying away." It is the leitmotif of sickness and decline, a parody
of Wagner's gigantic inventiveness, the music of a soul fascinated by its unfulfilled longing and watching its irresistible fall
into hell with absorbed and horrified interest.

Thomas Mann's concern with Hanno as a symptom of spiritual collapse is merely marginal. The description of his improvisation at the piano, however, is given at considerable length.
The character of parody is preserved: yet the theme that constitutes the essence of Hanno's musical imagining is expressive of
the sickness of the soul out of which this "pitiable invention"
grew: "The fanatical worship of this worthless trifle, this scrap
of melody, this brief, childish harmonic invention only a bar and
a half in length, had about it something ascetic and religious—
something that contained the essence of faith and renunciation.
There was a quality of the perverse in the insatiability with
which it was produced and revelled in: there was a sort of cynical
despair; there was a longing for joy, a yielding to desire, in the
way the last drop of sweetness was, as it were, extracted from the

melody, till exhaustion, disgust, and satiety supervened. Then, at last, at last, in the weariness after excess, a long arpeggio in the minor trickled through, mounted a tone, resolved itself in the major, and died in mournful lingering away."[28]

The morally equivocal nature of the musical experience remains Thomas Mann's preoccupation whenever music is mentioned in his work. His particular interest is at first with the young and yet unformed, the innocent searchers for truth, the grail seekers, the Parsivals from whom alone salvation may come. Yet education through music is the kind of spiritual adventure that only the morally strong can face. According to Settembrini in *The Magic Mountain*, music weakens and softens the moral fiber, its message is dubious, irresponsible, complacent. It is an opiate that sends the hearer to sleep, obscures his reasoning power, and encourages mental inertia and spiritual stagnation. Settembrini who tries to convince his young friend and admirer, Hans Castorp, to look upon music with suspicion as being "a gift of the Devil", indeed identifies music with disease because it does not serve the purpose of human progress. His antagonist, Naphta the Jesuit, equally concerned for the spiritual well-being of the simple-minded, innocent, and essentially normal young man, replies to these rhetorical outbursts by pointing out that life, and especially the life of the spirit, would be unbearably monotonous without the corrupting influence of the diseased, the fertilizing power of the irrational, the creative urge of the damned. For, he asks, "had not the normal, since time was, lived in the achievement of the abnormal?"[29]

Thomas Mann's position has always been that of "the bourgeois who has strayed into art" and who, as some of his characters, submitted to the attractions of the demonic in order to portray the better the blessing and the damnation that are involved in intense commitment to music. By cultivating a divided attitude he could not always avoid fighting on both sides of the fence. Unable to resist the blandishments of the irrational he yet speaks the language of reason and progress. Always ready to stand up in defense of the intellect and the word used to communicate its achievements among men, he willingly surrenders to the half-articulate, the invisible, the intangible which is the essence of music. Among twentieth-century novelists,

Thomas Mann is the one who has turned equivocation itself into an art.

The music which so powerfully attracts and repels these novelists and which they so insistently introduce into their fiction points towards chaos. Tolstoy is moved to tears and is morally outraged while listening to Beethoven's music. Thomas Mann's love for Wagner is consistently shown to clash with his admiration for the bourgeois virtues of moderation and self-restraint. Fascinated by the apparently irresistible appeal of Wagner's musical sensuousness, his belief in a moral order underlying all civilized conduct falters and is, ultimately, defeated by the music. D.H. Lawrence's creation of his flute-playing protagonist whose music conveys a melodic simplicity originating in some primeval age long before the invention of polyphony and counterpoint is rooted in a similar suspicion that the then fashionable surrender to musical dissolution may finally lead to self-destructive emotional anarchy.

Reality perceived through the eye rather than the ear evokes considerably less equivocal responses. Imagination absorbs what the eye sees, the mind defines it and gives it a name; although the portrait of a beautiful face or of a loving couple may arouse strong emotions of a distinctly erotic nature, these emotions are visually determined and, thus, like the paintings themselves two-dimensional involving little, if any, psychological ambiguity. A novelist who introduces a painting into a work of fiction may indeed "suggest the symbols, reveal the characters and emphasize the themes of his books". Analogies are readily available, for the visual element to which characters in the novel respond "matches and heightens the psychological significance of the action."[30] Assuming that the painting in question has no moral message to deliver, the characters will remain morally unaffected by it. At best the painting will teach them how to see, for as Virginia Woolf observes, "painting and writing have much to tell each other; they have much in common. The novelist after all wants to make us see."[31]

Lawrence is an instance of considerable interest. Throughout his life his natural inclination has been towards painting rather than towards music. He frequently tried his hand at painting and towards the end of his life exhibited some of his drawings in a London gallery. On grounds of immorality quite incomprehensible to us today, the police closed down the exhibition and confiscated the pictures. When Lawrence wrote about painting he stressed the kind of spiritual awareness which an adequate response to visual art should foster. "I believe," he says in an essay entitled 'Making Pictures,' "one can only develop one's visionary awareness by close contact with the vision itself; that is, by knowing pictures, real vision pictures, and by dwelling on them, and really dwelling in them. It is a great delight to dwell in a picture."[32] Lawrence never advised anyone to "dwell" in a piece of music. He must have realized the perils involved in too close a commitment to an experience of so intense and morally equivocal a nature.

There are many more paintings than musical pieces in Lawrence's novels. One of his earlier works, *The White Peacock* (1911) was inspired by a somewhat Pre-Raphaelite painting by the painter Greifenhagen (1862–1931) representing "a swarthy Pan figure, of great vigour and vitality" lifting "a pale . . . young woman off her feet" and pressing "her half-naked bosom against his own body." Actually, "the painting represents an ideal of 'splendid uninterrupted passion' [these are Lawrence's own words] that none of the characters in the novel is able to achieve."[33] The moment of inspiration occurred a few years before the writing of the novel when he first set eyes on the painting. The way it affected him is described in a letter to a friend: "As for Greifenhagen's 'Idyll,' it moves me almost as if I were in love myself. Under its intoxication, I have flirted madly this Christmas; I have flirted myself half in love."[34]

Lawrence "dwelt" in the painting until the novel was written. The passions this painting aroused could be satisfied—even if only partially—in a straightforward and unambiguous way. If there is emotional equivocation in the novel it is the one that Lawrence himself projected into the painting. Not the scene of "uninterrupted passion" but Lawrence's response to it and his way of using it in his novel may be open to psychological comment. But what would the response have been, had Greifenhagen been a composer rather than a painter: how would the novelist have been affected by the suggestive eroticism of this scene conveyed in terms of a musical vision of much greater intensity than any painting could possibly express? Passion communicated through sounds exacts from the listener a far more explicit commitment, the surrender to an inner experience immeasurably more demanding than whatever "dwelling in a painting" may do to a reader or to a character in a work of fiction.

The erotic and amoral appeal of music has been the object of studies since the time of Plato (who regarded it as an ethical discipline). Some of the most eminent novelists of our age carried the moral equivocation inherent in the musical experience to its logical conclusion: if human beings are attracted to music because it satisfies some of our most powerful instinctual drives, modern fiction, more aware of the association between musical and erotic arousal, attempted to portray and interpret this relationship in terms of the character susceptible to such arousal. The end may be either emotional chaos or the realization of a far deeper inner harmony than the experience of visual art could ever supply. The novelist's discovery that, in musical terms, no consonance could be achieved without a preceding dissonance provided him with a musical texture in the writing of his novel of considerable density and complexity.

Notes to Chapter Four

1. Hindemith, *A Composer's World.*
2. Roger Sessions, *The Musical Experience of Composer, Performer, Listener,* p. 67.
3. Deryck Cooke, *op. cit.,* p. 270.
4. Richard Wagner, *Beethoven,* pp. 55–56.
5. Leo Tolstoy, *What is Art?* (finished in 1897), p. 222; p. 248.
6. Quoted in *Beethoven: Letters, Journals, Conversations,* p. 89 (The authenticity of this letter has been disputed.)
7. Sergei Tolstoy, *Tolstoy Remembered–By His Son,* p. 226.
8. Leo Tolstoy, *The Kreutzer Sonata,* p. 214.
9. Leo Tolstoy, *ibid.,* p. 219. Tolstoy's own married life, soon after he finished writing *The Kreutzer Sonata* may be used as evidence either for or against the message so explicitly stated in the story. At that time Tolstoy noted down in his diary: "And what if another baby came? How ashamed I should be, especially in front of my children. They will compare the date of conception with that of publication of 'The Kreutzer Sonata'." His wife writing in her diary, adds her own sarcastic comment: "If those who have read and are reading 'The Kreutzer Sonata' could have a glimpse of Lyovochka's [Tolstoy's] love life, if they could see what makes him so gay and kind, they would hurl this idol down from the pedestal they have put him on."

(Edward Garden, "Tchaikovsky and Tolstoy", in *Music and Letters*, vol. 55, No. 3, (July 1974) 312).

10 From Max Nordau, *Degeneracy*, as quoted in Bernard Shaw's *The Sanity of Art* (1895), p. 327.

11. Leo Tolstoy, *What is Art?* p. 215.

12. Friedrich Nietzsche, *The Case of Wagner*, pp. 155–156; p. 164; p. 166 (author's italics).

13. Baudelaire, *Critique Littéraire et Musicale*, p. 364.

14. D. H. Lawrence, *The Trespasser*, pp. 27, 91, 143, 194.

15. D. H. Lawrence, "Pornography and Obscenity", pp. 36 and 39. See also Denis de Rougemont's chapter on *Tristan*, in his *Passion and Society*, a more elaborate condemnation of Wagner's opera and the "distressing morbidity" of its melodies which "disclose a world in which carnal desire has become no more than an ultimate and impure apathy of souls in process of curing themselves of life." (p. 230).

16. D. H. Lawrence, *Aaron's Rod*, p. 15.

17. *Ibid.*, p. 173.

18. *Ibid.*, p. 175.

19. *Ibid.*, p. 241.

20. *Ibid.*, p. 269.

21. From Middleton Murry's review of *Aaron's Rod*, published in *The Nation and Athenaeum;* quoted in Harry T. Moore, *The Intelligent Heart*, p. 366.

22. Thomas Mann, *Betrachtungen eines Unpolitischen* (1918), p. 32.

23. Thomas Mann, *Tonio Kröger*, p. 179. Compare this with Nietzsche's indignant exclamation: "Is a more profound, a *weightier* effect to be found in the theatre? Just look at these youths—rigid, pale, breathless! These are the Wagnerians—they understand nothing about music—and yet Wagner becomes master over them . . ." (*The Case of Wagner*, p. 172) (author's italics).

24. Quoted in Thomas Mann's *Adel des Geistes*, "*Leiden and Grösse Richard Wagners*", (1933), p. 421 (my own translation).

25. Thomas Mann, *Tristan*, in *Stories of a Lifetime*, p. 135.

26. *The Blood of the Walsung*, in *Stories of Three Decades*, p. 351.

27. *Ibid.*, p. 357.

28. *Buddenbrooks*, (published in 1901), p. 588.

29. *The Magic Mountain*, pp. 113–114; p. 587.

30. Jeffrey Meyers, *Painting and the Novel*, p. 31.

31. *Ibid.*, p. 2; from Virginia Woolf, *Walter Sickert: A Conversation*, London, 1934, p. 22.

32. *Ibid.*, p. 53; from D.H. Lawrence, *Phoenix II*, London 1948, p. 605.

33. *Ibid.*, p. 48.

34. *Ibid.*, p. 46; from a letter to Blanche Jennings, 31 December 1908, in D.H. Lawrence, *Collected Letters*, ed. Harry Moore, London 1962, p. 44.

V
The Musical Erotic

1

The full title of Kierkegaard's essay on *Don Giovanni* is: "The Immediate Stages of the Erotic, or, The Musical Erotic." It was written under the impact of Mozart's music which, as he wrote in his Journal of 1819, "has so diabolically gripped me that I can never forget it. It was the play that drove me, like Elvira, out of the cloister's quiet night."[1] What so overwhelmed Kierkegaard was the power of music to seduce the listener by what he repeatedly calls its "sensuous genius." As the musical experience transcends discursive thinking and is not amenable to the language of words, it may be described as "a species of the immediate," observes Kierkegaard, thus defining the "musical erotic" as part of a nonverbal reality. The mirror in which the sensuous is most faithfully reflected is, according to him, music. As all forms of speech are foreign to the musical erotic, Kierkegaard states that "Music everywhere limits language," evidently not because it says too little but because it says too much.

Music, accordingly, can only be defined in paradoxical terms —as a form of anti-language, as wordless speech, as meaning devoid of all intellectual content. Kierkegaard's analysis of *Don Giovanni* and *Figaro* thus makes use of metaphorical language abounding in erotic evocation such as "the sensuous awakening," the "dawning of desire," "intoxication," or "drunk with love." Moreover, and for obvious reasons, he is little concerned with the text of the two operas but almost exclusively with the music. Its effect on the hearer, according to him, must inevitably be a weakening of the moral fiber, a loosening of restraints, a surrender of "desire" at the very moment when the mind is lulled asleep and abandons itself to the ecstatic mastery of sounds. Kierkegaard's remarks—as Tolstoy's after him—have explicitly sexual overtones; for, says he, "our age does offer many horrible proofs of the daemonic power with which music may lay hold upon an individual, and this individual in turn, grip and capture a multitude, especially women, in the seductive snare of fear, by means of the all-disturbing power of voluptuousness . . . This art, more than any other, frequently harrows its votaries in a terrible manner."[2]

An uncontrolled response of the hearer's musical sensibility to the composer's creation of a world of eros may indeed be a harrowing experience. It is liable to produce psychic instability of a singularly violent nature especially in those who are more than ordinarily susceptible to emotional arousal through music. The previous chapter gave some instances from the work of Thomas Mann where Wagner's transmutation of myth into music led to powerful psychic disturbances characterized by distinctly erotic manifestations. Kierkegaard's attitude to music is more explicit still: there is no place for equivocation in his essay. It is Mozart, the very paradigm of all that is considered pure, wholesome, and uncorruptible in music, who is taken to be an embodiment of that principle of the sensuous to which Kierkegaard applies all the qualities of musical seductiveness. The aim of such seduction through harmonious sound may be assumed to be sexual arousal even if Kierkegaard does not say so in so many words. It is tempting to carry the argument to its unavoidable—if somewhat disconcerting—conclusion. In the words of a contemporary musicologist who, however, does not refer to Kierkegaard's essay, the ideal hearer of music will be the one who succeeds "to get inside . . . to 'enter into' the music so that it has some of the immediacy of carnal knowledge."[3] What happens to the hearer if and when he succeeds in achieving this total immersion into music may thus be compared to the sexual act where the hearer fulfills his musical function by getting to "know" the musical work as the feminine counterpart of his own psyche. The encounter between hearer and music may produce a paroxysm of such intensity that no musicological formula would be adequate to describe it. A description of such an encounter is, however, found in Berlioz's autobiography when he relates his reaction to a musical selection he especially liked: "My whole being seems to vibrate; at first it is a delightful pleasure, in which reason does not appear to participate at all.

The emotions increase in direct ratio with the force or grandeur of the agitation in the circulation of the blood. My pulses beat violently, tears which usually give evidence of the crisis of a paroxysm, indicate only a progressive stage, and a greater excitement and agitation is to follow. When the crisis is really reached there occur spasmodic contractions of the muscles, a trembling in all the limbs, a total numbness of feet and hands, a partial paralysis of the nerves of vision and hearing. I no longer can see and can hardly hear."[4]

As this is not the description of any particular musical occasion, it makes little difference whether it was the music of Mozart or Wagner that produced this shattering effect on him. Reactions of this kind can no longer be classified as being either normal or abnormal. They are of little clinical interest, as there is no evidence to indicate that Berlioz suffered from psychopathological disturbances when he responded to music the way he did. For the same reason it is of small interest that in the opinion of some pathologists epileptic fits can be cured by music while others have collected evidence to prove that such fits can be brought about by the playing of a tune on an instrument. All that can be said with some degree of certainty is that music may produce states of emotional agitation bordering on the compulsive, the ecstatic, or the insane. Kierkegaard, for instance, in opposition to most modern psychologists, did not believe in a cure of mental instability through the medium of music. For, in his opinion, "if one employs music, one uses entirely the wrong method, and makes the patient even more unbalanced."[5] If the loss of balance is due to an excess of pleasure following an experience of such overwhelming intensity as Berlioz describes in his autobiography, Kierkegaard's warning against musical overindulgence appears to be legitimate. The question that may be asked —and of which some modern psychologists are more painfully aware than Kierkegaard could ever have been—is whether a return to "normal" mental equilibrium is worth the loss of such musical ecstasis, in other words, whether the total surrender to the "musical erotic" and its bewildering effect on the psyche is not a very small price to pay for the paroxysm of fulfillment which is in store for the listener and which evidently lies outside the framework of reality as experienced by the non-listener. In such a relative context of evaluation as to what

constitutes a "normal" reaction to reality, psychological concepts such as mental stability, emotional balance, and resistance
to the "sensuous genius" of music, acquire a more than passing
ambiguity. For it is no longer moral equivocation that is involved but the overpowering longing for pleasure induced,
strengthened, and brought to a climax by music.

2

The assumption that musical arousal brings out specifically feminine psychic characteristics in man and that music is—among all
the arts—the most suggestive metaphor of femininity appears to
a considerable number of novelists to be self-evident. Though
Kierkegaard's essay limits itself to the "seductiveness" of Mozart's two operas only, there is reason to assume that music of
any kind and by any composer may invite similar conclusions. In
order to express the "erotic" genius of music in a work of fiction
the writer will make use of images where the tendency of music
towards the amorphous, the intangible, the immeasurable is
fused with suggestions of continuity and rhythmic recurrence.
As language lacks those elements of polarity which could express mutually contradictory musical qualities, novelists have recourse to metaphors of water, flowing or stagnant, using a diversity of images evoking the sea, lakes, rivers, and rain. Implied in
the metaphor is an image of the listener who by immersing himself in music, "melts" into it, "dissolves," and finally, "drowns"
in it. The associations such metaphors arouse are related to a
sense of relaxation and stability. Equally suggestive are images
of transparency, of timelessness, of the regular coming and going of waves. The calm surface of the sea, the unruffled expanse
of lakes, or rivers quietly flowing across parched landscapes
thirsting for rain are associated in the writer's mind with images
of abundance and fertility, the return to some primordial element of being, the very essence of femininity, the cradle of all
life.
    Thus, Proust describes the effect of Vinteuil's "little phrase,"
played on the violin, with the help of sea-images when he speaks
of the melody "trying to surge upwards in a flowing tide of
sounds," while the piano part is "multiform, coherent, level, and

breaking everywhere in melody like the deep blue tumult of the sea."[6] Young Jean Christophe, in Romain Rolland's novel of a musician, imagines Mozart as belonging "almost always to water. He was a meadow by the side of the river, a transparent mist floating over the water, a spring shower, or a rainbow."[7] Young Stephen Dedalus, in Joyce's *Portrait*, listening to the voices of people singing in unison associates the song with the flow of water "over the fantastic fabrics of his mind, dissolving them painlessly and noiselessly as a sudden wave dissolves the sandbuilt turrets of children."[8] In his dreams music comes to him once more as a power that soothes his mind, and restores his strength to live, "O what sweet music! His soul was all dewy wet. Over his limbs in deep pale cool waters waves of light had passed. He lay still, as if his soul lay amid cool waters, conscious of faint sweet music ... A spirit filled him, pure as the purest water, sweet as dew, moving as music."[9] The final and most revealing passage occurs towards the end of the novel. Here the feminine nature of the music he hears in his mind is directly related to the body of his beloved, "Yes, it was her body he smelt; a wild and languid smell: the tepid limbs over which his music had flowed desirously and the secret soft linen upon which her flesh distilled odour and a dew."[10]

When Virginia Woolf listens to an early Mozart string quartet she translates the sound of the music into "fountain jets; drops descend ... washing shadows over the silver fish." And, later on, evidently referring to the second movement, visualizes "the melancholy river [that] bears us on ... the green garden, moonlit pool, lemons, lovers, and fish are all dissolved in the opal sky."[11] Spandrell, in Huxley's *Point Counter Point*, listening to Beethoven's A-minor quartet, thinks of a river "stretched away into the hot haze." For the music seems to him "like water in a parched land." And later on, "It was an unimpassioned music, transparent, pure and crystalline, like a tropical sea, an Alpine lake. Water on water, calm sliding over calm; the according of level horizons, a waveless expanse, a counterpoint of serenities ..."[12] Perhaps the least stereotyped passage occurs in a book where one would least expect it. Henry Miller's novels have achieved their equivocal reputation for the frank portrayal of a large variety of sexual activities mixed with pseudo-psychological reflections devoid of any musical connotation whatever. In the best-known of all his novels, in the very midst of descriptions that deal explicitly with sexual arousal, there occur a few remarkably evocative lines. The writer is sitting at a concert, not because of any particular love for music, but apparently to quieten and distract his mind from the embarrassing multitude of sexual encounters that fill his otherwise aimless existence, and listens to some orchestral music: "After what seems an eternity there follows an interval of semi-consciousness balanced by such a calm that I feel a great lake inside me, a lake of iridescent sheen, cool as jelly; and over this lake rising in great swooping spirals, there emerge great flocks of birds, huge birds of passage with long slim legs and brilliant plumage. Flock after flock surge up from the cool still surface of the lake and, passing under my clavicles, lose themselves in the white sea of space."[13]

The water metaphor comes naturally to the novelist in search of an image which would best describe the "flooding" of consciousness by music. The listener having "drowned" in the harmony of sounds is pleasantly aware of the loss of his consciousness amid the rising "waves" of modulated tonalities. This encounter between consciousness and music remains incomplete as long as the mind does not submit to the seduction of the feminine. The fusion between the two leads to a reenacting of the composer's creative urge in the listener's own act of response. The "child" of the union is, in effect, the meaning the musical work acquires through this self-perpetuating encounter between the mind of the hearer and the sounds which flow into it. If, as Jung says, consciousness is symbolized by the eye rather than by the ear, the mode of seeing being itself symbolical of the act of self-realization, while water stands for the primordial, the maternal source of all living things, then this meeting between hearer and music may, indeed, be described in the language of metaphor as the fertilizing encounter between the active element of conscious generation in the composer and the passive element of unconscious receptivity in the listener. Listening to music is thus a singularly "erotic" activity where the femininity latent in the listener's psyche and the masculinity implied in the very act of "performance" are fused into an all-encompassing experience of affirmation through the senses, in which the distinction between the sexes, between "active" and "passive" participation in the musical experience, is no longer of any psychological validity.

3

Kierkegaard's "musical erotic" exercises its perilous influence on composer, performer, and hearer alike. They are equally transformed by the powerful magic of musical seduction. It matters little who is the victim, who the seducer. Metaphorically speaking, father, mother, and child are interchangeable; for no one can say with precision where to draw the line between seduction and surrender, between the musical conception and the act of creation, or between the performance and the response it evokes. By identifying himself with the work, the performer reenacts the creative moment though he may be unaware of its existential origin in the composer's experience of life. The hearer by responding to the music immerses himself in what may well seem to him a music expressive of ultimate bliss and fulfillment. For the moment when the composing of sounds acquires universal significance occurs when the hearer becomes aware of the transcendent nature of the music. This miracle of transmutation is the work of the performer, be he a soloist, a whole orchestra, or the conductor interpreting the work in question. What is being interpreted as a quietly flowing river, the rise and fall of waves, the smooth surface of a lake, the purling rain on a parched landscape, may be all that remains audible of the composer's experience which conceivably was one of anguish, torment, and a desperate search for fulfillment. The most erotically seductive of his musical compositions, the most "feminine" of his works, may be the result of conscious self-discipline imposed on the shaping and patterning of sounds, the application of the ordering intellect on the musical chaos out of which a melody is born. Had the hearer known the secret source from which the music sprang he might well have questioned the validity of the "erotic" implications of an experience the very essence of which seems to undermine the foundations upon which his rational life as a thinking human being is built.

Two of the most distinguished novelists of our age placed fictitious composers as central figures in their imaginary—or partly imaginary—universe. Marcel Proust created Vinteuil who, as a "character," is entirely the offspring of Proust's imagination, while as a composer, he appears to be an unlikely combination of several musical figures with whose compositions Proust was familiar. Thomas Mann created Adrian Leverkühn, an entirely fictitious invention, both as a character and a musician; his only link with reality is the historical context into which he is placed but which, for the time being, is of no concern to us here. Now, both these figures are shown in situations of extreme "erotic" ambiguity as part of their musical identity. Vinteuil as well as Leverkühn are exposed to violent emotional upheavals because of erotically unconventional and deeply disturbing relationships which impinge upon their consciousness and stimulate their musical creativity with singular and frightening intensity.

It is in keeping with Kierkegaard's assumptions (and Thomas Mann in his short account of the origins of *Doctor Faustus* acknowledges the resemblances between the portrayal of Leverkühn's surrender to the "musical erotic" and Kierkegaard's initial thesis) that both composers in these two novels fall victim to a form of "seductiveness" which overwhelms them at the very moment of intense musical creativity. By transforming into music what must at first sight appear to the reader of the novel as a form of explicit erotic deviation, they gave to their works a tenderness and subtlety from which the grossness of all sexual evocation seems to be excluded. If anything at all meaningful can be asserted about the dictates of the "musical erotic" in the work composed under the impact of such experiences, it is that their music at that moment in their life represented their escape from conscious awareness of psychological deviation into the inviolate purity of sound.

The dilemma they face, each in his own way, is indeed erotic in a disturbingly ambiguous way. Vinteuil's anguish concerns his daughter and her lesbian relationship with a friend. Marcel who listens to Vinteuil's last composition with a more than merely "musical" ear realizes that this musical work originated in suffering caused by what to the composer was an incomprehensible relationship between his daughter and her friend, and that by a not altogether surprising coincidence, this particular composition was preserved from total loss and oblivion by that very

same lesbian friend whom Marcel also suspects of having seduced his present mistress, Albertine—whose real name in life
was more probably Albert—a realization which turns the performance of Vinteuil's music for Marcel into a bewilderingly
"erotic" revelation. Moreover, the violinist who plays the "little
phrase" with more than ordinary expressiveness is the deceptively acquiescent participant in M. de Charlus's homosexual adventures which Marcel himself has previously, in singular and
distressing circumstances, witnessed. This, however, does not
diminish but rather heightens the pleasure derived from
Vinteuil's music. The psychic disorder arising from sexual deviation which contributed in such a large measure to the creation
of this music, is now being reenacted within the context of
social pretense and "erotic" parody. Marcel's recognition of the
link between Vinteuil's very real genius and the intricate erotic
entanglements which inspired the creation and the performance
of his music, indicates Proust's own awareness that—insofar as
the composition of music is concerned—normal codes of sexual
conduct are not to be trusted and that (though he was in all
likelihood unfamiliar with Kierkegaard's essay) the "musical
erotic" dictates its laws regardless of man's formal conventions
as to what constitutes right and proper conduct in the relation
between the sexes. The question implied in the following lines
refers to the nature of musical genius itself about which Kierkegaard had given his explicit comment some decades earlier.
These are the thoughts that pass through Marcel's mind while
listening to Vinteuil's music at its most expressive: "Anyhow the
apparent contrast, that profound genius (talent too and even
virtue) and the sheath of vice in which, as had happened in the
case of Vinteuil, it is so frequently contained, preserved, was
legible, as in a popular allegory, in the mere assembly of the
guests among whom I found myself once again when the music
had come to an end . . . the proximate, immediate cause of their
presence lay in the relations that existed between M. de Charlus
and Morel . . . the remoter cause which had made this assembly
possible was that a girl living with Mlle Vinteuil in the same way
as the Baron was living with Charlie had brought to light a
whole series of works of genius."[14] Sexual inversion which plays
so large a part in Proust's work appears as a constant counterpoint to Vinteuil's music. To be able to "enter into" these

compositions, to immerse oneself in them, to absorb them the
way they wished to be absorbed, required on the part of the
performer and hearer a similar disposition, a reversal, as it were,
of sexual ethics, where masculinity and femininity no longer
have any absolute validity but are subject to modification for the
sake of increased pleasure or what Kierkegaard called "voluptuousness." M. de Charlus who loves Morel, the violinist, and
whose love may be said to be unreasonable and to most men
incomprehensible, inspired the performer to give of his best; M.
de Charlus, the lover, is in Proust's own words, doomed to
become infatuated precisely with "that type of man who has
nothing feminine about him, who is not an invert and consequently cannot love them in return, with the result that their
desire would be for ever insatiable, did not . . . their imagination
end by making them take for real men the inverts to whom they
had prostituted themselves."[15]

Music as a metaphor of the feminine here acquires an ambiguity which, though never intended by Vinteuil, appears to be an
element inseparable from the experience of composer, performer, and listener alike. Even though none of the participants
in this experience may be conscious of the reversal of sexual
ethics implied in the creative act of the composer and its mirror,
the performer, nor in the process of immersion that the listener
undergoes, it determines the singular nature of musical "seduction" which Kierkegaard commented upon after having listened
to Mozart's *Don Giovanni* and of which Marcel Proust became
uncomfortably aware as being an ominous undercurrent to the
gentle expressiveness of Vinteuil's "petite phrase."

Thomas Mann's fictitious composer, Adrian Leverkühn, is an
exceedingly more vivid and thus more complex figure than
Proust's rather colorless Vinteuil. He comes alive in every page
of the book while Vinteuil throughout the novel is merely a
shadowy, remembered presence, seen, as it were, through a mist
and at a considerable distance from the events of the fictitious
present. During most of the novel he is already dead and the
anguish of his previous existence emanates from his music only.
Yet just as Vinteuil composes his music against the background
of erotic deviation of a peculiarly harrowing kind, Adrian
Leverkühn, no less of a hermit than Vinteuil, is exposed to
attempts at "seduction" at that point in the story where he is

shown to be most susceptible to offers of friendship from a man in whom the "musical erotic" is more than commonly manifest.

In Thomas Mann's fictitious universe the artist's love is, by definition, "unreasonable" because it is without hope and does not conform to the sexual ethos of the majority. This is true of Tonio Kröger's ambivalent tenderness for Hans Hansen, Aschenbach's desperate passion for the boy Tadzio, Hans Castorp's remembered infatuation for the boy Hippe at school—later on metamorphosed into his equally hopeless love for Claudia Chauchat, and Leverkühn's relationship with the violinist Rudi Schwerdtfeger. Among these only the writer Aschenbach and the composer Leverkühn are creative artists. But all of them have in common the need for human relationships which would raise their existence above the level of the trivial and commonplace and yet provide them with satisfactions which themselves derive from their love for what Thomas Mann, in the earliest of these stories, calls the blond and blue-eyed, the mediocre and the conformist.

Leverkühn's attempts at establishing relationships with women fail for reasons inherent in the artist's psychological make-up. He always returns to the seclusion of his cell, devoting himself to musical composition without apparently being disturbed by the absence of any contact with the opposite sex. Yet the "musical erotic"—in Kierkegaard's sense of the term—is one of the basic motifs of this novel. Twice Leverkühn visits a brothel. The first time against his will, being brought there by a somewhat questionable individual whom he had requested to guide him to an eating-place, the second time deliberately and with disastrous consequences. We are concerned here with the former, Adrian's first and unintentional encounter with the feminine. It is described, not without a great deal of self-mockery, in a letter to his friend, the narrator of his life. When he realizes the kind of place his guide had brought him to, he reacts in a characteristic way: "I see an open piano, a friend, I rush up to it across the carpet and strike a chord or twain, standing up. I wot still what it was, because the harmonic problem was just in my mind, modulation from B major to C major, the brightening of a semitone step, as in the hermit's prayer in the finale of the *Freischütz*, at the entry of the timpani, trumpet, and oboes on the six-form chord of G."[16]

This escape from the crudely sexual to the musical romantic, from the sense of complete alienation experienced at the brothel to the only "friend" available at this moment, the musical instrument, establishes an unexpected and yet perfectly reasonable relation between eros and music. Music is welcomed as a release from the comedy of mistaken identity resulting in unforeseen attempts at sexual seduction. On the other hand, the modulations he plays on the piano are indicative of the kinship of music and eros in an unmistakably sexual context. One cannot help recalling that two other figures—one taken from real life, the other from fiction—both artists and musically inclined, behaved in a very similar manner in equally disconcerting circumstances. When Nietzsche unexpectedly found himself in a brothel surrounded by "half a dozen apparitions clad in glitter and gauze" who looked at him full of anticipation, he "instinctively walked over to a piano, the only being endowed with a soul in this company, and played a few chords. This saved me from my rigidity and I escaped into freedom."[17] That Mann remembered Nietzsche on more than one occasion when he wrote his novel is well known. James Joyce makes Stephan Dedalus behave in precisely the same manner when—together with Leopold Bloom—he visits the redlight district of Dublin. For when, surrounded by the prostitutes and the habitués of the brothel, he discovers a pianola, he approaches it and with two fingers "repeats once more the series of empty fifths . . ."[18] which apparently saved his mind from completely surrendering to the riot of the senses that threatened to engulf him at that moment.

The archetypal escape of the artist from the "normal" life of his contemporaries into the seclusion of music, into the voluntary isolation of the hermit, is merely another aspect of the musician's predilection for the genius of the "musical erotic" in preference to the cruder conformity of bourgeois existence. The few chords played on a piano have a liberating effect precisely because they express, in the insidious language of musical modulation, the inarticulate yearning of the artist for what cannot come to be: the ideal and complete union of two human beings free of the grossness of mere bodily contact. The freedom they acquire through musical expression constitutes, in the context of Kierkegaard's essay, the privilege of the artist to expose himself to the "musical erotic" which, in turn, implies a growing vulnerability to nonconformist seduction through musical arousal.

Thomas Mann refers to Kierkegaard's essay, which he seems to have read for the first time while writing *Doctor Faustus* in his autobiographical sketch about the origins of his novel. He finds the novel's congruence with Kierkegaard's theories on music "remarkable." But a few pages earlier he relates an episode from one of Stendhal's letters (which he was also reading at about the same time as Kierkegaard's essay) which affected the writing of his book in no less a significant way. The incident in Stendhal's letter refers to a meeting between Stendhal and a young Russian officer. Thomas Mann was particularly struck by the description of this experience because the author of *Le Rouge et le Noir*, himself a personality of undoubtedly masculine characteristics, admits that he dared not look at the young man for fear "that passion would seize upon me if I [i.e. Stendhal] were a woman."[19]

Adrian Leverkühn's relationship with the violinist Rudi Schwerdtfeger suggests a latent homosexuality in the composer which, in view of the foregoing remarks, reflects the ambivalent nature of the creative act itself. Rudi himself lacks all those qualities of masculine creativity which distinguish the composer from the performer. He was indeed commonplace in a singularly unaware and, as it frequently happens with adults who have never outgrown their childhood, embarrassingly articulate manner. Zeitblom, the narrator of Adrian's troubled life, speaks of his "blue-eyed mediocrity," but adds that he was one of those people "who always have to touch and feel—the arm, the shoulder, the elbow." It is this "fanatical male coquette" (another of Zeitblom's designations for the young violinist) who offers his friendship to the solitary composer. His intrusion into the hermit's cell constitutes the origin of emotional disorders in Leverkühn's life. For the offer of friendship is accompanied by perfectly innocent manifestations of physical intimacy, and, soon after, is followed by the suggestions of artistic collaboration, the writing of a violin concerto by Adrian for his friend to whom it would be dedicated and who would be the first to perform it in public. The language in which this suggestion is couched is metaphorical in an erotically seductive manner and touches the composer where he is most vulnerable—his longing for human warmth and contact. No other passage among the novels under discussion evokes the implications of Kierkegaard's "musical erotic" more suggestively than this: "I would ... love every note like a mother," says Rudi, "and you would be the father—it would be between us like a child, a platonic child—yes, *our* concerto."[20] The violin concerto is duly composed. The first movement is inscribed "andante amoroso" and, in the narrator's words, is "of a dulcet tenderness bordering on mockery."[21] Just as in Proust the element of mockery is present as a reminder that the "musical erotic" has more than one facet when it is reflected in the musical composition and later on in the performance and the diversity of responses it may evoke. Both composer and performer succumb to the attraction of a situation which may well be called "erotic" in so far as the masculinity of the former is in need of the femininity of the latter in order to establish the necessary link between creativity and performance. The composer is both seducer and the one who is being seduced, the performer both victim and joyful participant. While the composer submits to the "musical erotic," he is mocking himself, having surrendered to what he knows to be his own human frailty, his love for the uncomplicated, the healthy and the unaware.

Adrian Leverkühn, at the end of the book, in his madness, faithfully relates the true story of this "seduction" to an appalled audience of invited guests. His breakdown has finally loosened his tongue. Having left his cell in order to perform what he had previously composed, he, as if under some inner compulsion, reveals the distressing circumstances that led to the composing of the violin concerto, with its fusion of the sentimental and the ironic. The relationship with the young violinist is remembered as something that deeply disturbed the quiet of his hermit's existence by introducing into the tranquility of his creative life the temptations of sensuousness musically perceived and recreated. Adrian uses archaic language, a concoction of medieval German and the feverish speech rhythms of a disintegrating mind: "I had well thought that, as devil's disciple, I might love in flesh and blood what was not female, but he wooed me for my thou in boundless confidence, until I granted it."[22]

Proust and Thomas Mann place their fictitious composers in

similar contexts of emotional upheaval. Vinteuil evokes little
sympathy in spite of his very real suffering. The level of social
reportage of which Vinteuil and the response his music evokes
are a part is not conducive to the arousal of such emotions as
pity or terror, admiration or even contempt. We come to know
of Marcel's various musical illuminations as a matter of psychological interest. Our attention is engaged while our sensibility
remains uninvolved. The musical erotic as it affects Vinteuil's
compositions, their performance, and the response they inspire,
serve the purpose of a *leitmotif* accompanying Marcel's story
from beginning to end until it becomes the main theme tri-
umphing over all others and embracing all the various manifestations of the artistic impulse in Proust's work. Yet it first has to
pass through his mind and be meticulously analysed before it is
absorbed in the total texture of his novel.

Thomas Mann's treatment of the composer's defeat at the
hands of the "musical erotic" arouses the reader's compassion
to an incomparably greater extent. As a "devil's disciple" Adrian
Leverkühn—much more than the unfortunate Vinteuil—is conscious of the attractions of the flesh, especially when it appears
in the shape of innocent, blue-eyed sensuousness. And when he
is compelled to speak about it to a crowd of uncomprehending
and bewildered well-wishers, the conventional words that men
use to communicate among themselves fail to say what his music
had so tenderly and so mockingly expressed in the past. Kierkegaard's dictum that "music everywhere limits language" is no-
where as true as when the mad composer attempts to put into
words the impact of the "musical erotic" out of which his music
sprang.

4

Kierkegaard's description of the "musical erotic" as a form of
evil which the composer transmutes into harmonious music,
thereby inviting the listener to identify with a musical message
of considerable ambiguity, is the result of a personal and harrowing experience: it is too closely related to Kierkegaard's
idiosyncratic attitude to music, and to Mozart's *Don Giovanni* in
particular, to permit far-reaching generalizations. Certain composers and listeners to music may react differently. The amor-

phous nature of all music may induce a sense of blessing rather than of malevolence. What in Proust and Mann is seen to be the artist's ineluctable damnation may become a manifestation of recovery and fulfillment. The ambivalent eroticism which serves both novelists as a source of anguish and torment is reflected in the music which originates from it, that fusion of contraries in Vinteuil leading from the tender melodiousness of his sonata to the sudden assertion of violence and strength in his septet, of over-sweetness and self-mockery in Leverkühn's violin concerto. It is a music inspired by a vision of self-consuming duality composed by men who found no peace in their creative work but merely an escape from emotional distress that could not be otherwise expressed in the society of men. The solitude in which they lived provided no other form of personal salvation but through the language of music written for the ears of a few initiates only. By transforming their inner torment into sound, they expressed all that could be said, without committing themselves to the vulgar speech of the multitude.

The assumption that the creative act performed by the artist originates in his bisexual disposition does little to explain the intricate psychic processes that lead from the initial inspiration to the execution of the work of art. The fluidity and flexibility of musical modulation may, in effect, evoke associations regarding the supposedly innate femininity of the creator of music. The final product, on the other hand, the composition itself, may exhibit strongly pronounced masculine features. Any deliberate distortion of the "musical erotic" into mere feminine sensuousness embodied in either men or women, would limit the musical experience to the presumably few whose singularly ambivalent psychic constitution would permit an intelligent and sensitive response. Possibly something of the kind was in Kierkegaard's mind when, in his essay, he expressed a warning against the seduction of the "musical erotic" while simultaneously admitting the overpowering impact of Mozart's music. This apparent contradiction between subjective surrender and rational negation of the musical experience is characteristic of most philosophical arguments about the relation between man's consciousness and the effect of music on it: the amorphous nature of harmonious sound, its liquid transparence, its seductiveness through sensuous evocation, and, in particular, its refusal to be verbalized, are shown to be symptoms of man's willing submission to the mindless, the amoral, and the demonic. At the same time the musical experience is being defined as the nearest approach to perfection in man's perception of the beautiful, a manifestation of some divine essence, the very rhythm of life itself echoing what the ancients called the universal music of the spheres.

Hermann Hesse's early novels may serve as a wholesome antidote to the hypothesis of isolation and inner division upon which Proust's and Mann's portrayals of musicians are based. At the time Hesse wrote these novels he himself was passing through periods of spiritual distress, the result of personal afflictions he could not come to terms with, but also of the growing realization of social and political chaos in the whole of the civilized world for which he saw no solution but through individual attempts at self-recognition. It is in terms of the individual, then, that his early novels try to cope with contemporary life. For this, if not for any other reason, the musical experience holds a predominant place in the fictitious universe he built around his heroes. It is the very stuff of which the knowledge of self is made.

The first of these novels, *Demian*, published in 1919, deals with the growth of the protagonist, Sinclair, from childhood to adolescence. Two influences are at work in shaping his personality, his friend Demian, a somewhat mythical figure with an almost hypnotic influence on young Sinclair who by his very existence illustrates the possibility of completeness and maturity latent in all men—and the musician Pistorius whose organ-playing reveals to the young man a whole universe of "inner voices", at times "a violent wrenching loose, a burning harkening to one's own dark soul, an intoxicating surrender,"[23] at other times an "unusually intimate, self-absorbed, music that seemed to listen to itself, that comforted me each time, prepared me more and more to heed my own inner voices."[24] Demian and Pistorius, though clearly distinguished figures in the story told by Hesse, have a tendency to blur into one another in their capacity as guides and admonishers who help the young man to discover his true nature. Occasionally it almost seems as if the musician were an incarnation of Demian, as if this quasi-mythological overlife-size "daimon" who, in truth, resided in Sinclair's own soul, had achieved a kind of materialization through the magic of music. This is of particular interest if one remembers that the character of Pistorius, the organ-player, was indeed taken from life, the portrait of a Jungian psychotherapist whom Hesse befriended at that time and who helped him to extricate himself from his difficulties. That Hesse found it possible, or even necessary, to transform a practicing psychologist into a musician and to put this musician into his story which is essentially a tale of recovery from inner division and of self-realization is of considerable interest to the student of Hesse's early work and what was to grow out of it in later years. For both, Demian the figure out of myth, and Pistorius the music-maker out of life, serve the same end: to transform the many into the one, to bring what has been split and divided back to the primordial unity from which it had sprung.[25] In this metaphysical rather than psychological sense *Demian* is a "musical" novel. For what Hesse is concerned with is not the composer, the performer, or the listener, but man growing from the darkness of incomprehension to the light that comes from the awareness of self through music. The love emotion which music so powerfully suggests is of the very essence of this growth.

One hesitates to speak of love relationships when considering Sinclair's attachment to Demian, to Demian's mother, to Pistorius and to his music. Once again one returns to Kierkegaard's coinage of the "musical erotic" as the most expressive formula though, in this case, devoid of all sexual implications. Sinclair's love is never described in explicit terms. Hesse employs a technique he must have learned from the psychotherapeutic methods of Jung and his disciples. It is through dreams, hallucinations, visions, and the patient's attempts at interpreting them through self-analysis that Sinclair gradually comes to understand himself. Some of these dreams are fairly obvious examples of the dreamer's undifferentiated erotic impulses revealed in sleep through images of astonishing and frightening vividness. Thus Sinclair sees his friend Demian in a dream, but the image "despite its strength . . . was completely feminine. This form drew me to itself and enveloped me in a deep tremulous embrace. I felt a mixture of ecstasy and horror—the embrace was at once an act of divine worship and a crime . . . Its embrace violated all sense of reverence, yet it was bliss.''[26] Demian's mother, a kind of *Magna Mater* with all the equivocal attributes that myth has created around the image of the Mother of all things, appears to him in a dream of a very similar nature. For frequently he dreamed that he was entering his house and, wanting to embrace his mother, he, instead, "held the great, half-male, half-maternal woman in my arms, of whom I was afraid but who also attracted me violently."[27] Pistorius himself is described as combining in his personality both masculine and feminine features. This is true both of his external appearance and of his music: "All his masculinity and strength were concentrated in eyes and forehead, while the lower part of the face was sensitive and immature, uncontrolled and somehow very soft.''[28]

It is the same Pistorius who interprets Sinclair's dreams in terms of the dualism that his music had already revealed. He tells the young man of the bliss and the damnation that appear as dream images in our sleep or as artistic creation in our waking life. The God whose name is Abraxas [29] may be worshipped in either darkness or light. He does not impose any restrictions as to whom to love or what kind of music to compose. For "your dreams", the organist tells Sinclair, "are the best things you have . . . When you know something about Abraxas, you cannot [violate your dreams] any longer. You aren't allowed to be afraid of anything, you can't consider prohibited anything that the soul desires."[30] The things we see in dreams, he also tells the young man, are the things that are within us. And thus the meaning we apply to music is also the meaning we project from within ourselves on to our life. Should this meaning be endowed with either masculine or feminine features, or with both at once, it is because by following the dictates of our inner being we are subject to no conventional social norm as to what constitutes proper or improper erotic fulfillment. Sinclair listens attentively to Pistorius's advice. At last he attempts to express one of his dreams through a painting; it is the portrait of his own soul which, having passed through the multiple mirrors in which all living things are reflected, has found peace in a newly acquired sense of harmony. The painting "was woman, girl, a little child, an animal . . . it was so much part of me that I could not separate it from myself, as though it had been transformed into my own ego."[31] Had Sinclair tried his hand at musical composition rather than at painting, the result would have been the same—a fusion of the masculine and the feminine, his creative consciousness transforming the amorphous unconscious into organized sound, not a metaphor of sexual dualism and deviation into the abnormal, but of completeness achieved through the inevitable descent into hell. In this immature painting damnation and blessing have become one as they had always been in Pistorius's music and in the horror and bliss of the dream-image of Demian himself.

Hesse's vision of hell resembles Mozart's in the last act of *Don Giovanni*. It is also like Michelangelo's fresco of the Last Judgment—a place of horror, torment, and a solitude beyond words. Fear and trembling are man's only companions. Having been cast out from the world of men he has become accustomed to the icy air of open spaces and inhabits a no-man's land of blurred distinctions where all dividing lines between sanity and insanity, love and lust, holiness and crime, have been eliminated from men's minds.

In order to enter such a place man must have an innate capacity for suffering and a knowledge of the ineluctability of pain. Otherwise damnation would pass him by and he would issue from his ordeal his soul unpurged and his body unchastened. To be worthy of purgatory he must be rich in nature's gifts of body and mind, but he must be more deeply aware than other men of a sense of insecurity which prevents him from being one of them. Most important of all, he must share in a child's innocence, such innocence as would be mistaken for foolishness and despised by others, an innocence which is also that of the artist and possibly that of the saint. From within the context of normality hell appears as a bottomless pit into which are thrown the unrepentant and the unredeemed. From the soul's inner perspective it is the natural habitat of those who are simple in mind and thus are ignorant of statistical norms, the laws regulating conditioned reflexes or the need for social adaptation. The only freedom that hell grants them is the freedom to be themselves.

Hesse tells the story of Haller's descent into hell, his purgatory, and final liberation, in his novel *Der Steppenwolf*. The local habitation and name are provided by a small provincial town in Southern Germany. The setting is bourgeois to the smallest

detail. The intellectual range of the people living there is restricted to the obvious and predictable, any scope for adventures of the mind or the body nonexistent. Haller's self-chosen
exile into the commonplace provides a suitable background to
the inferno which his thoughts create and his imagination elabo-
rates. Against this background of hollow philistinism Hesse
constructs a musical counterpoint which serves the purpose of a
purgatory and finally releases Haller from his suicidal escape
into moral dissolution.

Haller's relation to music is part of his essential innocence.
This, at least, is the first impression the reader receives when he,
through the eyes of a nondescript narrator, is permitted to
observe Haller at a concert where a little symphony by
Friedemann Bach is being performed. For this outcast who, in
the words of the speaker, had within himself "an ingenious, a
boundless and frightful capacity for pain" gave himself up to the
music with so much abandon, so much happiness, that the
observer could not help paying "more attention to him than to
the music."[32] Haller, some pages later, describes the effect of
this simple and, indeed, innocent music on his tortured mind in
the language of a saint who, though in hell, had seen a vision of
indescribable holiness in the midst of darkness. "After two or
three notes of the piano the door opened all of a sudden to the
other world. I sped through heaven and saw God at work. I
suffered holy pains. I dropped all my defenses and was afraid of
nothing in the world, I accepted all things and to all things I
gave up my heart."[33] Haller, the wolf of the steppes, is no
practising musician, no expert in musicology, no experienced
listener to music. But what distinguished him from so many
other hearers of music that have been dealt with till now is his
innate capacity to extract from the music he hears elements of
personal resurrection. That it shoud be music rather than any
other form of art, is of particular interest for our study of the
"musical erotic": for as Haller's familiarity with the various
aspects of the erotic grows in the course of the novel, so does his
comprehension of music as an art whose primary function in the
life of man is to "seduce" the senses by widening their range of
response until indeed all distinctions between seducer and seduced are eliminated in the totality of the musical experience.

In order to understand this inner growth, Kierkegaard's essay with which Hesse in all likelihood was unfamiliar, once more proves prophetically relevant. Two musical realms impinge upon Haller's consciousness: jazz as embodied in the figure of Pablo, "a dark and good-looking youth of Spanish or South-American origin", who, a few pages later, is also called "this beautiful exotic demigod of love"; and German classical music represented by the immortals, in particular Mozart and his opera *Don Giovanni* which, in Haller's or rather Hesse's own words, is "the last great music ever written". Pablo and Mozart are not always clearly defined and distinct figures in the story as told by Haller in the "biographical" part of the novel. Mozart, at first, is regarded through "bourgeois eyes". His supreme and special gift is not so much the outcome of his immense powers of surrender and suffering nor of his assumed indifference to the ideals of the philistine or of "his patience under the last extremity of loneliness which rarefies the atmosphere of the bourgeois world to an ice-cold ether."[34] Repeatedly Haller-Hesse refers to Mozart's "cool, bright, austere, and yet smiling wisdom,"[35] to "the radiance of this cool starry brightness and the quivering of this clearness of ether."[36] It is out of this "steel-bright gaiety" that Mozart's laughter can be heard, "shrilly and wildly and unearthly". It was indeed "a cold and eerie laugh! It was noiseless and yet everything went to smithereens in it."[37]

The common denominator which makes this encounter between Mozart and Pablo possible, is the innocence of their sensuousness and their complete devotion to their art. According to Haller neither of the two, the "immortal" and the jazz musician, has any opinion to express about music. They have no theories, no conventions, no formulas which might be applied to their compositions. They live in the present only, but their awareness of the fragility of time is so intense that all temporary duration becomes meaningless in their music-making. Their compositions, even their improvisations, transcend the moment of creation and become fused in the ever-present rhythm of life perpetuating itself in eternity. Thus, towards the end of the book Haller can write, ". . . he was Mozart no longer. It was my friend Pablo looking warmly at me out of his dark exotic eyes. . . . One day I would learn to laugh. Pablo was waiting for me, and Mozart too."[38]

Yet Pablo stands for all those elements in music which Haller-

Hesse had been taught to reject in the past. When he first visits a dance-hall and listens to jazz, he recognizes in it a "raw and savage gaiety" expressive of "an underworld of instinct" which "breathes a simple honest sensuality." Though his mind tells him that it is a "music of decline," it yet had "the merits of great sincerity". For it is "amiably and unblushingly negroid" and expresses "the mood of childlike happiness."[39] The encounter between the music of heaven and that of hell is very subtly portrayed in the imaginary meeting between Mozart and Pablo, but also in the discovery, made by Haller in the course of his musical adventures in the "Magic Theatre", that music is erotically undifferentiated, that the fluidity of musical harmonies permits either a masculine or a feminine interpretation and that, finally, its seduction contains the germs of both holiness and damnation, a life of godlike simplicity and a life dedicated to the works of the devil all in one.

Haller's rebirth into a new life takes place on these two levels: the musical and the erotic, the one, almost imperceptibly, passing into the other. Just as Mozart and Pablo become finally almost undistinguishable in Haller's imagination, so are those that are associated with their music as performers or listeners. Hermine whom he meets in a bar over a bottle of wine reminds him of his childhood and his early attempts at establishing human contact outside any erotic compulsion. Looking at Hermine one day, Haller, with a sudden shock of recognition, realizes, "It was a boy's face . . . I saw something in her face that reminded me of my own boyhood and my friend of those days. His name was Herman." And a few pages later, "Her boyishness welled up from time to time like a breath of life and cast a spell of a hermaphrodite."[40] Psychological interpretations of such daydreams offer a partial insight only into Haller's resurrection from damnation. It is not the presumed bisexuality of either seducer or seduced that matters but the recovery of his alienated self from inner division. The metamorphosis is hastened by the uninhibited sensuality of those whom Haller meets through mutually shared musical experience. For behind Pablo and his friends stand the immortals watching, as it were, over the precision and craftsmanship of their musical execution, the expressiveness of their art. But, above everything else, it is the innocent eroticism of the music-makers and music-listeners that finally cures Haller and brings about what Hesse evidently considered his redemption. There is, for example, Maria, Pablo's girl-friend who also loves Hermine. When Haller is with her he cannot forget that she had also held Hermine in her arms just as she held him, "that she had felt, kissed, tasted and tested her limbs, her hair and skin the same way as mine."[41]

Traditional psychoanalytical terminology may be singularly unhelpful when applied to the creative work of either musician or novelist. Was Haller attracted to Pablo because of possible homoerotic tendencies? Was Hermine when she gave herself to Maria as well as to Haller, a hermaphrodite? To whom did Maria surrender when she accepted Haller's caresses, the lover of Hermine or the lover of his school-friend Herman? Questions such as these lower the significance of Haller's reawakened will to live to the therapeutic level of psychoanalytical diagnosis. Such an approach to his relation with Pablo, that "demigod of love", would falsify Hesse's intentions. For like Demian in the previous novel, Pablo radiates a sense of wholeness which takes no account of erotic differentiation but stands for that sense of total involvement with life of which civilized living and philistine hypocrisy has deprived twentieth-century man.

At one time Haller experiments with drugs as a kind of short-cut to complete living. Later on feeling exhausted and unwell, Pablo places him on a bed and gives him some drops, "and while I lay with closed eyes I felt the fleeting breath of a kiss on each eyelid. I took the kiss as though I believed it came from Maria, but I knew very well it came from him."[42] There is nothing prurient, unsavoury, offensive about the relationship between these four, Haller and Hermine, Hermine and Maria, Maria and Pablo, Pablo and Haller. Though they might have deviated from the bourgeois norm, they re-established thereby a new innocence where surrender to seduction through eros and music is the only intimation of immortality that human beings are capable of. The spell of love under which they had fallen facilitates the transformation of desire from one plane of erotic fulfillment to another without arousing any sense of guilt or shame.

Thus, Haller's dreams of the immortals and his attempts to achieve his own rebirth with their help comes to an end. It is throughout accompanied by the music of Mozart's *Don Giovanni* as, indeed, it could not be otherwise. For though, after reading Hesse, it is no longer possible to agree with Kierkegaard's misanthropic conclusions as to the effect of the musical erotic on the hearer, his was a prophetic voice proclaiming that through music, alone among the arts, men become conscious of the power of Eros to shape and give meaning to their inner life. What Kierkegaard did not know and what his philosophy precluded him from knowing was that, though one may, in effect, listen to Mozart's music in fear and trembling, it may also show the way towards salvation, from the divided, self-centered and alienated ego to the full individuation of the conscious self.

Notes to Chapter Five

1. *Journal, 1839.* Quoted in Croxhall, T. H., *Kierkegaard Commentary*, p. 48. Here are two recent estimates of Kierkegaard's essay on *Don Giovanni*, one by Denis de Rougement, the other spoken by the Devil in Mann's *Doctor Faustus:* 1. "Kierkegaard's interpretation of Don Juan rivals Mozart's in its magnificence: it reinvests the drama's structure as though by a creation of intrepid logic. It imposes on us, by virtue of an unforgettable coherence, a triple and unique interpretation of the opera, the myth, and the essence of Western music." (*The Myth of Love*, p. 114). 2. "[Kierkegaard] knew and understood my particular relation to this beautiful art—the most Christian of all arts, he finds—but Christian in reverse, as it were, introduced and developed by Christianity indeed, but then rejected and banned as the Devil's kingdom . . . A highly theological business, music—the way sin is, the way I am. The passion of that Christian for music is true passion, and as such knowledge and corruption in one. For there is true passion only in the ambiguous and ironic. The highest passion concerns the absolutely questionable." (*Doctor Faustus*, p. 235).
2. Søren Kierkegaard, *Either/Or*, vol. 1, p. 72.
3. Gordon Epperson, *The Musical Symbol, A Study of the Philosophical Theory of Music*, p. 12. Contemporary composers, in particular, are fond of adducing bodily images to describe the perfect musical response. Thus, Pierce Harwell writes to Anais Nin in a letter: "The consciousness of sensation is not auditory alone, but the surge of the sound waves breaks like a tinkling surf aginst the responsive of our hair, our throats, our lips, our eyes. We should listen naked to music, with our pores, the littlest lanugo, the soles of our feet." (*The Journals of Anais Nin.* vol. 3, p. 257). And Stockhausen is reported to have said: "And the sound waves directly attack the whole skin, not only the eardrums. You can hear

through the whole body." (Jonathan Cott, *Stockhausen. Conversations with the Composer*, p. 28).
4. Quoted in Charles M. Diserens, *A Psychology of Music, The Influence of Music on Behaviour*, p. 191.
5. Søren Kierkegaard, *op. cit.*, p. 81.
6. Marcel Proust, *Swann's Way*, Modern Library Edition, New York, p. 298.
7. Romain Rolland, *Jean Christophe, Vol. I, The Dawn*, p. 97.
8. James Joyce, *A Portrait of the Artist as a Young Man*, p. 186.
9. *Ibid.*, p. 254.
10. *Ibid.*, p. 275.
11. Virginia Woolf, "The String Quartet", published in *A Haunted House and other Stories*, p. 25 ff.
12. Aldous Huxley, *Point Counter Point*, pp. 393 and 395.
13. Henry Miller, *Tropic of Cancer*, p. 78.
14. Marcel Proust, *Remembrance of Things Past*, vol. X (*The Captive*), Part II, pp. 78–79. See the following remark made in Michel Butor's *Les Oeuvres d'art imaginaires chez Proust*, p. 43: "The sexual deviant in the France of the early twentieth century is led, one day or another, to pass through the catharsis of the work of art; he cannot join the real object of his desire but by abolishing not only his own error, but what has provoked this error, thus changing reality in terms of a 'real voyage' which is the art-work." (My own translation).
15. Marcel Proust, *ibid.*, vol. VII (*Cities of the Plain*), p. 21.
16. Thomas Mann, *Doctor Faustus*, p. 139.
17. Quoted in Paul Deussen, *Erinnerungen an Friedrich Nietzsche*, 1901, in Heinz Peter Putz, *Kunst und Künstlerexistenz bei Nietzsche und Thomas Mann*, p. 107.
18. James Joyce, *Ulysses*, p. 492.
19. Thomas Mann, *The Story of a Novel*, p. 96. The original can be found in Stendhal, *Aux Âmes Sensibles*, Lettres choisies et presentées par Boudet-Lamotte, Gallimard, Paris, 1942, p. 138. The letter is dated 26 May 1814.
20. Thomas Mann, *Doctor Faustus*, pp. 338–9 (Italics in the original).
21. *Ibid.*, p. 393.
22. *Ibid.*, p. 480.
23. Hermann Hesse, *Demian*, p. 83.
24. *Ibid.*, p. 93.
25. All this is explained by Hesse in a letter addressed to Carlo Isenberg, dated January 7, 1926, quoted in *Materialien zu Hermann Hesse's "Der Steppenwolf"*, p. 58. The following observation made by Hesse one year before the publication of *Demian* is of some interest to the student of this novel: "What analysis recognized and formulated scientifically had always been known by the poets—yes, the poet revealed himself as the representative of a special kind of thinking that actually runs counter to analytical psychological thought. He was the dreamer; the analyst was the interpreter of dreams. Was any course left for the poet, despite all his interest in

the new psychology, but to dream on and to follow the summons of his unconscious?" (From an essay entitled: *Künstler and Psychoanalyse"*, "Artists and Psychoanalysis", in *Gesammelte Schriften*, VII, 137–143, 1957, first published in 1918; quoted in Ziolkowski, *The Novels of Hermann Hesse*, p. 12).

26. Hermann Hesse, *Demian*, p. 79.
27. *Ibid.*, p. 93.
28. *Ibid.*, p. 83.
29. C. G. Jung, in *The Seven Sermons of the Dead*, published anonymously in a private edition in 1925, defines Abraxas in terms of its duality, "the mother of good and evil", and "Abraxas begetteth truth and lying, good and evil, light and darkness, in the same word and in the same act." Also, "It is the hermaphrodite of the earliest beginning," etc. Quoted in Miguel Serrano, *C. G. Jung and Hermann Hesse. A Record of the Friendship*, pp. 94–96.
30. Hermann Hesse, *Demian*, p. 95.
31. *Ibid.*, p. 100.
32. Hermann Hesse, *Steppenwolf*, p. 23.
33. *Ibid.*, p. 38.
34. *Ibid.*, p. 76.
35. *Ibid.*, p. 84.
36. *Ibid.*, p. 181.
37. *Ibid.*, p. 246.
38. *Ibid.*, pp. 252–3.
39. *Ibid.*, pp. 46–7.
40. *Ibid.*, pp. 27 and 130.
41. *Ibid.*, p. 172.
42. *Ibid.*, p. 170.

VI
Musical Transcendence

1

The musical experience, in so far as it forms an integral part of the novelist's portrayal of contemporary life, modifies the tangible reality of everyday existence into something remote and yet familiar, open to sense perception and yet impenetrable to reason. In some of these novels music itself appears to originate in a psychologically and esthetically more satisfying context of reality than the one the listener is condemned to share with his contemporaries. The musical experience claims from him responsiveness to metaphysical ideas and a closer attention to spiritual significances of a nonconceptual nature than he would ordinarily devote to painting, sculpture, or poetry. It engages the whole of his psychic being in a manner comparable to the self-absorption induced by the discipline of meditation and the fulfillment consequent upon it. As his commitment to music increases, his capacity for differentiated sense perceptions and rational analysis diminishes. All intellectual activity becomes redundant when exposed to the hypnotic regularity of musical beat, while the mind still remains acutely responsive to modulations from one key to another, from initial discord to final harmony, the melting of tone into tone, the gradual and almost imperceptible transition from melody to silence.

The musical experience, at its most intense, thus resembles dream images expressive of some primordial harmony, the rediscovery of a lost paradise of human completeness from which all contradictory perplexities inherent in man's time-bound existence have been eliminated. Bergson makes a few illuminating remarks about this state of unresisting responsiveness to music.

According to him such a state induces in the listener a sense of remoteness from the reality of Nature which, in turn, enables him to confront the true nature of Reality. This ultimate "reality", Bergson repeatedly asserts, is to be found in Art alone. The musical experience, then, causes the responsive listener "to brush aside the utilitarian symbols, the conventional and socially accepted generalities, in short, everything that veils reality from us, in order to bring us face to face with reality itself."[1] The idea underlying Bergson's assumptions regarding the effect of music on man's consciousness corresponds to some archetypal vision of life according to which the artist, and in particular the musician, supplies a principle of wholeness to the fragmentary creations of nature. It is he who turns the transitoriness of all sense perception which take place in time into "a present which endures", and superimposes the conscious patterning of his mind on to the chaotic proliferations of nature. Bergson thus effectively questions the primacy of nature when he asks whether "in a certain sense art is not prior to nature" adding that "it seems more in conformity with the rules of a sound method to study the beautiful first in the works in which it has been produced by a conscious effort, and then to pass on by imperceptible steps from art to nature."[2]

The "study of the beautiful", in Bergsonian terms, however, involves considerable risks to the normal functioning of the human intellect. The first victim is the notion of a universe of thought insofar as it can be conceptually defined. For by endeavoring to immerse himself in the "beautiful" as conveyed through music the listener compulsively surrenders to a universe of pure sound. This, in effect, is the sole context of Being available to the listener at the moment of esthetic enjoyment as well as in the memory of it. Pure sound, like pure time, is not a measurable quantity and, thus, cannot be apprehended by reason. It does not lead to the creation of logically valid concepts, nor can it be designated as having any emotionally relevant significance. Pure sound has no more meaningful relation to everyday acoustic reality than pure time has to the measurable rhythm of the ticking of a clock. Susanne Langer, in her study of the effect of pure sound on human consciousness, employs a terminology which could equally well be applied to the analysis of dreams considered as creations of an invisible reality below the threshold of thought. "The mirror of the world, the horizon of the human domain, and all tangible realities are gone. Objects become a blur, all sight irrelevant . . ." Instead there is "a universe of pure *sound,* an audible world, a sonorous beauty taking over the whole of one's consciousness."[3]

The only logic of which music may be said to be an expression is the one that originates in the integrated universe of sound it creates. Thus, nothing is or need be eliminated from musical creation, performance, or response, whether it be of human or nonhuman significance. Its integrative power functions beyond the limited scope of man's consciousness. Though it is a temporal art, music suspends ordinary time, is, in the words of Monroe C. Beardsley, "the closest thing to pure process . . . to happening as such, to change abstracted from anything that changes."[4] Therefore what is called "musical time" constitutes an invisible reality to which criteria of measurement and structure, used in everyday life, are inapplicable. Susanne Langer calls it "virtual time" to distinguish it from "actual time" which men experience as duration, with its clearly defined sense of the past and anticipation of the future.

Such a universe of pure sound—insofar as pure sound can be said to possess any definable meaning at all—resides in the visionary power of the individual to transmute the invisible reality that music communicates to him into a source of inner knowledge, transcending the limitations imposed by the meddling intellect, into an awareness of "order liberated from all relation to things, pure order, bodiless, detached and free, not a mere concept, not as a dream, but as a vision beheld."[5] Such a "pure order" of things contradicts the very principle upon which a novelist's narrative is based, the rational patterning of plot, motivation, and character. As long as novelists use language and—in spite of James Joyce's adventures into the writing of literary "scores"—they persist in doing so, the creation of a sense of psychological continuity founded upon a conscious perception of the universe around them will be their main concern. For the artist in words, as distinguished from the artist in sounds, is, according to Henry James, "in the perpetual predicament that the continuity of things is the whole matter, for him, of comedy and tragedy; that this continuity is never, by the space of an instant or an inch, broken and that, to do

anything at all, he has at once intensely to consult and intensely
to ignore it."[6]

While the novelist's concern is with time experienced, the
musician's is with time contemplated. But contemplation is outside time, does not involve a sense of duration, embodies no
rhythm but that of eternal recurrence. Contemplation is, indeed,
like a melody, "a beginning, a question asked, a listening into a
distance."[7] Introducing such a melody into a novel is a subtle
and often ironical reminder of the fragility of the human intellect and of man's faith in human perfectibility through reason.
By calling the reader's attention to that other reality which is not
to be found "in nature" but in art, contemplation is substituted
for experience and the principle of continuity may, at last, be
not merely "intensely ignored" but abolished; for when contemplation takes over, not the sequence but the togetherness of
things alone matters. In this metaphorical sense all contemplative response induced by music constitutes a turning away from
visible and tangible reality, from measurable duration in time,
towards an extra-human awareness of some primordial truth
which music alone is predestined to reveal. The paradox with
which the novelist is faced concerns the tenuous relation between pure sound and contemplation, on the one hand, and
words used to communicate this relation, on the other. For the
natural domain of contemplation is silence. When the melody is
over and has been absorbed in the deepest recesses of the
hearer's consciousness, the metamorphosis from pure sound
into spiritual essence occurs in a realm where speech does not
enter.

When Proust attempts to translate the inexpressible into
words he appears to be in search of a terminology which literary
tradition had not yet developed. Possibly he remembered some
of Bergson's remarks regarding the effect of music on the hearer's consciousness though he consistently refused to acknowledge any direct influence on the part of the philosopher on his
work. But Swann and Marcel realize the power of music to
reveal to the hearer states of consciousness resembling those
trancelike experiences described by mystics which culminate in
moments of ecstasy and complete surrender to the unknown.
Such experiences transcend the limitations of the everyday vocabulary employed by the novelist. Reason cannot name them

nor can they be designated by the emotive terminology derived from conventional responses to the other arts. This inability to invest what appears to be "pure" sound with meaning is both frustrating and exalting. After Swann has listened to Vinteuil's "petite phrase", for example, he realizes that musical motifs may conceivably express "actual ideas", but, he adds, "of another world, of another order, ideas veiled in shadows, unknown, impenetrable to the human mind." And some time later he speaks of the astonishing wealth of invention, indeed of "ideas"—as he repeatedly calls them—which the composer reveals to us after they had lain "hidden, unknown to us, in that great impenetrable night, discouraging exploration, of our soul which we have been content to regard as valueless and waste and void."[8]

The second passage which occurs several volumes later is spoken by Marcel. It reads almost like a summing up of Bergson's main ideas about the effect of music on the hearer, its revelation of an inner reality, which has little to do with "Nature" but pertains to Art alone; for, by implication, the meditation that Vinteuil's music suggests to Marcel lifts him up beyond the confines of what is "natural" and fuses his whole being with the music of which Vinteuil—by an accident of art—is the creator: "In Vinteuil's music, there were thus some of those visions which it is impossible to record, since, when at the moment of falling asleep we receive the caress of their unreal enchantment, at that very moment in which reason has already deserted us, our eyes are already sealed, and before we have had time to know not merely the ineffable but the invisible, we are asleep."[9]

The "pure sound" of Vinteuil's "petite phrase"—and here we are not concerned with its thematic structure but with the extraordinary effect it created in the hearer's mind—reflects a reality to which Proust applies a variety of names. It may at times stand for "the essential nature" of the composer himself[10] or be the expression of some "supraterrestrial joy"[11] which the music communicates to the listener. At other times Proust, looking in vain for a material explanation of the effect of this music on him, speaks of the music's "profound equivalent, the unknown and highly colored festival ... the mode in which [Vinteuil] 'heard' the universe"[12] or of "that extra-temporal delight" which the melody caused him so that Marcel's response to Vinteuil's phrase suggested to him "a presentiment of something more supraterrestrial still,"[13] indeed an evocation of pure sound divorced from any contamination with measurable and rationally explicable reality.

Proust's repeated reference to the purity of Vinteuil's music as opposed to the defiling moral squalor out of which it grew is an illuminating instance of his inclination to idealize man's creation of beauty above anything made by nature. In historical perspective Vinteuil's "petite phrase" was certainly far from being "pure sound". From what we know of the actual origins of this musical motif from Proust himself, it was inspired by two sonatas for piano and violin, one by Saint-Saëns ("a musician I do not love") and another by César Franck, while the "tremolos" which cover the little phrase had been suggested to Proust by the Prelude to Wagner's *Lohengrin* and even by "something out of Schubert."[14] Proust must have been well aware of the contradictions implied in the relative "impurity" of the music performed and the ultimate effect created in the hearer's mind. The transformation from the sentimentally impressionistic music played at the Verdurin's salon into the pure sound heard in Marcel's imagination occurs below the surface of conscious thought. Neither the plot of the narrative nor Marcel's own character have any part in this remarkable metamorphosis from the remembrance of past impurity to the resurrection of the quintessence of pure sound in the present. This is why Samuel Beckett could speak of music in Proust's work as "the catalystic element [which] asserts to his unbelief the permanence of personality and the reality of art." Through his music, Beckett continues, the composer made an "ideal and immaterial statement of the essence of a unique beauty, a unique world, the invariable world and beauty of Vinteuil, expressed timidly, as a prayer, in the Sonata, imploringly, as an inspiration, in the Septuor, the 'invisible reality', that damns the life of the body on earth as a pensum, and reveals the meaning of the word: 'defunctus'."[15]

Pure sound, a symbol for some ultimate and nonhuman order and unity, pertains to no particular class of music. The process of integration it provokes in the listener stands in contradiction to everything that the declining civilization which Proust so vividly describes in his work represents. As an "extra-temporal" and "supra-terrestrial" phenomenon of the spirit and as an "invisible essence" it belongs to no time and is confined to no particular space. It is the only true essence of Being that men, in moments of heightened consciousness, can dimly perceive beyond the distorting mirror of their senses.

2

Any attempt at defining pure sound must ultimately turn away from the Western tradition of polyphonic music and consider a system of atonal homophony commonly met with in Far Eastern cultures. Music as part of religious ritual in India, for example, requires no orchestral volume, no contrapuntal development of theme within theme, no programmatic leitmotifs. It is essentially nondramatic since it expresses a sense of unity with a universal Being rather than the emotional conflicts of a composer or performer. It is at peace with itself, performing a circular movement originating in a realization of man's nothingness which is its beginning and its end. The vanity of human wishes in the face of a universe that is largely indifferent to man's fate is its main theme. The cycle of the seasons, the immutability of fate as it affects men or nature, the life-death-rebirth pattern to which all living things are subject, the willingness of man to submit uncomplainingly to a pattern that the gods have devised for his benefit, are expressed in various *ragas,* a word that may be translated by "moods" expressive of the various times of the day, the change of the seasons, the correspondences relating music to the never-ceasing ritual of living. Thus, "selecting the appropriate *raga* [the performer] subordinates his individual creative power to it, yet he must be more creative than the western performer who is simply a channel for expressing the composer's ideas. The performance is affected by his own mood and the reactions of the listeners with whom he is in intimate contact from moment to moment. The composer-performer-listener relationship is thus in fact quite different from that of the West."[16] Such "moods" are, of course, not determined by mere personal joys or sorrows but are rooted in a musical tradition which has grown from pre-historic times as part of a code of religious rituals which no individual is privileged enough to question. The king as well as the beggar listened to the same music and it spoke to them in one and the same language. Distinctions of caste and class might have, from time to time, interfered in this universality of the musical appeal. But, like prayer and worship, the music belonged alike to everyone and to no one in particular.

The artificial distinction between composer, performer, and listener is thus largely meaningless in such ancient musical traditions. The solo voice of the singer may have to follow the traditional *ragas* in as rigid a manner as tradition has laid down, but there is much place for individual improvisation within the limits set by the ritual. While the performer may improvise for hours together, the listener participates in the rise and fall of the voice with an intensity of identification quite unknown among concert-goers in the West and, in most cases, considered by them a shocking display of uncontrolled emotions which the European listener to music has long ago been conditioned to avoid. A single voice singing for hours with what must appear to Western ears a total absence of "melody" is likely to have a soporific effect on any but Indian listeners. To the Western mind attuned to the changes in tempo, key, volume or pitch, the effect is one of unbearable monotony. On the other hand, to the Indian listener, the rise and fall of musical volume produced by a crescendo or a decrescendo are alien elements violently disturbing the even measure of the singing voice. Whatever modulation may occur in the course of the singing does not only depend on the singer's emotional involvement in the music but on the strict structural principles of development inherent in the *raga* that happens to be the subject of the song. Therefore "[a piece of classical Indian music] can only be understood in terms of Indian philosophical thought. This thought . . . is essentially contemplative . . . The tonic . . . is no separate element, but the ever-present guide; in the language of music it expresses the timeless, eternal unchanging background of all things,—their origin, sustainer, and goal . . . Thus it is that the *ragas*, like the *mantras* or sacred formulas, are regarded as aspects of and hence as approaches to . . . the Absolute (Brahman) conceived as sound."[17]

The absence of any attempt at producing polyphonic effects gives this music a "purity" of sound that cannot, in any "programmatic" way, be related to nonmusical reality. It exists in

isolation, as it were, independent of the objects that constitute
the natural environment of musician and listener, apparently
divorced from any physical substance or temporal condition,
having no definable beginning, middle, or end, ignorant of the
relative validity of minor or major scales, its demi-tones ignor-
ing with complete indifference possibilities of consonance or dissonance—a music the best description of which would be one
that claims the formlessness of infinity as its sole characteristic
feature while the musician combines within himself the qualities
of creator, performer, and listener, all in one. Where all man-
made distinctions are abolished, man's song may, indeed, become either a revival of some primeval musical chaos or an
experience of subliminal non-music: the only "pure sound"
possible in the impurity prevailing in nature.

In E.M. Forster's *A Passage to India* there occurs an incident
which may serve as an illustration for the clash between a human
voice meditating in musical terms and the total incomprehension of Western listeners to what the music purports to convey.
A Hindu Brahmin, Professor Godbole, is called upon by a
number of English visitors to sing a song. The request is made
out of genuine curiosity to know more about Indian music.
Possibly the "mysterious East" might become more intelligible
through a musical experience which, the English assume, will
open up new vistas onto a civilization in which they are aliens,
however reluctant they may be to admit it. The events that
follow are described by Forster in a language which is meant to
convey the ironic implications inherent in this encounter between two opposing musical traditions: "His thin voice rose, and
gave out one sound after another. At times there seemed
rhythm, at times there was the illusion of a Western melody. But
the ear, baffled repeatedly, soon lost any clue, and wandered in
a maze of noises, none harsh or unpleasant, none intelligible. It
was the song of an unknown bird. Only the servants understood
it. They began to whisper to one another. The man who was
gathering water chestnut came out of the tank, his lips parted
with delight, disclosing his scarlet tongue. The sounds continued and ceased after a few moments, as casually as they had
begun—apparently half through a bar, and upon the sub-
dominant."[18]

The listeners, eager to know what the song "meant", overwhelm Professor Godbole with questions. His replies are non-committal and evasive, for the ritual out of which the music originated *is* its "meaning". The song, according to Godbole, addresses the god Krishna inviting him to come. It is a "milkmaiden" that makes this request. But the god refuses to come. He, as Godbole puts it, "neglects to come" in spite of the repeated entreaties of the girl. It is a *raga*, he adds, "appropriate for the present hour, which is the evening." The *raga*, we are given to understand, also deals with the presence or absence of love which may again be either human or divine, and man's relation to the god; in all likelihood it also concerns life and death, and the near impossibility of distinguishing between the two, in short, the song "means" nothing as definite as the Western hearers had anticipated. It is not a call for freedom or justice or equality. It does not express, in so many words and sounds, the longing of the lover for his beloved. Nor does it concern itself with the yearning of the solitary wanderer for human company or with the nostalgia of the city-dweller for the delights of nature. It is expressive of nothing but its own small-scale musical universe. The story it tells is without any definable plot. The god of which the song speaks is both here and no-where, pertaining to the past, the present, and the future. The music, unsupported by any harmonies, unaccompanied by any instruments, floats in vacant space, only to come down to earth when the sound can no longer uphold the nothingness of which it sings. The end is no end but a beginning; it makes no assertion but leaves the listener with a feeling that, as no prom-ise had been made, none had been broken. What should have been an end remains a question-mark.

The words used by Forster in his description of the song sung by Professor Godbole have a familiar ring to readers of the novel. What the Western hearers think to be the beginning of a melody turns out to be an "illusion", just as various objects in the Indian landscape or the Indian character are revealed as being illusory because they are either nonexistent or are mere projections of Western expectations. If the ear is "baffled" by the absence of melody so is the mind throughout the novel by the absence of any recognizable order in the Indian way of thinking or any definable sense of the logical to which the Western mind could respond. The word "maze" is the most revealing of all. Throughout Forster's story people wander around and lose their way in a labyrinth of sounds and sights which, if taken literally, is an exact description of the incidents in the Malabar caves or, if taken symbolically, represent the failure of the characters in the novel to make out each other's meanings or intentions.

Professor Godbole's singing performance holds a significant place in the structure of the novel. Slight and casual as the incident appears to be at first reading, it provides a clue to Forster's own commitments and sympathies. In the story told by Forster in *A Passage to India*, Godbole holds a middle position between the extremes of Western intolerance represented by the average British empire-builder and his associates, and the Muslim point of view, represented by Aziz who, in vain, tries to establish a friendship between himself, the oriental, and the schoolteacher Fielding, an outsider in the English colonial society. The monotheistic attitude of mind of the Christian and the Muslim are equally confounded by the polytheistic "maze" of Hindu worship, Hindu art, and Hindu mythology. Naturally enough, the Christian and the Muslim are astounded at the multiple diversity of divine manifestations which seem to ignore all order of precedence, any generally accepted scale of hierarchies, nor submit to any intelligible separation between right and wrong. Hindu polytheism by acknowledging the necessary existence of many parallel possibilities of worship, affirms the One and Indivisible as a true symbol of transcendental reality which has found expression in the ancient architecture of their temples, their sculpture, and, finally, in a synthesis, startling to Western eyes, of eros and religious worship, illustrated in their various arts, not least of all in their music.

Godbole's singing voice is indeed a counterpart to the sense of unity and order as expressed in the "mosque", at the beginning of the story, and to the Christian civilization of Europe to which Fielding returns at the end of the novel. His song prepares the reader for the episode in the Malabar caves where, in the darkness of some primeval chaos, everything and anything may happen and, where, we are given to understand, actually nothing happens at all. Godbole, the only figure in the novel capable of comprehending the transcendent and of expressing it through song, is also the one who alone knows of the illusory nature of objective reality and therefore believes in the existence of eternity where the many will be as one, and the love of things both great and small the only pursuit worthy of man. Though he knows all this and even tells his uncomprehending listeners about it in his song, he cannot realize his knowledge through action. His intuition of love and compassion, of the universal sympathy of all men for all men, remains incomplete. Forster's description of the comedy being enacted during the Hindu festival, his ironic comment on the fallibility of all the three religions to come to terms with one another, the satirical description of the Hindu religious ceremony over which Godbole—reduced to life-size dimensions—presides, all of them indicate the prevalence of the sceptical Western view (which was Forster's own) over oriental "muddle". Yet, he makes Godbole, during the ceremony at the temple, sing a different kind of song in which his love "for all men" is expressed, merging for a moment "into the universal warmth" which includes both the human and the nonhuman universe and reaching out towards "completeness . . . not reconstruction". For he, Godbole, in the ecstasy of musical worship "was (he imagined) imitating God" through song and dance.[19]

Forster's inclusion of Godbole's transcendent musical meditation in his novel is both moving and slightly absurd. His song about the milkmaid and the god Krishna represents the most characteristic contribution of an amorphous polytheist civilization to the concept of pure sound. As an instance of musical abstraction, its ironic implications are painfully manifest. Placed within the framework of deeply rooted Western preconceptions as to the "meaning" inherent in musical compositions, and measured against the assumed cultural superiority of colonial administration over their subject-peoples, it has little chance of evoking any but a condescending and uncomprehending response. Its impact is, finally, lost amidst the confusion of the caves which follows soon after, in the preposterous maze of Hindu religious ceremonies, and, not least of all, in what the Western mind considers to be the superstitions of the illiterate, the ignorant, and the uncivilized. But within the total context of the book Godbole is the only one who reminds us of "how vast the effort for totality must be; nothing is excepted, the extraordinary is essential to order. The cities of muddle, the echoes of disorder, the excepting and the excepted, are all to be made meaningful in being made one." Frank Kermode who wrote these lines in praise of Forster's novel sees Godbole's unselfconscious attempt at conveying to his listeners through his song the only truth worth communicating—that though "love cheats, and muddle turns into mystery", true wholeness resides in art, "our one orderly product."[20]

3

To the novelist as well as the musicologist pure sound is a philosophical rather than a musical concept. In its absolute sense it can no more be heard than silence can be perceived by the ear. In the novel it may be synonymous with dreamlike contemplation, as indicated in Proust's work, or with transcendental meditation, as suggested by Godbole's song in Forster's novel. Yet neither the human voice nor the strings of an instrument can reproduce the ultimate purity of sound: thus, the metamorphosis from sound modulation into the self-contained wholeness of the human mind is doomed to remain incomplete. The hypnotic effect that music induces lacks absolute insubstantiality, for it may be merely the result of nervous exhaustion or physical strain. The meditation suggested by the singing voice does indeed convey the need for detachment from anything material and egocentric: it is still remote from that ultimate silence where musical reality meets the mind of the listener in a still unmoving point in time.

While musicologists are legitimately sceptical as regards such final musical consummation, the novelist whose main business is with men rather than with concepts continues his search for the experience of total fulfillment induced by music. Some novelists regard such a possibility of reaching out beyond the borders imposed by time and space which music offers to those who are susceptible to its influence as within the scope of their fictitious universe. Among the earliest to attempt a portrayal of such a shattering experience was Aldous Huxley who, at the conclusion of *Point Counter Point*, describes Spandrell's reaction to Beethoven's A-Minor quartet in considerable and—as has been shown in chapter 3—somewhat absurdly impressionist details. Of course, Spandrell was the last character in the novel one would have expected to make the shift from the esthetic-musical to the metaphysical that the whole episode suggests. Huxley, many years later, tried to justify his failure in consistency by pointing out that his initial mistake was to identify the esthetic with the metaphysical, an identification which—considering the fallibility of human nature and of Spandrell's emphatically repulsive character, in particular—simply did not work. Not only did his "meditations" on Beethoven's greatest music reflect a trivial mind incapable of profound metaphysical thought, but—to judge by a letter Huxley wrote in 1945—it was Beethoven himself who failed to bring about that final transformation from musical statement to metaphysical meditation. Though Huxley's apology for his own failure as a novelist sounds somewhat unconvincing, it is worth quoting here as it constitutes the starting point for other reflections on music that were to follow some ten years later. He begins by stating that the musical episode at the end of *Point Counter Point* "is the concentrated expression of that kind of aesthetic mysticism which runs through the book and which is the analogue on another plane . . . of the ultimate, spiritual mysticism." After such large claims, Spandrell's meditations on Beethoven's quartet and his violent death a few seconds later, appear to be a mockery of whatever metaphysical intentions Beethoven might have had in mind when he composed the movement which had so profound an effect on Spandrell. Thus Huxley blames Beethoven's art rather than Spandrell's incapacity for profound thought for the lamentable conclusion of the episode. In Huxley's words "even the highest art was not good enough, that if this was all, it was a pretty poor thing to man's final end."[21]

The reader rightly suspects that Huxley's apology for the awkwardness of his conclusion rests on a fallacy. It was evidently not Beethoven's music that failed, but man. What is to be condemned as insufficiently "pure" is not Beethoven's *Dankgesang* but the listener's ego-centered response, his ulterior motives in offering this music to his friends, his inability to forget his self and immerse himself in the metaphysical universe that Beethoven's musical meditation evokes. Huxley's declaration is the more surprising as initially he had no doubt at all as to the metaphysical nature of the music he introduced at the end of his novel. In a letter to Paul Valéry, written in 1930, he mentions

the A-Minor quartet as among Beethoven's "profound philosophic works, subtle and by all evidence *true.*"[22] In the same
year, in another letter, he declares that "the most perfect statements and human solutions of the great metaphysical problems
are all artistic, especially, it seems to me, musical,"[23] and again
refers in particular to Beethoven's A-Minor quartet. Huxley
went even further than this when, at the same time, he mentions
Wilson Knight's *The Shakespearian Tempest* and compares the
effect produced by the playing of the quartet on the stage (in a
dramatic adaptation of *Point Counter Point*) to "Shakespeare's use
of music whenever he wanted to produce or emphasize some
mystical effect."[24]

Huxley's failure to make this episode musically as well as
metaphysically convincing did not discourage him from experimenting further with the possibilities of creating heightened
states of consciousness through music. These experiments are
of more than passing interest to the student of the modern
novel. As the novelist was increasingly driven into introspection
and into an analysis of the psyche at moments of estrangement
and consequent loss of personal identity, the time seemed ripe
for a breakthrough that would enable the hearer to turn from
the reality of the objective world to the psychic reality of an
inner universe which the musical experience was best qualified
to reveal. No one realized more deeply than Huxley the perils
confronting the soul once it undertook this voyage into the
unknown. But Huxley's curiosity as to what alteration might be
produced in man's consciousness under the combined influence
of psychedelic drugs and music originated in his creation of a
world of fiction in which man's striving for completeness constitutes one of the main themes. It is thus not by chance that some
of the experiments he performed upon himself concerned the
effect of mescalin on his ability to respond to music. The results
provided the required evidence that the pure sound of absolute
music was not the result of mere wishful thinking but a level of
"reality" attainable through an altered and heightened consciousness. The music he thus heard did not come to him in
sleep or in dream but in a state of alert wakefulness, intensely
absorbed in self-observation. What he heard under the effect of
a small dose of mescalin is described in an essay published in
1954. It is a musical landscape of the mind which opened the

doors of heaven as well as hell, combined consonance with dissonance, chromaticism with the most perfect concord of pure sound. A record of Gesualdo's madrigals provided the musical raw material for the experiment.

Huxley's choice of Gesualdo to test a mescalin-induced musical experience reveals an unusual musical intelligence. For these madrigals exhibit many of the symptoms of mental instability and emotional anguish which find expression in violent chromatic modulations, unexpected shifts from minor to major keys, and an uninhibited use of dissonance. Gesualdo's strikingly "modern" chromaticism may be taken to be a musical reflection of some deep-rooted inner division, the affective character of which is illustrated by Gesualdo's own turbulent and violently unbalanced emotional life. Later composers—classic or romantic—made ample use of such chromatic progressions whenever they wished to portray a sense of emotional ambiguity, the result of suspense and uncertainty or unrelieved anguish and unresolved conflict situations. In historical perspective chromaticism came into being as part of the humanist emphasis on the exclusive validity of individual consciousness. Wilfrid Mellers calls chromaticism "Shakespearean" and speaks of its "humanist pathos" through excessive introversion, melancholia, and the death-oriented associations it evokes. He also suggests that the increasing use of chromaticism in the music of the age is symptomatic of the disintegration of the personal life "under the intensity of its passion", implying that the growth of dissonance reflected a disturbing awareness of man's inability to face the reality of his spiritual uprootedness with equanimity.[25] His conclusion—no less relevant for the Jacobean age than it is for ours—refers chromaticism to the emergence of the dramatic instinct which, in its turn, is closely related to a sense of the lateness of the times, of impending decline, of inescapable doom. It is in such a civilization in transition that Gesualdo holds a singularly fitting position. For, again, according to Mellers, he "is the first 'romantic', the ultimate triumph over the medieval attitude of the more individualistic attitude of the Renaissance culture: we may see him in relation to the melancholia and perplexity of Shakespeare's *Hamlet*. Man, with his passions and desires, has become the center of the universe rather than a contributory cog in the universe of God."[26]

When Huxley asked his friends to play a record of Gesualdo's madrigals while he was under the influence of mescalin he did not know what was in store for him. For the "startlingly chromatic" music of the "mad prince" revealed to his altered consciousness an atonality resembling that of late Schönberg and thus brought him back with a pang of recognition to the reality he had hoped to leave behind. Indeed, Gesualdo's madrigals were "a kind of bridge back to the human world" because not only did the music apparently lack any focus of inner organization but it evidently expressed a deep psychological disintegration of a very personal kind. Thus mescalin acted in a twofold manner. On the one hand, the sudden changes from dissonance to consonance, from sustained chromaticism to the least predictable major chord, produced a sense of what Huxley calls "a Higher Order" which prevailed not merely in spite of but even and especially because of the preceding disintegration. Huxley continues his description with the following revealing words: "The totality is present even in the broken pieces. More clearly present, perhaps, than in a completely coherent work. At least you aren't lulled into a sense of false security by some merely human, merely fabricated order. You have to rely on your immediate perception of the ultimate order."[27] Conversely, Gesualdo's music created an emotional dilemma not altogether dissimilar from the one the schizophrenic faces when he has to make a choice between two equally unattainable realities—his own, which he rejects as incompatible with his aspirations, and the reality of a "Higher Order" created by Gesualdo's music; for if, as Huxley puts it, the schizophrenic's "sickness consists in the inability to take refuge from inner and outer reality . . . in the home-made universe of common sense", then indeed, "the schizophrenic is like a man permanently under the influence of mescalin and therefore unable to shut off the experience of a reality which he is not holy enough to live with."[28] Placed thus between two perspectives on reality, that of commonsense and that of Gesualdo's chromaticism resolving itself into "pure sound", the listener under the influence of mescalin may well find it impossible to respond to either of the two with anything but a divided mind. Instead of the revelation of a "higher order" which Gesualdo's music no doubt implied, the hearer was violently and painfully reminded of the disintegration out of which this order grew. The effect of mescalin on the hearer's consciousness consisted in his deeply disturbing realization that though the personal neurosis of the "mad prince" suggested certain musical accomplishments far beyond any achieved by his emotionally more stable contemporaries, the chaos that lay at the root of the "higher order" may finally destroy the purity of the musical illumination it had made possible. The haunting spectre of increased division after listening to the revelation of a "higher order" of things did not encourage further experiments with Gesualdo's amazing madrigals under the influence of mescalin.[29]

But Huxley did not give in. Experiment followed experiment, and Gesualdo was finally replaced by Bach. Once again this was a natural choice. Where if not in polyphonic and contrapuntal music could the One and Indivisible be found and full integration be achieved, provided of course the drug was powerful enough to induce a state of consciousness where musical illumination, without the danger of schizophrenic division of mind, could be attained. A year after the experiment with mescalin and Gesualdo's madrigals Huxley listened to Bach's B-Minor suite under similar laboratory conditions, having previously taken 75 micrograms of LSD. On this occasion his hypothesis was fully corroborated: man when effectively drugged could in effect intensify the power of his awareness to "supraterrestrial" dimensions (as Proust would have said) with the assistance of Bach's music.

The implication is fairly obvious: as LSD could produce a heightened state of musical consciousness, the hearer—if at all susceptible to spiritual illumination—is enabled to experience a sense of infinity and timelessness, while at the same instant achieving full integration of his psyche with the objective reality around him. The dichotomy between the two planes of perception, the inner and the outer, no longer interfered with the newly acquired consciousness of transcendence. Huxley described this unconventional musical experience in a letter to Humphrey Osmond. The relevant passage deserves to be quoted in full: "I had the same kind of experience as I had on the previous occasion—transfiguration of the external world, and the understanding, through a realization involving the whole man, that Love is the One . . . We played the Bach B-Minor suite and the

'Musical Offering'. Other music seemed unsatisfactory. Bach was a revelation. The tempo of the piece did not change; nevertheless they went on for centuries, and they were a manifestation, on the plane of art, of perpetual creation, a demonstration of the necessity of death and the self-evidence of immortality, an expression of the essential all-rightness of the universe—for the music was far beyond tragedy, but included death and suffering with everything else in the divine impartiality which is the One, which is Love, which is Being, which is *Istigkeit* . . . One can imagine a ritual of initiation, in which a whole group of people transported on to the Other World by one of the elixirs [e.g. LSD] would sit together listening to, say, the B-Minor suite and so being brought to a direct, unmediated understanding of the divine nature.

It has been a long journey from Proust's musical *salon* at the Verdurins where a variety of specially invited guests listened to Vinteuil's "petite phrase" and at least one among them felt compelled to note down the inner transformation his consciousness underwent under the impact of the newly discovered musical reality. The guests who listened to Professor Godbole's ritualistic tune were treated to a "petite phrase" of a more demanding nature, for the singer's musical meditation put their whole code of esthetic and religious values into question and thus required of them an effort of the imagination of which none of them was capable. The "purity" of the sound passed them by—not being absorbed by their conscious mind. Huxley's suggestion of a ritual of initiation with the assistance of a dose of LSD acting upon the music of Bach and thus creating the perfect condition for the heightening of consciousness that would enable the invited hearer to experience the ecstasy of the saint confronted by visions of holiness—thereby assisting those who have been initiated into the mystery of transcendence to overcome all dichotomy and, therefore, all existential anguish— appears like a short-cut to ultimate bliss, an apparently fully satisfying ritual of collective paradise regained.

Those who followed Huxley's perilous experiments, among them many of his younger disciples, discovered soon enough that neither music nor drug-taking need be limited to special occasions—such as experiments under laboratory conditions— nor need they be considered separate aspects of an experience that, Huxley had said, involved *the whole man*. Kenneth Leech, in his book *Youthquake*, describes this synthesis of drugs and music in the underground culture of London, between 1967 and 1969, in language strongly reminiscent of Huxley's description of his experiments with LSD. In a review of his book we read: "The association between hallucinogens and music was almost indissoluble: people got high to appreciate music more, and listened to music to get high. The high of music and hallucinogens was in turn seen as a form of spiritual experience *in itself* . . . As the terminology suggests, music was thought to act like a drug, altering consciousness and changing society."[31]

The social angle given to these experiments is not surprising. Music has at all times been considered either as an opiate to alleviate the suffering of the majority or as a stimulant to inspire doubts and questions among the few who knew what doubts to express and what questions to ask. Some of them, undoubtedly a minority among the few, discovered a confirmation of their doubts and an answer to their questions in music. But never before has it been proclaimed in language intelligible to everyone—within the context of the increasing vulgarization of metaphorical speech through the media of mass communication—that all music is politically and socially significant; and that, as *Youthquake* proclaims, "When the mode of music changes, the walls of the city will crumble."

Notes to Chapter Six

1. Henri Bergson, *Laughter*, p. 162.
2. Henri Bergson, *Time and Free Will*, p. 14.
3. Susanne Langer, *Feeling and Form. A Theory of Art developed from "Philosophy in a New Key"*, p. 104.
4. M. C. Beardsley, *Aesthetics*, pp. 338–9.
5. Victor Zuckerkandl, *Sound and Symbol*, p.242.
6. Henry James, Preface to *Roderick Hudson* in *The Art of the Novel*, p. 5.
7. Martin Foss, *Symbol and Metaphor*, p. 160.
8. Marcel Proust, *Remembrance of Things Past*, vol. II, pp. 180–185. See the following, quoted in Jean Brincourt, *Les Oeuvres et les Lumières*, p. 40: "I have tried to make unconscious phenomena, completely forgotten and situated in the remote past, visible to consciousness. This, perhaps, as a form of reflection, may have made me encounter Bergson, for there has not been as far as I am aware of it, any direct influence." (From a letter to C. Vettard,

written a few months before his death, In: *Correspondance Generale de Proust*, tome III, p. 195.) The translation is my own.

9. *Ibid.*, vol. X, part II, *The Captive*, p. 233.
10. *Ibid.*, p. 67.
11. *Ibid.*, p. 74.
12. *Ibid.*, p. 234.
13. *Ibid.*, vol. XII, p. 224.
14. From a letter to Jacques de Lacretelle, n.d., quoted in Benoist-Mechin, *La Musique et l'Immortalité dans l'Oeuvre de Marcel Proust*, p.18.
15. Samuel Beckett, *Proust and Three Dialogues*, pp. 91–92.
16. Peter Crossley-Holland, in *The Pelican History of Music*, ed. by Alec Robertson and Denis Stevens, chapter I/3, "India", p. 35.
17. *Ibid.*, p. 36.
18. E. M. Forster, *A Passage to India*, p. 77.
19. *Ibid.*, pp. 281-2.
20. Frank Kermode, "The One Orderly Product", first published in *Puzzles and Epiphanies: Essays and Reviews 1958–1961*, 1962. Republished in *E.M. Forster, A Passage to India, A Casebook*, edited by Malcolm Bradbury, p. 223.

    Forster's attempt to define the Hindu vision of things is given, again, through Godbole, in an oblique reference to his song: "Good and evil are different as their names imply. But, in my own humble opinion, they are both of them aspect of my Lord. He is present in the one, absent in the other, and the difference between presence and absence is great, as great as my feeble mind can grasp. Yet absence implies presence, absence is not non-existence, and we are therefore entitled to repeat, 'Come, come, come, come.' "
21. Aldous Huxley, letter to Jean E. Hare, dated Llano, Calif., December 30, 1945, *Letters*, p. 538.
22. Letter to Paul Valéry, from 3 rue du Bac, Suresnes (Seine), dated January 4, 1930, *Letters*, p. 323.
23. Letter to Scudder Rice, from 3 rue du Bac, Suresnes (Seine), dated January 6, 1930, *Letters*, p. 324.
24. Letter to Robert Nichols, dated February 17, 1930, *Letters*, p. 329.
25. Wilfrid Mellers, *Harmonious Meeting*, pp. 19, 23, 39, 47.
26. Wilfrid Mellers, *Music and Society*, pp. 60–63.
27. Aldous Huxley, "Doors of Perception" (1954) in *On Art and Artists*, p. 111.
28. *Ibid.*, p. 115.
29. See also Huxley's essay, "Gesualdo: Variations on a Musical Theme," in: *Tomorrow and Tomorrow and Tomorrow*, 1956, *Ibid.*, p. 286.
30. Letter to Dr. Humphrey Osmond, from 740 North Kings Road, Los Angeles 46, Ca., dated December 23, 1955, *Letters*, p. 778. In the same letter there occurs the following passage: "Only polyphony, and only the highly organized polyphony . . . can convey the nature

of reality, which is multiplicity in unity, the reconciliation of oppo-
sites, the not-twoness of diversity, the Nirvana-nature of Samsara,
the Love which is the bridge between objective and subjective,
good and evil, death and life."
31. From a review of Kenneth Leech, *Youthquake*, Sheldon Press, by
Jerome Palmer, *The New Statesman*, January 25, 1974, pp. 120–1.

VII
The Music Master

1

While Huxley was conducting initiation experiments aimed at a heightened state of consciousness through the effect of music on the nervous system, altered by hallucinogenic drugs, other novelists derived little comfort from an artificially induced awareness of oneness with a Higher Order of Being. Anyone who cares to trace Huxley's development as novelist as well as thinker, will be struck by the ever-recurring theme of the perfectibility of the human mind, and its countertheme, the relapse into barbarism and moral chaos, both being part of an evolutionary curve which, once the supremacy of awareness over unawareness has been established, will finally promote the conquest of the fragmented and divided intellect by the unified human personality.

It is an inspired vision of the future, no less exalting for being utopian. In this vision of the individual mind integrated in a society of initiates, total musical response, whether drug-induced or experienced as part of an exercise in meditation, plays a not inconsiderable part. From first to last, in novels or essays, Huxley reiterates his conviction that through a combination of music and contemplation the individual can attain an awareness of the indivisibility of all Being. The initiation ritual thus acquires religious, indeed mystical, overtones.[1] What is originally experienced as music, need no longer be defined in terms of sounds heard, but of life-giving values entertained by the conscious mind.

The ideal of the contemplative life for the multitude was outside the scope of Huxley's perennial philosophy. Its teachings do not address the unitiated who, indeed, may seek salvation by "getting high" on drugs and music (as the quotation at the end of the last chapter so clearly illustrates) and by dabbling in "transcendental meditation", inducing thereby a vision of personal bliss and a sense of freedom from the compulsions imposed by the expediencies of contemporary life and by the conformist standards of social behavior. Huxley would, in all likelihood, have repudiated most of his self-indulgent disciples who took the short-cut to "complete living" without ever having experienced the trial of intellectual anguish which initially led him to experiment with mescalin.

Huxley's vision of a future where it might be possible to initiate a group of individuals into a Higher Order of Being through a greatly intensified musical experience is portrayed as the central focus—not without its ironic overtones—in the development of man's mind towards self-realization, in Hermann Hesse's last, and most mature novel, *The Glass Bead Game*, set in a German-speaking country with a non-German sounding name (Kastalien–Castalia in the English translation) and narrated in an even more remote future age. In this "pedagogical province", the individual is, first of all, instructed in the discipline of subordination. Only after he has achieved complete adaptation to the intellectual hierarchy which constitutes, in terms of absolute obedience to the rules laid down by the Order, the framework within which teachers and pupils live, is he initiated into the various branches of knowledge that will make him, at some future date, an adept at the "game". The discipline of subordination is, by way of conscious training, absorbed by the individual through the study and the exercise of music and the contemplation induced by it. The ideal of the musical life is so closely allied to the acceptance of an intellectual hierarchy within the "province" that musical response cannot and, indeed, need not any longer be separated from voluntary submission to an ethos of social values. Being one and indivisible, the discipline of music and that of intellectual discrimination provide the foundation upon which alone the ideal of the fully integrated individual may be built.

Conceivably Hesse derived his ideal of education through music from Goethe's description of a "pedagogical province" in his *Wilhelm Meister*. The discipline and training to which the young have to submit is, in Goethe's novel, formulated in terms of a musical metaphor. "Would the musician permit his pupils," asks the writer, "to rove wildly on the strings or to invent intervals according to his own inclination and liking? What is most noticeable [in this educational scheme] is that nothing should be left to the arbitrary choice of the student; the basic subject which will determine his future work is clearly given, the tools he will have to handle are passed on to him, even the manner in which he will have to make use of them ... through this disciplined collaboration [gesetzliches Zusammenwirken] the impossible will be made possible." Thomas Mann who, in 1922, quotes this passage in his essay "Goethe and Tolstoy" justifies Goethe's musical metaphor. "It is not by chance," he observes, "that the authorities of the province choose music as the paradigm [of all education]; for is it not truly the spiritual symbol of all 'disciplined collaboration' of the manifold constituents [in human life] with a view to achieving a cultural aim worthy of human dignity ... in brief, just as agriculture is the natural element of education, music constitutes its spiritual counterpart," for from it [in Goethe's words] "identical paths lead in all directions."[2] Once only, in his novel, does Hesse explicitly refer to Goethe's vision of an ideal education when he reminds the reader that "in the old days [it] used to be called, in the poet Goethe's phrase, 'the pedagogical province'."[3] But Goethe's age, and the centuries that preceded and followed it, are only vaguely remembered by the narrators of Hesse's story (always an anonymous "we"), situated, as these ages are, in an almost prehistoric past. Long before this, one may dimly recognize layers of an even remoter age which can no longer be recaptured except in the form of legends transmitted from generation to generation, and traditionally kept alive by the few wise men who, in order to give meaning to the present, resuscitate the past. Hesse's anonymous narrators thus call themselves the heirs of "a reformation which began in the twentieth century". What came before pertains to the dark abyss of time.

Like Mann and Joyce before him, Hesse is attracted to the mythological roots of the universe he creates. Each one of these novelists in his own way reveals below the surface of present appearances as yet unexplored significances within an everrecurring archetypal scheme of things, as if he wishes to stress the vulnerability of the foundations on which man's own awareness of the present is built. Hesse's "General Introduction" to the story refers the reader, eager for information about the origin of the Glass Bead Game, to the ancient Chinese, to Pythagoras, and the Hellenistic Gnostic circles, to "several pinnacles of Arabic-Moorish culture", to Scholasticism and Humanism, to the academies of mathematicians of the seventeenth and eighteenth centuries, and, perhaps the most revealing of them all, to "the runes of Novalis's hallucinatory visions."[4] Well-known figures in the history of ideas such as Abelard, Leibniz, and Hegel, are mentioned side by side with less familiar and partly legendary thinkers, such as Nicholas de Cues, Plinius Ziegenhals, and Bastian Perrot of Calw who is presumed to have been the actual inventor of the "Game". The historical and the legendary share a common relevance. There is nothing in the story, as told by Hesse, to divide fact from imagination, knowledge based on empirical experiment from knowledge based on creative intuition. Though the narrators use a plain and unadorned, if somewhat archaic, language, theirs is a post-twentieth century view of things.

The present, considered as a structural component of Hesse's story, is virtually nonexistent: the historical past melts into the fictitious future. The present instant in time is buried beneath various layers of consciousness which are uncovered, as in an archeological dig, in the course of the novel: here are side by side Bergson's "present which endures", embodied in the musical compositions of the seventeenth and eighteenth centuries, the present during which the Glass Bead Game flourished (possibly some time during the first half of the twenty-first century), the present of the narrators who tell their story after the decline and reorganization of the Game, the present of the reader which may lie anywhere in a not-to-be-defined future. In addition, there is the writer's own present, the decade during which he conceived and wrote the novel, between 1933 and 1943, and which includes his views on the cultural disintegration which, according to him, took place in the first half of the twentieth century and is characterized by artistic and psychological deviation.

The narrators call that remote time which is Hesse's and the reader's own "The Age of the Feuilleton" when "men came to enjoy an incredible degree of intellectual freedom, more than they could stand". Ignorant of the tremendous scope for good

or evil that this freedom conferred upon them, they debased and
betrayed their own reasoning power by selling it to the daily
newspaper, "a major source of mental pabulum for the reader in
want of culture", by substituting virtuosity for true erudition,
and the "irony of desperation" for a positive code of values. The
games they played were innocuous enough, but "they sprang
from their deep need to close their eyes and flee from unsolved
problems and anxious forebodings of doom into an imaginary
world". The lectures they attended were "entertaining, impassioned or witty", full of fashionable phrases, catchwords, and
"fragments of knowledge robbed of all meaning." The most
ominous cultural feature of that far-away period (which is the
first half of the twentieth century) is what the narrators desig-
nate as "that dreadful devaluation of the Word", whether in
speech or in print, in private or in public, in parliamentary
debates no less than in literary work. It was, indeed, an age of
"busy productivity", but also an age of dread at what the poet
Yeats foresaw as "the second coming". Prior to this fateful
retrogression into barbarism and as a symptom of the coming
darkness, the poet had, as early as in 1919, realized that "the
best lack all conviction, while the worst are full of passionate
intensity". The narrators, in Hesse's novel, recognize the same
symptoms and diagnose the same disease: "Among the good
there prevailed a quietly resigned gloom, among the wicked a
malicious pessimism."[5]

In the context of hollow intellectual pretense, the individual,
with a sort of hectic eagerness, admitted the absurdity inherent
in his own existence, while simultaneously adapting himself to
what fashion, dictated by the majority, expected of him. Twentieth-century writers and, especially, biographers, described the
essence of a personality as residing in his "deviance, abnormal-
ity, uniqueness" with a characteristic stress on the pathological
as being the touchstone of all originality. Idiosyncrasy of any
kind seemed preferable by far to what "the moderns" (as the
narrators at times call themselves) look upon the individual's
most challenging pursuit in life, "the greatest possible integration into the generality, the greatest possible service to the
suprapersonal."[6] The study and practice of music provides a
valid criterion by which to judge the singular deterioration of
the human psyche during that period. The narrators speak of

the twentieth-century "mania for dynamics and *gradazione*" in the performance of music, its merely "intellectual veneration" for the art of music, "all too frequently tainted by melancholic resignation" and finally refer, in particular, to the wrong-headed emphasis on "the conductor's execution and 'conception' ", rather than on the music itself.[7] If the Word suffered "devaluation", so indeed did music, when it adapted itself to the fashionable style of the day and when the public considered originality of performance to be an end in itself. As opposed to this, the narrators speak of "the naïvety and chasteness" of an earlier musical age and those "happier times" when "the charming, simple-hearted delight in music making"[8] required no adherence to the passing fashions of an ignorant multitude, but grew out of a tradition, "both child-like and superior, as all good music must in the midst of the unredeemed muteness of the world."[9]

2

As the narrators wander backward and forward in time, anxious to place the Glass Bead Game within a time dimension comprehensible to the present-day reader (which may be any time from the early twentieth century to some remote future when the Glass Bead Game itself would already be almost forgotten), they use music as a yardstick by which to measure the political stability and spiritual vigor of civilizations or to predict the inevitability of their downfall. The ambiguity of such terms as "modern", "recent", or "contemporary" applies to all elements that contribute to the rise and fall of civilizations, not least to music. A sense of contemporaneity need not be the result of a conscious realization of what is being experienced as "the present". The true contemporary may find himself at home in the civilization and music of some past age, not merely listening to it with a mind attuned to that far-away time, but performing the music as though no time at all had elapsed between the actual composition in the remote past and the "contemporary" performance in the present. Such an experience is not identical with the fashionable resurrection of some past musical fashion but reveals an unselfconscious indifference to the time-bound mutabilities of musical taste and the changes in conception and performance consequent upon it.

The narrators refer, in particular, to the League of the Journeyers to the East among whom there were supposed to be
"itinerant instrumentalists and minstrels" who could perform
the music of earlier periods, such as a piece of music composed
between 1600 and 1650, "exactly as if all the subsequent modes,
refinements, and virtuoso achievements were still unknown".
When, the narrators continue, an orchestra of the Journeyers
performed a suite by Handel as it must have been heard by
Handel's own "contemporaries", some of the listeners, brought
up as they were in the musical dilettantism of the "Age of the
Feuilleton", had the impression that they were hearing music
for the first time in their lives."[10] As past and future are inextricably interfused in Hesse's story, the only continuity of which
the reader of this novel is aware is, as in Proust's and Joyce's
work, that of a fictitious present "which endures". What to Joyce
was a day in the life of Leopold Bloom and to Proust a lifetime
of remembered experiences, expands backward into prehistory
and forward into utopia in Hesse's novel. Music is the catalyst
which resolves past and future into one. In that sense all music is
"contemporary" with the one who has acquired the knowledge
of how to perform it and how to listen to it.

Individual composers, if they are at all mentioned, provide the
scenario for this musical universe. Composers who lived after
1700 are hardly ever referred to by name. Beethoven, Schubert,
Brahms, and the Romantics (or Hesse's own musical
contemporaries) are either passed over in silence or receive a
cursory mention. The eighteenth century is called "a time of
incipient degeneration", while the musical style of the fifteenth
and sixteenth centuries is admired for its unalloyed purity and
for the curious fact that "among the vast quantities of music
written at that time we fail to find a trace of anything bad." [11]
While Bach is unquestionably one of the "immortals" among
the Glass Bead players in Castalia, a piano-sonata by Purcell,
certainly not a major work by this composer, plays a not inconsiderable part in the musical education of the hero of the novel.
Throughout, the merely subjective elements in a composition
are frowned upon and treated with distrust. What matters is not
the musical idiosyncrasy of composer or performer, nor the
acquired taste for a particular style on the part of the listener,
but the context of significances within which music is placed in
any given culture.

Already in the "General Introduction", the narrators refer to fables and legends which originated in the formative years of all great civilizations and which ascribe to music powers far greater than those of a mere art—the capacity to control men and nations. More specifically they mention "the legendary China of the Old Kings," where it was generally assumed that "if music throve, all was well with culture and morality and with the kingdom itself." Conversely, if music decayed, and "forbidden, diabolic, heaven-offending keys" were used, the decline of music was reflected in the government of the country, "the walls trembled and collapsed", and all order and unity in the state was overturned. Examples of such declining music are given by the Chinese sage Lu Bu We in his book *Spring and Autumn*. It resembles the music of the "Age of the Feuilleton" (though the narrators do not say so explicitly) by striving for new and rare tonal effects, thus departing from the essence of music which is serenity. This "tempestuous" and "magic" music had its inevitable effect on the life of the common people: they were dissatisfied and rebelled. For, says the Chinese sage, "The music of a restive age is excited and fierce, and its government is perverted. The music of a decaying state is sentimental and sad, and its government imperilled." The narrators, in their eagerness to trace the origin of the power of music over the minds of men, go even further back in pre-historic times when music was used as a device "for putting large numbers of people 'in tune' with one another, engendering the same mood . . . encouraging them to invoke and conjure up the eternal powers, to dance, to compete, to make war, to worship,"[12] all this in view of an innate desire among all men to submit to some Higher Order of Being by subordinating their individual will to the abstract ideal of wholeness, unattainable to man except through complete absorption in and identification with a work of music.

This ideal of wholeness is embodied, the narrators observe, in the Game played by the initiates who have been instructed in its rules and who are ready to submit to the discipline of the quasi-monastic order into which they have been accepted by a process of strict and somewhat patriarchal selectivity. Starting at the bottom of the hierarchy, they undergo an exhaustive training in the various intellectual accomplishments the playing of the Game demands. The "instrument" on which the Game was initially played resembled a child's abacus, "a frame with several dozen wires" on which glass beads could be strung, an arrangement which corresponded to "the lines of the music staff" while the various-sized beads stood for the time-values of the notes. It was a primitive handmade mechanical contrivance on which musical themes could be "played" or improvised, variations invented, counterpoints established, and so forth. At a much later date, this purely musical discipline on which the original game was based was expanded to include many other arts and sciences. The playing of the game led to the development of a sort of universal language, with a special emphasis on music and mathematics, and an extension of these two into symbolic formulas applicable to all arts and all sciences. In this way each additional discipline created its own symbolic language and its own combination of meanings and counter-meanings, its relations, analogies, and correspondences. The narrators call the Game, after it has reached its ultimate perfection, a *unio mystica*, or "a form of concentrated self-awareness for intellectuals". The encyclopedic knowledge which was required of the masters of the Glass Bead Game made such a search for a common denominator which would embrace *all* arts and sciences an intrinsic part of the Game itself. This common denominator provided an esthetically satisfying solution, but by no means the only possible solution, to the problem the player had set himself. For, considered as an exercise in mental concentration, there were as many solutions as there were possible "combinations" of esthetically or intellectually meaningful formulas.

The means used to obtain such solutions was contemplation. It is only by meditating on the essence of things, and by transcending all ready-made formulas and transitory correspondences, that the ideal of intellectual perfection could be attained. As each field of knowledge creates its own symbols by which it alone can be understood, the player was required to devote a considerable effort to the exercise of meditation. For the meaning of symbols eludes discursive thought and mere intellectual analysis: as the basic principle of the Game resided in the search for perfection, the various symbols, whether pertaining to music, to mathematics, or to any other realms of human knowledge, had to be fitted into a framework of significances "beyond all images and multiplicities", a perfection which would embody, in the narrators' words, "pure being, the fullness of reality."[13]

It is characteristic of Hesse's conception of the Game and its most gifted players that at the end of the "General Introduction" the narrators should conclude their historical survey with a remark supposedly made by Joseph Knecht, the hero of the novel and the future *Magister Ludi*, on the meaning of perfection in human rather than scientific terms. His criterion is taken from western classical music, and the attitude of mind underlying this musical tradition. Speaking to his pupils, he describes the essence of this music as expressing "knowledge of the tragedy of the human condition, affirmation of human destiny, courage, cheerful serenity." In addition to this, in works composed by the greatest among the classical composers, may be heard "death-defying intrepidity, a gallantry, and a note of superhuman laughter, of immortal gay serenity."[14] This is the language of Harry Haller, the Steppenwolf, listening to Mozart's dread-inspired chords which accompany Don Giovanni's descent into hell and which are followed by the composer's "shrill, wild, unearthly laughter". Is Joseph Knecht then, perhaps, a reincarnation of the Steppenwolf who, on one occasion, after getting drunk on a bottle of wine, dreams of the intimacy of a candlelit baroque music-room where a small chamber orchestra would be playing select pieces of classical music, while he, under the effect of his momentary intoxication, "would have sipped the cool and noble music as gods sip nectar"?[15]

Anyone familiar with Hesse's way of thinking will see in the concept of reincarnation one of the main creative principles at work in the writing of his novels. He actually added three more "lives" of the protagonist of *The Glass Bead Game* to his story, supposedly written by Joseph Knecht himself, of which the first, *The Rainmaker*, takes place "thousands of years ago" and tells a story of service and sacrifice—not so much for the sake of the primitive matriarchal tribe of which he is the spiritual leader, but as an expression of allegiance to the life of the intellect. The second "life" is placed "in the days when St. Hilarion was still alive" and describes the sacrificial search of "Joseph" for true faith in an age when Christianity was still rooted in pagan rites and rituals, while the third "life", historically of even greater ambiguity, occurs at a time "when Vishnu, or rather Vishnu in his avater as Rama, fought his savage battles with the princes of demons" and "one of his parts took on human shape and thus entered the cycles of forms once more." It is the story of a dream, of the illusion of love requited and yet unfulfilled, and, lastly, of the return of the hero to reality embodied by his "master" who receives him back to life with sympathy and understanding, and teaches him the meaning of self-discipline and service.

Basically, Hesse never deviated from the path that his own inner nature had pre-ordained. The various literary reincarnations of the hero of *The Glass Bead Game* correspond to the psychological reincarnation that lead from Sinclair to Demian, from Mozart to the jazz-player Pablo, from Narziss and Siddharta to the most mature and most controversial figure of them all, Joseph Knecht, first as a young man in search of perfection and later on as *Magister Ludi*, as a player and teacher but, more than anything else, as quester, and ultimately as rebel against the very principle of perfection upon which the Game was built. Each reincarnation, a step towards greater self-knowledge, but also towards a more demanding commitment to a life which acquires whatever validity it possesses through the ideals of service, discipline, and sacrifice.[16]

3

What is true of the idea, and the embodiment of that idea in the hero, is equally applicable to the art-form which accompanies the reader from novel to novel. The various human activities related to music, creation, performance, and response, undergo a process of transmutation, of ascent from mere emotional commitment unencumbered by metaphysical thought to complete spiritual absorption where the music-maker and his music are one and indivisible. The creation of music, itself a form of reincarnation, is an integral part of Hesse's contemplative view of the human condition. In his novels—at least in those that are the object of this study—the music played by Pistorius on his organ (in *Demian*), Pablo on his saxophone (in the *Steppenwolf*), and by the Castalian music master on his piano (*The Glass Bead Game*) establish a musical continuity out of time, a kind of common denominator in musical terms where the organ-playing

Pistorius acquires the spiritual features of a Jungian psychotherapist, Harry Haller's fantastic vision of the saxophone-play-
ing Pablo resurrects a gaily laughing Mozart, while, lastly, the
piano-playing music master in *The Glass Bead Game* who instructs
Joseph Knecht in musical meditation, completes the circle of
reincarnation by teaching his pupil the art of communing in
silence with what the infinite articulateness of music expresses in
a language which is neither that of human speech nor that of
nature.

The figure of the music master is, in effect, central to the
understanding of Hesse's novel. It is he who introduces the still
undeveloped mind of Joseph Knecht to music as "the joy-giving
harmony of law and freedom, of service and rule" by playing out
to him a theme, taken from an old song, and developing it into a
fugue which, simple as it is, makes the young boy see "the whole
cosmos guided, ordered, and interpreted by the spirit of music."[17] At a later stage in his musical instruction, Joseph Knecht
is taught the art of meditation through the discipline of self-
awareness induced by the musical experience. The music master, together with his pupil, explores this ever-renewed synthesis
between the musical and the contemplative life. The first exercise in meditation is described in full: it all begins with a sense of
void. Then, as the theme played by the music master reaches the
young listener's conscious mind, he experiences it "as a dance, a
continuous series of balancing exercises, a succession of smaller
or larger steps from the middle of an axis of symmetry." Later
on, when the music master leaves him to meditate on what he
has just now heard, he asks his pupil to draw what he has "seen"
in his meditation on a piece of paper. At first Knecht tries to
express his inner vision as a line with small tributary lines
moving off diagonally from it; later on, the line curves into a
circle with the same tributary lines radiating from it "like flowers
in a garland". When, finally, he falls asleep, he dreams of the
bright quadrangle of the school "contracted into an oval and
then spread out to a circle, a garland, and the garland began
turning slowly, until at last it was whirling madly and burst,
flying apart into twinkling stars."[18] This is the nearest that
Hesse's novel comes to a symbolic representation of the Self,
not embodied in the intellectual/esthetic game of ideas upon
which Castalia is built, but as a still point, a core of primordial

meaning, around which life turns in ever-expanding circles of luminosity. What the meditation, induced by the playing of a fugue, reveals to the dreamer is not the perfection of intellectual relationships between various conceptual systems but the impenetrable depth of the human soul surrounded by perpetually revolving light, the eternal return of life to its own source.

The music master's profoundly ambivalent attitude to the Glass Bead Game as practiced in Castalia is best exemplified in his old age and death. Already during Knecht's first meeting with him, he had warned him against the temptations of the Game as a fruitless intellectual exercise alienating the mind of the player from the true reality of being which resides in man's Self rather than in the subtle combination of ideas and the esthetic pleasure that the playing of the Game affords. As the music master grows in age, he not only becomes a stranger to the Game itself but increasingly turns inward, as if listening to sounds that can no longer be heard by human ears, towards the inaudible quintessence of music, "away from ideas and towards unity". At the time of his death, the music he had practiced all his life permeates his whole being. There is little left of his physical presence, of his musical memory, and of his musical skill. He has, at last, become what he was always meant to be, "a symbol, or rather a manifestation, a personification of music."[19]

Knecht's encounter with Castalia thus takes place on two opposing symbolic planes, that of the "Game" as a symbol of abstract intellectual perfection and that of the music master as a symbol of human excellence born out of the synthesis of the language of music with the art of meditation. That this ideal of human wholeness should have taken the music master "away from people and towards silence, away from words and towards music", indicates the initial doubt that entered Hesse's mind, while he was writing this novel, as to the validity of mental training carried on in an existential void, however illuminating the results of these exercises of the mind and however esthetically satisfying the pure structurality of the Game.[20]

While the narrators of Knecht's life are at great pains to tell the story of his rise in the "pedagogical province" from pupil to *Magister Ludi* as if their main concern was to provide the reader with convenient formulas for an understanding of his growing mastery of the arts of music and meditation, the accomplishments deriving from it, such as serenity of mind and a cheerful disposition, acquire, in the course of the narrative, an increasingly hollow ring. In a conversation between Knecht as the Master of the Glass Bead Game and his rebellious friend Designori, the former defines music as "an act of courage, a serene, smiling, striding forward and dancing through the terrors and flames of the world, the festive offering of a sacrifice."[21] This is already a significant departure from the music master's teaching. Knecht's definition of music as a "dance" of defiance against the brutishness and the nastiness of the world reveals his own awareness of the symbolic polarity existing between the supremacy of the esthetic ideal as cultivated in Castalia and the "reality" of the outside world, spiritually crippled and threatened by retrogression into chaos. For the first time the narrators of Knecht's life hint at the contradiction inherent in the assumption of man's spiritual life as a game—however esthetically relevant the rules which lead to the creation of a sense of ultimate harmony in the player's mind—and in the opposing reality of "terrors and flames" surrounding the ivory-tower over which Knecht presides. The irony implied in man's striving for perfection in an imperfect world is never explicitly stated by the narrators of *The Glass Bead Game*. They, after all, write with hindsight, long after Knecht's sacrificial death and the inevitable compromise in the playing of the Game between the extremes of esthetic exclusiveness and the historical processes which took place outside Castalia. Joseph Knecht's ultimate rejection of Castalia and his return to the world of ordinary men, supplies an additional symbolic dimension to the story, that of time regained at the price of a paradise lost. What has, so ironically, been regained is an awareness of the impurity of all living processes and of the need to redeem the world for ever anew, not by isolating oneself within the seclusion of an intellectual elite of master-players, but by service and sacrifices; not by dedicating oneself to a life of esthetic and intellectual integrity, but to the more demanding virtues of humility and compassion.

4

Anyone who reads Hesse's last novel as a parable rather than as literary fiction will not find Knecht's desertion of Castalia for the "terrors and flames" of the world in the last part of the book an inconsistent *volte face*, or, as has been said, a recantation of all the ideals he was supposed to embody, a change of mind almost in the nature of an apostasy. Throughout Knecht's rise to mastery over the intricacies of the Game, the narrators of his life story insist on the religious fervor with which he devoted himself to the study of the various arts and sciences, but above all to the practice of music and meditation. The ideal of the *Magister Ludi*, in effect, resembles that of the saint, "in whose soul-state," according to Hesse, "the chaos of the world is turned into meaning and music."[22] But Knecht, considered as a reincarnation of so many other imperfect heroes in Hesse's previous work, is no saint. In the course of the story he comes to realize, not his shortcomings as a master of the Game, for therein he has achieved perfection, but his shortcomings as a human being who, by cutting himself off from the "world", from history and from time, denies the existence of chaos. He also becomes aware of the need of more sacrificial courage than music and meditation call for, and of a humble, less self-conscious serenity than life among the "immortals" permits him to cultivate. By returning to chaos at this stage in his life, Joseph Knecht confronts reality with his eyes open, no longer an overlife-size figure of superhuman intellectual dimensions, but a man among men, a teacher of the young, placed in historical time, only more aware than any one of his contemporaries of the true core of his being which, amidst all the chaos of the world, must remain unalloyed by the sickness of the age.

As a parable rather than a novel, Hesse's last work has indeed a message to deliver. Mental integrity equals sterility if it is not put into the service of life; the artist who has achieved such a completeness of vision must, if he wishes to relate his art to life, translate his sense of inner wholeness, indeed his "serenity", into creative activity within the limiting context of life's unredeemable chaos. This may be achieved through music; but there are other avenues of creation open to him, all those which would enable him to transmit his own personal integration to others. Hesse's last work is indeed no longer "fiction", but an allegory of the ascent of man from mere intellectual mastery to complete individuation.

In musical terms this shift from the artificially controlled harmony prevailing in Castalia to the uninhibited chromaticism echoing through the chaos of the world, is hinted at whenever Knecht's Castalian friend Tegularius appears in the story. Conceived as a Nietzschean figure, he is described as a man "of low vitality" who intermittently suffers from "periods of insomnia and nervous aches", yields to "spells of melancholia", and probably plays with thoughts of suicide. In addition to all these "deficiencies" (as seen through the eyes of his Castalian contemporaries) he is a man of brilliant intellectual gifts who "has mastered the technique of our game like a great musician his instrument". Yet, when Knecht studies some of the games composed by his friend, he discovers an originality in style quite alien to the spirit of Castalia. Actually they contradict everything that the glass bead game essentially stands for, being, as Knecht describes them, "true literary productions . . . little dramas, in structure almost pure monologues." Tegularius offers no solution; instead, each game is "like a perfect elegy upon the transitoriness inherent in all beautiful things and the ultimate dubiety immanent in all soaring flight of the intellect." Yet, these games,—in terms of their "musical" composition—"were so extraordinarily beautiful that they brought tears to one's eyes."[23]

Knecht's willful and brilliant friend represented an element of "chaos" in which his various "games", musical and otherwise, originate. Subordination, discipline, and the practice of meditation were rejected by him as incompatible with his strongly developed individuality. Though utterly unhierarchic, he was accepted in Castalia, simply because his way of organizing his thoughts corresponded to the highest level of culture demanded of a true Castalian. Knecht was fascinated by this outsider, this solitary genius who, in spite of all warnings and admonitions, played with "bold, forbidden, intrepid ideas" and also represented in the eyes of the *Magister Ludi*," a small open window that looked out upon new prospects", and yet at the same time, a portent of the demoralization and downfall of that same Castalian culture which Knecht's mastery of the game symbolized. Tegularius was, indeed, a "forerunner" of something that was still nameless, recognizably pertaining to the past and yet also indicative of the tenuous dividing line between what was and what will be. Within the context of Hesse's worldview every new cultural departure constitutes a return to chaos, and thus an affirmation of the individual (rather than of a hierarchy) as the ultimate creator of values.

In Knecht's letter of resignation to the "Board of Educators" the metaphor of fire threatening the foundation upon which the institution of the Glass Bead Game is built, is very much in evidence. While he is occupied with the "delicate, sensitive instruments" which help him to solve the abstruse problems of the human mind, his instinct tells him "that down below something is burning, our whole structure is imperilled, and that my business now is not to anaylse music or define rules of the Game, but to rush where the smoke is."[24] The tone in which this letter is written is one of exasperation and impatience. Exasperation with a ritualistic hierarchy which insists on the preservation of the purity of the Game, the rules that have to be followed, the intellectual sterility which results from irresponsible toying with associations and ideas, worthless in themselves, though of considerable structural interest. Impatience with Castalian elitism which refuses to acknowledge the need for suffering, the inevitability of personal tragedy whenever artistic creation rather than intellectual manipulation is at stake. The musical analogy which accompanies Knecht's rise to the status of *Magister Ludi* acquires a more relevant significance in the context of his resignation from Castalia. One of his early friends had defined the true nature of this analogy when he told Knecht, "We analyse the laws and techniques of all the styles and periods of music . . . but produce no new music ourselves."[25] The creation of music would indeed involve the musician in "chaos", the suffering caused by the clash between the pure aspirations of the Game and the impure reality of the world. There is no place for creative activity of any kind in Castalia: the artist as opposed to the thinker would constitute a real threat to the ideal of uncommitted "serenity" and "cheerfulness", and finally destroy the efficacy of meditation in the attempt to master man's intellectual universe.

Knecht's new ideals, expounded in his last conversation with the President of the Order, described the life he wishes to lead after his departure from Castalia in musical terms, not as an ascent towards increasing abstraction from reality, but as a progression "from theme to theme, from tempo to tempo, playing each out to the end, completing each and leaving it behind, never tiring, never sleeping, forever wakeful, forever in the present."[26] In Knecht's mind the static immobility of musical meditation, as part of the self-imposed discipline of the Master of the Game, is replaced by the restless mutability of musical invention, a constant renewal of themes within a dynamic musical structure leading from the serene past to a chaotic future, a symbolic musical composition, both in time and out of time, speaking the language of the present as well as that of eternity.

It is rather moving to find that, when Knecht leaves Castalia for good, a toy flute is the only personal possession he takes with him on his journey to the capital. Leaving behind him the "delicate, sensitive, instruments" on which the most intricate musical themes could be recomposed and related to one another, this flute now serves him as a homely reminder of the kind of music which may, if all goes well, bring back serenity and cheerfulness to the world of chaos towards which he is going. Thus he blows a melody on the flute, simple and full of faith, and while listening to "the serenely devout song ringing out in the sweet notes of the flute", he experiences a new vivid feeling of being "at one and content with the sky, the mountains, the song and the day."[27]

Knecht's wish to become an ordinary schoolteacher in a school outside Castalia remains unfulfilled. Instead he accepts the invitation of his former classmate Designori who had left Castalia long before him, had married and settled in the world, to become his son's private tutor. He undertakes this task the more willingly as he sees in the child's readiness to be taught the promise of a maturity still to come. It is not by chance that Knecht tests his pupil's responsiveness by playing out to him an andante movement of Scarlatti's which, not long before leaving Castalia, he had himself used as a basis for one of his glass bead games. The child listens attentively to the music and to Knecht's explanations, dimly realizing that this is no ordinary music lesson, but rather an exercise in contemplation by a man "who had acquired a subtle, exacting art and practised it with a masterful hand" and that this art, this delicate balance between music and meditation, which Knecht himself has learnt from his old music master, "seemed to be deserving of full devotion and to call forth all the powers of an integrated personality."[28]

Joseph Knecht's death with which the story ends contributes one more dimension to the musical analogy which accompanies him throughout his life. When he plunges into the ice-cold water to follow his pupil Tito across the bay, he finally commits himself to that element in nature most akin to the "cool starry brightness ... frozen into space", which is Hesse's favorite symbol for the music of the "immortals". Just as his music-master, in his death, had become one with the inaudible, with a silence which is beyond all speech, so the former *Magister Ludi*, in his hopeless attempt to overtake the boy swimming out into the bay, plunges into the chilling water which at once surrounds him "with leaping flames" rapidly consuming his body and dragging it down into the depths of fiery dissolution.

Knecht's death by fire and water is a subtle metaphor of his striving for perfection. For what causes his death is the serene, and yet deceptively calm, surface of the water, the burning terror of its transparent brightness, the unruffled silence of its luminous expanse. It is an act of faith, this musical death of the master of the game; for when his heart ceases beating, the progression of themes and counterthemes comes to an end, and he returns to that same silence beyond speech which was his music master's last "musical" credo. He also, like his own teacher, leaves behind a transfigured soul, his pupil Tito, a reincarnation of his own self, but no longer a Castalian in spirit, but a pure mind in an impure world, vaguely conscious of the significance of his master's sacrificial death. Realizing for the first time that sacrifice may be a form of perfection and thus an expression of the ultimate humility before life, "there came over [Tito] with a premonitory shudder of awe, a sense that this guilt for his Master's death, would utterly change him and his life, and would demand much greater things of him than he had ever before demanded of himself."[29]

When Tito assumes responsibility for Knecht's death, he does so, as a commitment to the ideals embodied in his master's life. In the last resort, the young boy, instead of becoming a Castalian in order to accomplish even greater wonders in the playing of the game, will, following the dictates of his own inner nature, remain in the world of "terrors and flames", valiantly struggling against chaos, the reincarnation of his teacher's heroic sacrifice in an unheroic world. Is it too far-fetched to assume that his striving for harmony, in both the musical and psychological connotation of the word, will be defeated by the controlled dissonance and the mathematically regulated chromaticism which constitutes his (and Hesse's as well as the reader's) musical present?

Notes to Chapter Seven

1. See the following two passages, separated by a thirty years' interval:

   a. "Only music, and only Beethoven's music, and only this particular music of Beethoven [the 'Benedictus' from the *Missa Solemnis*] can tell us with any precision what Beethoven's conception of blessedness at the heart of things actually was." ("Music at Night", 1931, in: *On Art and Artists*, p. 317).

   b. "The nearest approach to a demonstration of the doctrine of the Trinity is a fugue or a good piece of counterpoint." (From Huxley's Preface to *On Art and Artists*, p. 7, written in 1960).

2. Thomas Mann, "Goethe und Tolstoy" (1922), in: *Adel des Geistes*, p. 292 (My own translation). Thomas Mann, in the same essay, also quotes Luther who considered the study and exercise of music an integral part of the education of the young. "I do not accept," Luther is supposed to have said, "a schoolmaster who cannot sing."

3. *The Glass Bead Game*, p. 61.

4. *Ibid.*, p. 19 (This interweaving of various time-perspectives is one of the most characteristic structural devices used by Thomas Mann in his *Doctor Faustus*—see chapter VIII).

5. *Ibid.*, pp. 22–27.

6. *Ibid.*, p. 16.

7. *Ibid.*, pp. 28–29.

8. *Ibid.*, p. 30.

9. *Ibid.*, p. 154.

10. *Ibid.*, p. 28; Hermann Hesse's *Die Morgenlandfahrt (The Journey to the East)* was first published in 1932 at the time of the inception of *The Glass Bead Game*. The narrator of the story, a dream-like parable of the soul's search for truth, used to be a musician before he sold his violin because he mistakenly thought of his music as a mere "game", unworthy of the more serious pursuits of life. In a letter, written in 1947, Hesse permits himself the following fanciful observation: "As far as I am concerned, I have never lived in Castalia, I am a hermit and have never belonged to any association [Gemeinschaft], except for that of the Journeyers to the East, a league of the faithful, whose manner of life is very similar to that of Castalia." (Letter addressed to "A Reader of *The Glass Bead Game*", September 1947, *Briefe (Letters)*, p. 242 (my own translation).

11. *Ibid.*, p. 30.
12. *Ibid.*, pp. 30–32; see also Hesse's letter to Otto Basler, dated 25 August 1934, in *Briefe (Letters)*, p. 122 in which, at the time of the writing of *The Glass Bead Game*, the Chinese sources are quoted in full. In the same letter also occurs the following observation: "My theoretical interest in music is very limited and it would have little value since I am not a practising musician. I am interested in counterpoint, the fugue, the change of the harmonic modes; but behind these purely aesthetic questions there are others that also engage me: the actual spirit of true music, its morality." (Translated by Theodore Ziolkowski, and quoted in his *The Novels of Hermann Hesse*, pp. 192–193).
13. *Ibid.*, pp.33–41; many years after the publication of the novel, Hesse describes the origin of Castalia and its Glass Bead Game in less abstract terms than used by the narrators in his "General Introduction" to the story. According to a letter, written in 1955, Castalia symbolized for him during the years before and during the Second World War "a spiritual space . . . in which I could breathe and live, in spite of the poisoning of the world, a refuge and a fortress." The invention of the Monastic Order of the Players was meant to express the "resistance of the spirit against the forces of barbarism." This is why, Hesse writes, his novel had to be utopian in character while "the evil present was banished into a past that had to be overcome." In this way Castalia did not have to be "invented". It was there, within him, long before he put the concept of an ideal community of thinkers on paper. "And thus was found the desired breathing space," he concludes. Letter to Rudolf Pannwitz, January 1955, *Briefe (Letters)* p. 438 (my own translation).
14. *Ibid.*, p. 44.
15. *Steppenwolf*, p. 45.
16. Hesse considered the concept of reincarnation to have been the guiding principle which, initially, inspired him to write *The Glass Bead Game*. It was, according to him, the only form of expression which could convey a sense of stability and continuity in the midst of the constant flux of history. The creation of Joseph Knecht, was thus an attempt at transcending the temporal, while still adhering to criteria of individual characterization, at combining the impersonal with the personal, the historical with the archetypal. (See the letter quoted above, written in January 1955, *Briefe (Letters)* p. 436).
17. *The Glass Bead Game*, p. 54.
18. *Ibid.*, pp. 75–77; possibly Hesse remembered when he wrote this passage the many dreams and drawings of mandalas referred to by Jung in his discussion of the Self as an archetype. The symbol that went to the making of a mandala in Jung's own dreams, are all contained in Joseph Knecht's vision of a circle expanding outward with a luminous light in the center. Jung, in his *Memories*, traces his own development in the understanding of the mandala-archetype.

Realizing that mandala symbols originate in the unconscious, he concludes that "everything, all the paths, I had been following, all the steps I had taken, were leading back to a single point—namely, to the mid-point. It became increasingly plain to me that the mandala is the centre. It is the exponent of all paths. It is the path to the centre, to individuation." (C. G. Jung, *Memories, Dreams, Reflections*, p. 196.) This can be compared to the music master's advice to Joseph Knecht after he had drawn his mandala-dream on paper: "Those who direct the maximum force of their desires towards the centre, towards true being, towards perfection, seem quieter than the passionate souls because the flame of their fervour cannot be seen." (*The Glass Bead Game*, p. 79); on the other hand, Hesse, in a letter to Jung, draws a clear distinction between the function of the psychotherapist and that of the artist, referring in particular to musicians. It is they, the masters of classical music, Hesse writes, who "without being at all aware of it, have transferred their instincts [Triebe] on to a sphere (namely that of music) in which they—in view of this genuine 'sacrifice'—achieved perfection." He calls classical music "a school of wisdom, of courage, of the art of life," and adds "Because of this, psychoanalysis for artists is difficult and dangerous as it may prevent the one who takes [such treatment] seriously from ever realising his artistic gifts [Künstlertum] ... As you possess your secret in alchemy, so I keep the analogy with music to myself," he concludes. (Letter to C. G. Jung, Küsnacht, September 1934, *Briefe (Letters)*, p. 127) my own translation).

19. *Ibid.*, pp. 241 and 244.
20. Hesse traces the development of his own ideas while writing *The Glass Bead Game* in a letter, written some years after the publication of the novel. He distinguishes between three phases. First, probably in the early thirties, came the idea of creating "the ideal secular monastery", similar to the Academy of Plato, a wish-fulfillment which accompanies and effectively characterizes the history of man's ideas from age to age. At a later stage, Hesse realized the need of embodying the "inner reality" of Castalia in one outstanding personality, "the figure of a spiritual hero and sufferer", Knecht as a paradigm of human perfection; lastly, during the second half of the decade and under the growing pressure of political events in Western Europe, came the realization that this same heroic figure must find his way back to life since, as Hesse writes, "a perfection alienated from the world" cannot provide a sense of ultimate fulfilment." (Letter to Siegfried Unseld, Tübingen, 1949/50, *Briefe (Letters)*. p. 287 (my own translation).
21. *Ibid.*, p. 297.
22. Quoted in Mark Boulby, *Hermann Hesse, His Mind and Art*, p. 164.
23. *The Glass Bead Game*, pp. 137–140.
24. *Ibid.*, p. 322.

25. *Ibid.*, p. 92; in connection with the poems which Joseph Knecht, in his capacity as *Magister Ludi* could only write in utter secrecy, the narrators observe: "For while Castalia has in general renounced the production of works of art (even musical production is known and tolerated there only in the form of stylistically rigid composition exercises) writing poetry was regarded as the most impossible, ridiculous, and prohibited of conceivable acts." (p. 101).
26. *Ibid.*, p. 369.
27. *Ibid.*, p. 380.
28. *Ibid.*, p. 318; musical instruction acquires symbolic dimensions whenever Joseph Knecht remembers his various meetings with the music master. For the relationship between the old man and the young boy involved them in an interplay of psychic forces, only remotely concerned with the teaching of music. Thus Knecht's memory of these meetings centered in an image where "the Master and the boy followed each other as if drawn along the wires of some mechanism, until soon it could no longer be discerned which was coming and which going, which following and which leading, the old or the young man." This memory leads to the insight that "this courtship of wisdom by the young, of youth by wisdom, this endless, oscillating game was the symbol of Castalia." (p. 207).
29. *Ibid.*, p. 395.

VIII
The Devil's Disciple

1

One of the first to receive a copy of *The Glass Bead Game*, early in 1945, was Thomas Mann. He had by then written most of his *Doctor Faustus*, begun a year after Hesse had concluded his parable of the life, death, and the various reincarnations of Joseph Knecht. The chronological sequence is of more than merely biographical interest.[1] For Thomas Mann started his story where Hesse had left off. The worldly context in which the protagonist of *Doctor Faustus*, the fictitious composer Adrian Leverkühn, receives his musical education is that of cultural breakdown and anarchy, the same to which Joseph Knecht returns when he deserts the "pedagogical province" of Castalia to lead a life of service and humility in the midst of the "terror and flames" of a civilization on the decline. The reader of the two novels is aware of an uncanny sense of continuity which leads from the spiritual certainty of the former novel to the cultural nihilism of the latter, from affirmation of musical tradition to denial of any stable cultural values whatever, from the grace which resides in the acceptance of a principle of subordination to the damnation which the creative artist carries within him, an inescapable heritage of his privileged condition as transformer and innovator, magician and prophet, most subject to temptation because least conscious of social obligations and the need to distinguish between moral good and moral evil. The way from Joseph Knecht to Adrian Leverkühn leads from the blessedness that lies at the heart of all self-denial to the curse of demonic self-immolation, from the true heroism of humility to the false heroism of conceit, from serenity to suffering.

Neither Hesse, who wrote his book in the seclusion of a small village in the Italian-speaking part of Switzerland, nor Mann, who wrote *Doctor Faustus* in California as a political refugee from Nazi Germany, knew of their respective fascination for fictitious biography at that time. The war had effectively closed all frontiers. It was, thus, with considerable surprise that they discovered striking similarities in the imaginary life histories of their protagonists. There was, first of all, their common concern with the need to preserve what could still be preserved of the cultural heritage of Western Europe, and, secondly, an equal emphasis on the significance of music in the life of the community.

Thomas Mann's first reaction to Hesse's book is remarkable on several accounts. In a letter to his friend he speaks of a certain "sportiveness" (Verspieltheit) which, he believes, is the most congenial form of investing imaginary characters and events with a life which transcends the limitations imposed by the historical present. In his opinion Hesse's novel is, in itself, a kind of "glass bead game". He compares it to an improvisation, performed by a master musician on an organ: Hesse's novel thus resembles a piece of music which embodies the gradual development of its thematic material from the particular to the universal, from the subjective to the objective, and, finally, adds Thomas Mann, back again, from transcendence to ironic aloofness. For the artist's inevitable defeat at the hands of an environment which constitutes the only historically valid universe in which he lives, calls for an attitude of self-mocking detachment. This, at least, is a clear implication of Mann's comment after first reading Hesse's novel.

Hesse himself was, in all likelihood, less aware of the ironic dimension which Mann, so characteristically, projected into Knecht's life story. His own fictitious biography, Mann explains in the same letter, is "the tale of a man's selling his soul to the devil. The 'hero' shares the fate of Nietzsche and Hugo Wolf, and his story, told to us by a pure, good-hearted humanistic soul, has strong anti-humanistic elements:—intoxication and paralysis. Sapienti sat. Nothing more unlike your book can be imagined, and yet the similarity is striking—as it happens now and then among brothers."[2]

Several years later Mann, in his *Story of a Novel*, returns to what he considers to be the remarkable similarity between the two books. He once more emphasizes the elements of parody which the writing of fictitious biography entails as well as the common concern with musical tradition which defines the two writers' approach to the threatening disintegration of cultural values. Again he refers to Hesse's "playful" treatment of his subject-matter, while his own is "more pointed, sharper, more soaring, more dramatic (because more dialectical), more topical, more direct."[3] What appears to have struck Thomas Mann above everything else is Hesse's relative unconcern with the "present", with what is not fiction but reality, as well as Hesse's naïve acceptance of the function of the novelist as a spiritual guide, instructing his readers in the difficult virtues of serenity and cheerfulness growing out of the training and practice of meditation. For though a return to the "terrors and flames" of reality is possible, Hesse implies that no purpose would be served unless it also led to dissociation from the esthetic intellectual sterility of the "Game" as well as from the material preoccupations of the outside world. Hesse, in support of his view, quotes (though without acknowledging the source of the quotation) an observation made by the famous nineteenth-century historian Jacob Burckhardt, one of Hesse's own spiritual guides while writing his *Glass Bead Game*, at the end of Joseph Knecht's letter of resignation: "Times of terror and of deepest misery may come. If, however, there is to be any happiness in the midst of misery, it can be only a spiritual happiness: facing backward for the preservation of the past and facing forward towards the serene and undismayed representation of the spirit in a time that might otherwise capitulate wholly to material concerns."[4]

These are indeed brave and prophetic words. Thomas Mann whose main concern in his novel is to portray these "times of terror and deepest misery" would have wholeheartedly approved of Burckhardt's far-sighted comment on a future which has, in the meantime, become an inescapable present. Thomas Mann realized the irony of an act of self-sacrifice performed in a present possessing none of those inner resources which would make such a sacrifice spiritually significant. Knecht's death by drowning must have appeared to him a willing surrender to the ironic principle of nothingness which reaches beyond innocence and experience, and thus eludes all definition in terms of good or evil, happiness or misery. What meaning (Thomas Mann might have thought) could his master's self-chosen death convey to young Tito whose own spiritual growth was going to be determined by the world of "terror and flames", by historical processes taking place in a present equally contemptuous of the intellectual intricacies of the "Game" and the spiritual happiness advocated by Burckhardt? For in the eyes of those that will instruct the young boy after the death of his teacher, the transcendence of spirit over matter will, however desirable in itself, always appear as a somewhat idiosyncratic accomplishment, reserved for the few who are ready to pay the price, but of utmost irrelevance within the historical context of cultural devaluation which both Hesse and Mann, in their respective novels, had placed in the first half of the twentieth century.

Hesse not only admits these "dissimilarities" between his and Thomas Mann's approach to the problem of integration in our time, and in particular of musical integration, but finds his own theories vindicated by Thomas Mann's emphasis on the artistic chaos that must inevitably result from the social and political anarchy which leaves its indelible imprint on the work of art. On reading the very detailed analysis of Leverkühn's various musical compositions, he is reminded of the figure of Tegularius in his own novel whose "games" always revealed a tendency to deviate "into melancholy and irony". But what strikes him as a real literary *tour-de-force* in Mann's novel is his daring attempt to transfer the musical analysis of purely fictitious works of music from the abstract realm of musicology to emotions evoked by these works in historical time—"that you do not allow this pure extract, this ideal abstraction to soar out into an ideal realm, but that you locate it in the midst of a realistically visualized world and time."[5]

Several months later, again in a letter to Thomas Mann, he, more specifically, views the world into which the composer Adrian Leverkühn is placed as a microcosm, strongly reminiscent of the figures, divine or mortal, which people Indian mythology. What fascinates Hesse in artistic representation of Hindu myths is the bewildering osmosis (itself a key-word in Thomas Mann's novel) between the sublimity of human thought which went to the creation of this art and "the wildness, lewdness, and grotesqueness" by which the sublime is transformed into the monstrous.[6] The analogy with Indian mythology is not as remote as it may appear at first sight. For though the Devil, a

Christian embodiment of evil and negation, is absent from the phantasmagoria of Hindu religious art, elements of the demonic, the brutal, and the prurient are its most striking esthetic features. It is as if the unconscious itself had been given human shape, the irrational translated into patterns of astonishing sensuous beauty, all man's hidden impulses immortalized in an unequivocal exhibition of lust at its most uninhibited and violent.

The decline from nineteenth-century estheticism to the cultural barbarism of the present is the basic theme of Mann's novel. This theme is embodied in a musical genius whose compositions illustrate the profoundly amoral nature of the twentieth-century artist's concern with reality. This has been one of Mann's principal preoccupations whenever he wrote about the artist and his ambivalent attitude to society in his essays or when he made him the central figure in one of his stories. Aschenbach's infatuation with the boy Tadzio, in *Death in Venice*, for instance, was never meant to be read as a somewhat disconcerting case history of an aging writer whose suppressed homosexual tendencies find an unexpected though congenial outlet at the very moment of highest literary achievement and fame. Mann's portrayal of the gradual decline of the intellectual self-discipline which the writer had imposed upon himself in the past into a compulsive surrender to physical temptation, followed by the upheaval of instinctual urges of the existence of which he had till then been unaware and which are now metamorphosed into a dream of "barbarous" and yet infinitely attractive promiscuity, was merely a prologue to the history of Adrian Leverkühn's pact with the Devil.

When the psychologically equivocal is joined to the satanic, the Devil, in the novel's most revealing chapter, comes to bargain for the artist's soul. The temptation to surrender to the powers of darkness in order to make full use of the newly acquired freedom to be as "barbaric" as he pleases is hard to resist. For, in the Devil's words, "you will break through time itself, by which I mean the cultural epoch and its cult, and dare to be barbaric, twice barbaric indeed, because coming after the humane, after all possible root-treatment and bourgeois *raffinement*."[7] The Devil is sufficiently well versed in the ritual of unmitigated estheticism in cultural tradition as well as post-romantic late nineteenth-century music, to promise the young composer (who on several previous occasions had expressed the opinion that no "modern" music could be composed that is not a parody of something that had already been done much better in the past) a final liberation from the hollowness of a musical estheticism which, at the beginning of the twentieth century, had ceased to communicate anything but its own sense of exhaustion and vacuity.

This relapse into barbarism, as Thomas Mann calls it on several occasions, is a deliberate attempt to escape the trivialities of musical expressiveness no longer in touch with a communal mode of experience. What to the average concert-goer may well appear a frightening example of musical atavism, is merely the expression of the composer's sense of alienation from his own culture carried to its logical conclusion. One of Leverkühn's last works, his *Apocalypse*, incorporates primitive ritualistic rhythms, the savage beating of the drum by which the medicine-man of ancient tribes evokes magic ends, a music which combines a sense of anonymity with powerful individual expressiveness portraying the anguish of the human soul alienated from the past and anticipating no blissful resurrection in times to come. For music composed in hell calls for esthetic formulas combining the most heterogeneous elements into one paradoxical whole. No experience of any kind need be excluded from this new instrumental and vocal language, forged in the fires of a musical inferno. The listener who realizes "how near estheticism and barbarism are to each other: estheticism as the herald of barbarism,"[8] will be no stranger to this music. No rational interpretation will do justice to the elements of contradiction inherent in this new and terrifying musical synthesis. It indeed stands for "the beast in man as well as his sublimest stirrings", and serves as a reminder of "blood-boltered barbarism" allied to "bloodless intellectuality" which, in Thomas Mann's view of contemporary culture, constitutes one of its essential characteristics.

Leverkühn's use of the glissando, "this destructive sliding through the seven positions of the instrument", a musical device which the composer employs whenever images of terror are evoked in his *Apocalypse*, is of particular significance. Both the orchestra and the human voice are given themes reminiscent of, if not actually imitating in a most realistic manner, "the savage howling" of the damned. Special mention is made of "the acoustic panic" which results from "the repeated drum-glissando", the uncanny and shattering effect of the "frightfully shrieking human voices", when nature herself partakes of the final apocalyptic upheaval. Any traditional tonal distinction between a music of grace and one of damnation and their relation to the use of consonance and dissonance, becomes irrelevant when subjected to the test of the primitive, the barbaric, and the demonic. In the face of a middle-class audience, nurtured on what seemed to most of them an irreversible musical tradition, Leverkühn made the paradox come true that in this work "dissonance stands for the expression of everything lofty, solemn, pious, everything of the spirit; while consonance and firm tonality are reserved for the world of hell, in this context a world of banality and commonplace."[9]

Thomas Mann, in the course of the novel, characterizes this reversal of traditional musical values as a form of "dynamic archaism". Concepts such as this will be familiar to writers, a quarter of a century later, whenever the more sensitive among them will attempt a description of what happened to literature and the arts, in terms of an escape from hollow estheticism into an enthusiastic acceptance of barbarism as an end in itself.[10] In contrast to this, the imaginative recreations of uninhibited sensuality in Indian religious art of which Hesse was reminded when he first read *Doctor Faustus*, appear to be of an appealing aesthetic naïvety. The stone images which cover the walls of Hindu temples are expressive neither of self-indulgent aestheticism nor of crude and "archaic" barbarism. What they evoke is the principle of divine procreation rather than of satanic denial. It is an art that affirms nature in the innocence of its polytheistic faith. Leverkühn's music is an art which affirms nothing but its own alienation from the sources of all tradition. What, in the last resort, it *does* acknowledge is the defeat of "unaccommodated man" confronting his own inevitable damnation beyond all culture.

2

The "common reader", and in particular the English-speaking reader, may well find the reading of *Doctor Faustus* a challenging task. He must be ready and willing to subject himself to a test in general erudition which encompasses such diverse fields of knowledge as the theory and history of music, an understanding of the various religious controversies around the figure of the Devil as part of the Faust legend in folklore as well as in literature, a critical grasp of the history of Germany, from about 1890 to the end of the Second World War, a study of the lives of composers and men of letters who served Thomas Mann as models in the writing of his fictitious biography, among them, in particular, Beethoven, Hugo Wolf, Tchaikovsky, Schönberg and, above all, Nietzsche. He must be more than superficially familiar with the theory and art of fiction as practiced by Flaubert in France, Dostoyevsky in Russia, Fontane and Stifter in Germany, and Joseph Conrad and James Joyce in England. He should be a sympathetic student of the old-age works of Ibsen, Wagner, and Shakespeare. Last, but not least, a medical knowledge of the effect of syphilitic infection on the nervous system and, especially, the way it may affect artistic creation, has to be added as an indispensable scientific ingredient among the humane fields of knowledge which constitute the raw material of Thomas Mann's story.

While the reader is assumed to be a polymath, the narrator of the story is nothing of the kind. Though we are made to see the disintegration of cultural values through his eyes and though it is through his mind that the reader comes to realize the ultimate terror of the composer's insanity, preceded, as indeed it is, by increasingly violent outbursts of creative activity, the narrator's mental and cultural perspective is almost entirely free of personal idiosyncrasies. It represents, with an element of parody, nineteenth-century traditionalism as embodied in the educated middle-classes and their unquestioned conformism as regards existing esthetic and musical values. Simultaneously, the narrator provides Thomas Mann with a "voice", transcending the social limitations imposed by the age and the class in whose name he speaks, a voice of sanity and reasonableness, and yet also of growing anguish, in a world floundering in political anarchy, violence and the rule of unreason. Such a voice—and Thomas Mann must have been aware of this—guides the reader's response along well-defined channels: the narrator makes no secret of his sympathies, for he speaks in the name of all those whose acquaintance with the demonic and the insane is mainly of literary origin and whose pretension to understand and appreciate contemporary music is circumscribed by a conservative attitude to musical tradition. By letting *him* speak, Thomas Mann adds an ironic dimension—indeed, at times a comic distortion of the truth which the narrator hesitates to face in all its grotesque frightfulness and of which he can only speak with the shuddering revulsion of a man whose belief in human decency and artistic integrity is deeply rooted in his upbringing (the study of classical languages and literature), his social position as a member of an academically educated leisured class, and his choice of profession, that of teaching the young the languages and civilization of ancient Greece and Rome. He is, in its inevitably ironic assumption, a representative of those values and attitudes that the two World Wars have so successfully liquidated from the face of Europe. Thomas Mann's choice of the narrator reveals the need for a bifocal vision, one represented by the tradition-bound scholar's desperate clinging to social and artistic conformity, the other by the composer's wholehearted and, indeed, ecstatic dedication to the principle of negation, leading to the final rejection of any aesthetic criterion based on a definition of beauty which, by dwelling too much and too long on the trivial and the *déjà-entendu*, reduces the musical experience to the self-indulgent surrender to aesthetic wish-fulfilment. The mingling of the two perspectives may produce the dizzying effect of experiencing life on two opposing levels simultaneously. As we get progressively involved in the appalling story of the composer's pact with the Devil, Thomas Mann repeatedly reminds us of the "speaking voice" of the narrator through whose bewildered consciousness we are permitted to have a glimpse (and sometimes, indeed, a front-row view) of hell.

Serenus Zeitblom would not have been out of place among the less illustrious members of the Order of Glass Bead Players in Castalia. He represents (not without a touch of irony) that element of moderation, indeed of serenity (as his first name seems to indicate) without which no Castalian could become an adept at the Game. He calls himself a "humanist" and plays the viola d'amore in his spare time. Naturally reticent in company—neither his classical erudition nor his teaching profession provide sufficient material for small talk—he brings his instrument along whenever invited to do so to "regale the company" with ancient music played in a traditional manner such as "a chaconne or sarabande from the seventeenth century, a 'plaisir d'amour' from the eighteenth."[11] There is certainly nothing barbaric or demonic about him: he is a thoroughly civilized person who, until the rise of Hitler to power, felt very much at home in the educated bourgeois society of which he was a respected and well-adjusted member. His attitude to music is characteristically ambivalent: in this respect, he is a true successor of that other humanist, the Italian Settembrini in *The Magic Mountain*. Like most middle-class Germans brought up in the musical tradition of the late nineteenth century, he appreciates the educative and the intellectually elevating power of music, while suspecting it of "subversive" tendencies. At the very beginning of his story he admits that epithets such as "sane, noble, harmonious, humane" do not quite fit a description of the art of music whose "inarticulate language . . . does not seem to me to be included in the pedagogic-humanistic sphere."[12] Had he, indeed, been a member of the Castalian "pedagogical province", his glass bead exercises would have included only those musical themes which expressed "the beauty and dignity of reason", omitting, as in effect most players did, any musical evocation of the elements of irrationality in the composing of his games.

This "good, unheroic soul" represents more than an ironic device, or a "comic idea" (as Thomas Mann declares in his *Story of a Novel*), more even than the desperate attempt of the novelist to create a narrative medium which would be both self-portrait and self-mockery, a speaking voice of average sensitivity, conscious of his own lack of creative imagination, a sympathetic outsider in Leverkühn's inner life and scarcely qualified to pass comment on his musical creations. It is a homely and humane voice profoundly disturbed by the story it is compelled to tell in order to honor the memory of his departed friend, though possibly also in order to justify his own sense of legitimate mediocrity before the judgment of some "future reader" who may, in times to come, look for an explanation of Leverkühn's tragedy in the pages of his friend's biography. For if, as Thomas Mann informs the reader, the central idea of his novel is "the flight from the difficulties of the cultural crisis into the pact with the devil, the craving of a proud mind, threatened by sterility, for an unblocking of inhibitions at any cost, and the parallel between pernicious euphoria ending in collapse with the nationalistic frenzy of Fascism,"[13] while the place of music in the novel is "only a paradigm for something more general, of culture, even of man and the intellect itself in our so critical (sic) era,"[14] then poor Serenus Zeitblom is, in effect, a mirror image of the age but therefore no less significant than the protagonist whose life story he tells. From being a mere literary medium or well-worn structural device, he is seen to be a kind of unified consciousness symbolizing all that was left behind when the Third Reich collapsed and with it most of the Western cultural values that the writer of the novel himself had cherished all his life. In this sense his is also a prophetic voice which, though it hardly ever rises to a crescendo and avoids all the cheap rhetorical effects of what Hesse called "The Age of the Feuilleton", speaks in the name of a whole generation of writers who, more clearly than the reader ever could, foresaw the coming doom and were helpless to prevent it.

It is for this reason, Thomas Mann adds, that he could not give any detailed physical description of the two protagonists, the narrator and the composer, for they have "too much to conceal, namely, the secret of their being identical with each other."[15] Their identity, evidently, does not reside in the realm of demonic intoxication but rather in this two-fold acceptance of the secluded life, that of the scholar and that of the composer, the former because he distrusts the growth of "barbarism" among his contemporaries, the latter because he, deliberately and fully aware of the consequences, surrenders to the powers of unreason. Social isolation, is thus shown to be, in the last resort, a moral as well as an artistic necessity. The humanist scholar in an age of cultural dissolution withdraws into his study in order to escape from a chaotic present into an idealized past, there to dedicate the remaining years of his life to the writing of his friend's biography. The musician having been given twenty-four years of intense and ever-revitalized creativity, thereby forfeiting his more than ordinarily vulnerable soul to the temptations of a life entirely dedicated to the composing of music, retires into his own inner life which—by the very nature of his pact with the Devil—he cannot share with any of his contemporaries, so that he may compose in the seclusion of his quasi-monastic life those harrowing works which will terrify and appall his audience and will, finally, drive him into madness. Both protagonists, thus, reflect the exile, political as well as artistic, in which the novel was written. Thomas Mann, in effect, holds a mirror up to the reader, a kind of historical looking-glass in which can be seen Leverkühn and his friend, multiplied an infinite number of times, figures who, whether in times past, present, or future, are driven, by a combination of personal idiosyncrasy and social circumstances, into a life of exile and alienation. It is there, in the seclusion of their scholarly or artistic pursuits, that they strive to extract some meaning from an increasingly hostile environment. What defeats them in the end is the disproportionate degree of suffering this search for meaning involves. Thus Zeitblom and Leverkühn are twentieth-century embodiments of an archetypal polarity inherent in human nature, symbolized in the Faust-legend by the unimaginative, down-to-earth, prosaic friend and disciple, the eternal student Wagner who freely admits his unfamiliarity with demonic inspiration, though he envies Faust his conception of a metaphysically postulated universe. He does not know and could not possibly understand that Faust's pact with the Devil has given him knowledge, but without the compassion which should accompany it, a capacity for intense intellectual experience without the fertilizing emotion of love, an awareness of the multiplicity of existential phenomena which, in the absence of an ordering design, appear to the onlooker an expression of aimless and amorphous profuseness in nature and, finally, has provided him with the tools with which to express his knowledge and his anguish, tools forged in the fires of hell with which "to make music" fit for its inhabitants.

3

Adrian Leverkühn receives his education from a variety of teachers. Some, like his father and the American scholar Abercocke, instruct him in the natural sciences with an uncanny emphasis on the equivocal tricks that nature plays with man's sense perceptions by first undermining his conviction in the existence of an orderly and reasonable material universe and then by revealing to him a physical reality quite unlike the one that inductive science has proclaimed with so much deceptive certainty. Thus his father introduces him to tropical insects of fantastic beauty, only to declare that their splendid colors are no colors at all but the result of an optical illusion. Similarly, he tells Adrian about a butterfly, *Hetaera Esmeralda*, who, except for two spots of violet and rose, exists "in transparent nudity", and is, to all practical intents and purposes, invisible to the human eye. Adrian's father never tires of revealing to the boy other oddities in nature: snails which were used in secret practices by witches and sorcerers in the Middle Ages, ice-crystals which by their shape imitated the vegetable kingdom without in any sense of the term being "alive", a drop of paraffin in a bucket of water, or it might have been some other similarly equivocal liquid substance, which, when a glass-stick covered with shellac is introduced into the water, first, "swallows" it, then absorbs all the shellac into its own substance, and, finally, ejects the stick as being of no more interest to it.

Such experiments, performed before the child's inquisitive eyes, raise questions of considerable metaphysical interest: where, for example, does nature draw the line between the animate and the inanimate; can matter and its behavior be described apart from the way it is perceived by the human senses; is the real a mere by-product of the illusory, depending on whether man considers himself to be part of matter or an atom in some imaginary universal mind. Even more bewildering are those questions which refer to the behavior of all living organisms, apparently the result of what Adrian's father on one occasion, in his quaint terminology, calls "osmotic pressures", corresponding to metaphysical rather than biological or chemical processes, nature's irrepressible "will to live" and to reproduce at whatever cost, even if this involves the creation of "illusory" and virtually non existent mirror images of life. What Adrian learns from his father's curious experiments in life's chemical transformations, is a growing conviction of the deceptive nature of all sense perception and the devilish efficiency with which osmosis does its work by fusing the apparently incompatible, establishing links between mutually repellent materials, and, not least, by frivolously pretending to create "life" out of inanimate substances while actually doing nothing of the kind.

Osmosis is also the key to the instruction provided by that mysterious American explorer—it is never quite clear whether he ever existed in reality or was merely a figment of Adrian's imagination—who takes him down to the depths of the ocean in a "two-ton hollow bell" to reveal to him, in the electrically illumined darkness of "a new, unknown, irrelevant world", utterly foreign to our own, "the unlooked-at, the not-to-be and not-expecting-to-be-looked at". What the two, the mentor and his pupil, see is indeed an underworld of nature unrelated to the respectable surface existence of man, "frantic creatures of organic life" which inhabit the impenetrable darkness of a planet apparently millions of light-years away from our own, and yet part of the same "hollow ball", the same "drop in the bucket" in which men pass their life "on earth". When the American scholar, for a change, takes Adrian on a voyage among the heavenly constellations and explains to him the relativity of such terms as "finite" or "infinite", of "expansion" and "contraction", of "movement" and "standstill", the same sense of metaphysical dizziness, of equivocation emanating from the Absolute itself, overcomes the young composer.[16] For if light and darkness, air and water, height and depth are interchangeable, if not actually identical, having undergone a process of osmosis beyond the reaches of man's understanding, there is no more certainty to be had by merely thinking the Absolute into existence. For thought itself is seen to be the result of an osmotic process—as another of Adrian's "teachers" proves in his theological lectures at the university of Halle.

According to Professor Schleppfuss's "psychological" exegesis of biblical material "the demonic conception of God" is more acceptable to the modern scientific mind than the medieval separation between the satanic and the divine. In his well-attended lectures at which Adrian is a regular visitor in his own vain attempts to escape the temptations of music, the learned professor "received . . . the blasphemous and offensive into the divine, and hell into the empyrean" and "declared the vicious to be a necessary and inseparable concomitant of the holy, and the holy a constant satanic temptation."[17] No clear dividing line need be, indeed can be, drawn, between grace and damnation, for only in terms of a metaphysically legitimate osmosis is man enabled to experience the spiritual potentialities that lie within him. Only through the temptations of evil can he achieve a state of blessedness which will, in no essential feature, differ from a state of damnation. For only those that pass through hell are, in the professor's words, worthy of grace.

Adrian's nonmusical instruction in "osmotic pressure" through observation of nature or artificially induced laboratory conditions, leaves an indelible effect on his attitude to music and to musical composition. If animate as well as inanimate substances are controlled by the constant interfusion of the visible and the invisible, the audible and the inaudible, the strictly mathematical and the loosely intuitive, how much more is music exposed to acoustic ambiguity arising from the spurious separation between what can and cannot be perceived by the ear, for example the gradual sliding from key to key, the almost imperceptible modulation from major to minor modes, the interweaving of themes and counterthemes, the interpenetration of instrument and human voice, the chromatic subtleties of dissonance in a context of harmoniously sounding chords. Thus Adrian, very early in his musical education, tells his friend, "Relationship is everything; and if you want to give it a more precise name, it is ambiguity ... You know what I find?" he asked, "That music turns the equivocal into a system. Take this or that note. You can understand it so or respectively so, you can think of it as sharpened or flattened, and you can, if you are clever, take advantage of the double sense as much as you like."[18]

Musical osmosis, if such a term may be coined, opens up new vistas, as yet unexplored, for the young inquisitive composer. For if the same note, used in a diversity of musical contexts, either as flat or as sharp, produces different effects on the listener, the same intangible metamorphosis may be produced in chords converted into melodies, while a succession of sounds may be transformed into a chord, with the result that tonal identity may be established between what Leverkühn calls horizontal and vertical composing. Once again, by a process of osmosis, the successive and the simultaneous in music are shown to be identical.[19] Such a discovery, whether it derives from nature or from metaphysics, plays havoc with the conventional distinction between movement and immobility, time and no-time. Adrian, with characteristic single-mindedness, speaks of chords as merely "frozen" melodies, while single notes are

considered as latent chords, only waiting, so to speak, to be
linked to other notes in a process of musical fusion which may,
indeed, produce dissonance according to the polyphonic value
of the notes that find themselves related to one another in such
a chord. Complete musical interrelatedness thus claims that any
note or series of notes may constitute the basic element of a
melody, determined by a "horizontal" succession of sounds
which *is*, properly speaking, its time-element as well as by the
creation of "vertical" consonance (or dissonance) which would
control its progression in space. Adrian, in effect, develops what
he calls a technique of "strict" composition, "certain combinations and interrelations of the twelve semitones, series of notes
from which a piece and all the movements of a work must strictly
derive. Every note of the whole composition, both melody and
harmony, would have to show its relation to this fixed fundamental series . . . There would no longer be a free note."[20]

This sounds like a quotation from Schönberg, the inventor of
the so-called twelve-tone method. It is, however, only remotely
connected with it. Neither in spirit nor in basic concepts does it
reproduce Schönberg's view of the "row" and the place every
note holds in it. Yet Leverkühn's observation about "strict"
composition echoes various sayings about music by past and
present musicologists, including Schönberg, whose function in
Thomas Mann's novel is to prepare the way towards that final
musical osmosis which will incorporate the old in the new and
combine "harmonic subjectivity" with "polyphonic objectivity",
in short, to establish a musical universe which, in Zeitblom's
quaint terminology, "rests . . . on the curvature of the world,
which makes the last return into the first."[21]

The use of historical, biographical and musical "quotations"
in the writing of his novels, is one of Thomas Mann's most
deliberate literary devices. Just as in the novels of Proust, Joyce,
and Hesse before him, it enables him to shift the focus of his
narrative from one period to another, from character to character, from country to country, without ever losing sight of his
central concern—which is the life of the half-real and half-
fictitious figure of the composer whose personal disintegration
is paralleled by the break-up of political, moral, and artistic
values in Western Europe. On more than one occasion Mann
calls this device a "montage-technique", using a visual concept

familiar to photographers, graphic artists, and film-producers. When this method is applied to the writing of fiction, various layers of time are added to the central narrative, expanding it backward or forward according to the thematic structure of the plot, substituting one time dimension for another, portraying the central character as seen through various time perspectives, and, finally, enabling the reader to perceive meanings that lie below the surface of conventional language as used by the novelist.

This is a highly sophisticated procedure calling not merely for considerable powers of concentration on the part of the reader but for an awareness of the multiple layers of significance which constitute the structural and thematic body of the work. Fiction of this kind can no longer be a "straight" narrative but a weaving in and out of time, reflecting the apparent casualness with which the writer manipulates temporary and spatial dimensions, inevitably resulting in the rejection of any objective criteria by which duration can be measured.[22] *Doctor Faustus* provides instructive examples for this sort of procedure: Leverkühn's meeting with the Devil (one of the central chapters in the story) takes place at Palestrina, a small Italian village, birthplace of the sixteenth-century composer of the same name who served Mann as one of the models for Leverkühn's intellectual inhibitions in the composition of his early music. What attracted Mann to the figure of Palestrina long before the writing of *Doctor Faustus*, was the composer's musical dilemma at having to choose between two styles of composing, that of the plain chant used in Gregorian music during the Middle Ages and that of sixteenth-century polyphonic structures. Palestrina, like Leverkühn, was more deeply aware of the exhaustion which had overcome the music of the past and the need to recreate it anew in the image of a new age that has as yet little to offer in terms of renewed musical inspiration. Deeply pessimistic about the future of music, he yet becomes its "savior" by convincingly combining the old and the new in his church music. All this Mann had long before expounded, in an essay written in 1917, a few weeks after having attended the first performance of Pfitzner's opera *Palestrina*, on July 12, 1917, conducted by Bruno Walter in the Munich opera-house.[23] Now Pfitzner who was himself agonizingly aware of the destructive power of consciousness paralyzing the impulse toward creation, did not hesitate, when his inspiration failed him, to incorporate a quotation from Palestrina's music in his own opera, thereby providing Mann with a model for his "montage-technique" in music. The dialogue between the Devil and Leverkühn (chapter 25 of the novel) takes place in 1911 or 1912, that is long before Pfitzner's opera had been performed, but was actually begun in December 1944. Again, prior to these two dates, Thomas Mann and his brother Heinrich had stayed at Palestrina in 1896–98, so that the autobiographical, the histori-cal, and the musicological combine in this episode to form a fictitious texture of extraordinary and fascinating complexity, especially if one remembers that, throughout this episode in the village of Palestrina one more time-dimension has to be added to Leverkühn's story by the inclusion of the Faust-legend and its innumerable ramifications into myth, alchemy, literature, and psychology.[24]

This complexity in time-structure and in the use of thematic material whose origin lies in the remote past is one of the most characteristic features in Mann's earlier work. Its specifically musical application is, very largely due to the influence of the social philosopher and musicologist Adorno on Thomas Mann while he was writing his novel. This influence is acknowledged throughout the autobiographical sketch in which Mann de-scribes the genesis and the actual writing of *Doctor Faustus*. In July 1943 Adorno gave Mann his as yet unpublished manuscript *Zur Philosophie der Modernen Musik* (*Philosophy of Modern Music*, published in 1949) to read. The effect was instantaneous and far-reaching. Not only did Thomas Mann become familiar with Schönberg's theories on the twelve-tone method through this book, but he learned to look upon Schönberg's musical innova-tion through Adorno's critical, and, at times, disapproving mind. In addition, it is in this book that he found the musicolo-gist's justification for the use of "quotations". For, observes Adorno, anyone who attempts to compose music today will find his inspiration paralyzed by the fact that "no idea could be conceived that had not been thought of already. Composers therefore accepted the objective fact that their material had been exhausted and made that fact part of their subjective relationship to the material; they constructed their themes on more or less obvious 'quotations' achieving their effect through reiteration of the familiar."[25]

Thus Adorno by introducing Mann to Schönberg's musical

theories and, incidentally, also to Kierkegaard's essay on *Don Giovanni*, was also in part responsible for the description of Leverkühn's compositions, in particular his *Apocalypse*, which was, in effect, the result of extensive collaboration between the novelist and the musicologist. Mann first asked Adorno in a letter how *he* would approach Leverkühn's work "if you had a pact with the devil". What he had in mind, Mann writes, is "something satanically religious, diabolically pious . . . something that goes back to primitive, elementary levels of music."[26] Adorno is a willing, indeed enthusiastic, collaborator, provoking and stimulating the novelist's curiosity and contributing a great deal of information as to how to render this return to the barbaric musically valid.

Thomas Mann's preoccupation with "osmotic pressure" leading to the creation of a variety of musical reincarnations explains his concern with the immanent nature of esthetic innovation, whether it be in music or in any other art. Thus, it is possible to retrace, step by step, the history of Leverkühn's musical illumination back to the age of Palestrina, without thereby disturbing in any way the even flow of the narrative. This "remembrance of things past" is a form of musical evocation where it is not a "little phrase" that is being recalled but a particular *moment musical* in time which may refer to the development of Mann's own musical understanding, to the musical history of his hero, or to theories elaborated by musicologists or composers living in the first half of the twentieth century; reaching further back into a remote past, it encompasses such central figures in the musical life of the nineteenth century as Wagner and Bruckner, and, finally, comes to rest, as it were, in the timeless figure of a musicologically well-informed Devil who, by an alarming shift in time perspective, starts expounding musical theories familiar to any avant-garde twentieth-century musicologist.

In this way Adorno's interpretation of Schönberg's musical innovation is put into Leverkühn's mouth as if it were his own discovery, while Mann, surely, could not have helped realizing that the "tragically cerebral relentlessness of [Adorno's] criticism of the contemporary musical situation"[27] related him intellectually to his fictitious composer. On the other hand, Leverkühn's music teacher, Kretschmar, appears as an earlier reincarnation of a similar musical temperament, especially if one recalls that it was Adorno who, for the benefit of Thomas Mann, played out to him the two movements of Beethoven's last piano sonata, opus 111, which were to form the main topic of Kretschmar's lecture on the final disintegration of the sonata-form. After listening to Adorno's playing, Thomas Mann went home, and for three days revised his chapter on this most instructive of all Kretschmar's lectures.

This leads the story back to Beethoven himself as interpreted by Kretschmar, his struggle to liberate himself from conventional musical forms in order to give expression to the inexpressible, the working of his inner mind in opposition to what the age expected of the contemporary music-maker. But this, in turn, leads to an even earlier reincarnation of musical rebellion, a quaint and pious figure, Johann Conrad Beissel who, about the middle of the eighteenth century, had founded in Pennsylvania a Baptist sect named "Solitary Brethren and Sisters", a community of simple folk who, in Kretschmar's words, led a life "full of sacrifice and self-discipline". Beissel himself had followed "his inward voice" which made him work out a musical theory that was utterly unrelated to any music of the past. He, in effect, decreed "that there should be 'masters' and 'servants' in every scale. Having decided to regard the common chord as the melodic center of any given key, he called 'masters' the notes belonging to this chord, and the rest of the scale 'servants'." The music thus composed was extraordinarily effective; it was, said Kretschmar, "nothing more nor less than a foretaste of heaven", and in this sense it was also timeless, traditionless, and yet an imposition of an order and a discipline in the composition of sounds which appealed to young Adrian. For, remembering the stable-maid Hanne's instruction in the simple and all-too-human warmth of polyphonic music (while he was still a child), he is struck by the need, reexperienced from age to age, to enforce a discipline of "pure calculation" which, he tells his friend, is music's "penance in advance for her retreat into the sensual."[28]

Thus, Beissel, within the total structure of Thomas Mann's story, becomes the somewhat unexpected precursor of Schönberg, of Adorno, and of Leverkühn himself. He shares with them—as with Leverkühn's father, the American scientist Abercocke, and the theology professor Schleppfuss—a certain

melancholic inquisitiveness into the byways of art and life, a
quaint interest in the unusual and nonconformist, a very private
intoxication with an elixir of knowledge, difficult to come by,
but once obtained, leading to "exceptional beatitudes". In its
final analysis, this quest for the out-of-the-way and the extraordinary, whether in the biological sciences, in theology, or in
music, reflects a sense of intellectual insecurity, of spiritual
malaise, which drives Leverkühn, first into the arms of a prosti-
tute who, after having warned him of her diseased condition,
infects him with syphilis, and finally leads to the fateful "meeting" between the composer and his *alter ego*, the most equivocal
figure of them all, combining within himself all the ambiguities
that went to the making of Leverkühn's genius, the Devil as the
final embodiment of osmotic self-knowledge. It is the composer's own awareness of the need to abolish all musical pretense,
all romantic transformation of emotion into musical image, that
makes the Devil pronounce these alarming, and yet prophetic,
words: "Only the non-fictional is still permissible, the unplayed,
the undisguised and untransfigured expression of suffering in
its actual moment . . . the self-satisfied pretense of music itself
has become impossible . . . It is all up with it."[29] Who is the
speaker, one may well ask—Thomas Mann, the writer of fiction,
or Palestrina, Beissel, Beethoven, Schönberg or Adorno, the
Devil or Leverkühn himself?

The osmotic process is anti-historical. It works outside time. It
combines and dissolves the living and the dead. Once it is
elevated to the status of a metaphysical dictum, the creative act
will be seen to originate in "osmotic pressure,"[30] every beginning a departure into the unexplored, every discovery a revelation of a former beginning, every work of art a return to the
timeless, beyond culture and beyond history, and the man of
genius a reincarnation of some former self—a metaphor of life's
never-ceasing struggle at renewal, at the very moment of death
and apocalypse.

4

There is no knowing what may happen to language, either of
words or of sounds, under "osmotic pressure". The novelist
who sets himself the task of writing the biography of a fictitious

composer is constantly faced with the need of "musicalizing" his fiction or of verbalizing music composed in his mind alone, unassisted by instrumental or vocal media, a kind of free-floating music, heard, if heard at all, in the auditory imagination of the one who put it on paper, not as musical notation but through the medium of words. The reader is aware of unresolved tensions. The struggle between words and sounds is of the very essence of the story as conceived and told by Thomas Mann. But "strict composition" does not lend itself easily to verbalization. The "stricter" the sequence of sounds, the farther removed it is from language as used in non-musical communication. The final "breakthrough", a term applied by Thomas Mann to Leverkühn's last work, his *Lamentation of Doctor Faustus*, is, in musical terms, a return—beyond estheticism and barbarism—to simple harmony devoid of contrapuntal features where the melodic interest once more is the central focus of the music. This is not an atavistic regression but a form of musical "repentance", followed by a sense of redemption, a release in spirit, though not in body, from the horrors of hell. It is an extreme instance of "osmotic pressure" where the element of fire devours all the impurity that went to the making of the work, a momentary grace radiating forth in the midst of damnation. All this is beyond the language of words. That is why the onset of Leverkühn's madness is portrayed as a form of linguistic disintegration.

Having addressed his invited friends in the archaic language of the medieval Faust-legend, interspersed with expressions which reflect his growing inability to relate words and their meaning, but also a general loosening of grammatic syntax and texture, "with something doubtful and unregulated about it", as Zeitblom puts it,[31] he sits down at the piano to play extracts from his *Lamentations* to those few who have remained to listen. With tears running down his cheeks, "he attacked the keys in a strongly dissonant chord. At the same time he opened his mouth as though to sing, but only a wail which will ring for ever in my ears broke from his lips."[32] The "osmotic pressure" which should have led to a pure fusion of word and sound, was too great to be borne. The simple-hearted humanist narrator tries in vain to grasp the connection between this return to the purity and lucidity of Monteverdi and his friend's mental collapse. For

Zeitblom defines this new music as "the reconstitution ... of expressivism, of the highest and profoundest claim of feeling to a state of intellectuality and formal structure, which must be arrived at in order that we may experience a reversal of this calculated coldness and its conversion into a voice expressive of the soul and warmth and sincerity of creature confidence."[33] Yet behind this musical "breakthrough" stands the word, or, to be more exact, the language of lamentation. It is "expressiveness as lament" which, finally, issues from the lips of the mad composer as an inarticulate, anguished cry.

The last "word" is with Zeitblom, indeed an adept at languages, who finishes the tragic story of his friend's life in the way he had started it three years earlier. His narrative is, throughout, told in the leisurely and old-fashioned idiom of the nineteenth-century bourgeoisie, erudite and somewhat pedantic, characteristic of academic scholarship, so closely akin to the self-consciousness of moral respectability. It is the speech of one who has never had reason to doubt the innate stability of the universe his mind inhabits, who takes the essential reasonableness of the human world for granted, and consequently feels repelled by any form of intellectual or emotional deviance. His speech consistently expresses a classical balance of thought. It is firmly placed in the double-time context in which it occurs, that of Leverkühn's life and his own. The speech and rhythm of his narrative never change, whether he portrays his friend's secluded existence as a composer or the violent political upheavals that were undermining the very foundations of the civilization that had made the writing of such a book as his possible. However great his personal anguish, his narrative reads like a twentieth-century requiem for a past that never existed "in reality", except within the four walls of his book-filled study.

Thomas Mann who thought of Zeitblom as a kind of ironic self-portrait was too deeply versed in the art of fiction not to realize that the narrator's style of life and style of writing stood for a way of seeing the world incompatible with the subject-matter he had chosen to write about, the tragedy of the composer who had lost sight of "the world" except insofar as it was a vision of hell. The very leisureliness of Zeitblom's narrative rhythm, his constant digression, and apologies for having strayed from his friend's life story into philosophy, politics,

religious exegesis or musicology, and especially his growing
sense of failure in expressing what he, of all men, was least
qualified to express—the disintegration of a great and noble
mind—all this is part of Thomas Mann's own realization of
defeat, not only as a "humanist" but as an artist.

This sense of the failure of words represents a still more
profound awareness on the part of the novelist that the absence
of any social cohesion in the Europe between the two wars led to
a debasement of language itself, a cheapening of meanings
deriving from fashionable affectations in style, mannerisms of
speech and hollow public eloquence which precluded any meaningful communication between people belonging to different
social strata, professions, or educational background. This is
particularly evident whenever the two outsiders and friends,
Zeitblom and Leverkühn, are shown in the company of people
who are quite unaware of such difficulties and who, on the
contrary, use language in that glib, self-assured, and assertive
way common among writers of academic pretensions "who
wrote books on cultural history" and "other writers who wrote
nothing at all but made themselves socially interesting as spe-
cialists in the art of conversation, superficially, and without
tangible result."[34] There were others, no less articulate, who
had a real insight into the *malaise* of the age, but were too deeply
engrossed in performing linguistic acrobatics ever to translate
their insights into rational language. Instead they indulged in
paradoxes and intellectual equivocations to please their own
vanity and satisfy the expectation of their hearers. Such a one is
Breisacher, "a polyhistor, who knew how to talk about anything
and everything" and whose wit "was as amusing as it was repulsive."[35] Poets, in this society of pseudo-avantgardists, of reac-
tionaries who preached revolution, and revolutionaries who
sided with reaction, were infected with the desire to proclaim
some ultimate, yet paradoxical, truth. One of them was a familiar figure at the "Kridwiss evenings" where "informal discus-
sions for gentlemen" were regularly held and which Zeitblom
and Leverkühn occasionally attended, the poet Daniel zur Höhe,
modelled after Ludwig Derleth, one of Stefan George's disciples, whose only collection of poems had been printed on handmade paper, "a lyrical and rhetorical outburst of riotous terror-
ism, to which one had to concede considerable verbal power."

He inspired a particularly strong dislike in the sedate Zeitblom who speaks of this poet's "impudently detached, flippant, and irresponsible style" as being characteristic of an age where estheticism and barbarism met in a kind of witches' cauldron.

Throughout the novel the equivocal use of language by scholars and artists of social distinction is contrasted with Leverkühn's single-minded search for purity and lucidity which would place intellectual severity at the service of musical expressiveness. However disturbing his last achievement in musical composition may be when viewed from the perspective of cultural pathology, its tragic implications are manifest when contrasted with the glib linguistic ambiguity of those who believe they have something relevant to say *about* culture or music. There is, first of all, Fitelberg, musical producer and agent for prominent avant-garde musicians, who intrudes into Leverkühn's secluded study to offer him, in a characteristic mixture of demotic French and German journalese, publicity and fame, and whose "rapid-fire, slightly indistinct, always rather high-pitched voice"[36] paints before the composer a picture of social and artistic success founded on the sensational and controversial character of his music. For, says Fitelberg (now in the English translation), "society demands to be excited, challenged, torn in sunder for and against", it expects "diversion" and enjoys nothing better than "endless, endless chatter". Unable to appeal to Leverkühn's vanity, he exhibits before his mind's eye, a vision of cultural Europe, divided against itself, incapable of producing a unifying principle whether it be in music or in any other art. He calls this cultural division "tragic"—"because in my opinion the unhappiness of the world rests on the disunity of the intellect, the stupidity, the lack of comprehension, which separates its spheres from each other."[37] Who if not a musician of the stature of Leverkühn would be best qualified to reconstruct a unified artistic tradition which might still save Europe from its otherwise inevitable doom? Fitelberg's monologue, in chapter 32 of the novel, is a linguistic *tour de force*: intelligent and fully aware of what language can do when used assertively and without the slightest trace of self-doubt, hypocritically humble and digressive and yet never once losing control of the trend of the argument, he is a true representative of the public relations man, one whose disciplined eloquence is a necessary veneer for the shallowness of his erudition and the superficial cosmopolitanism of his opinions about music and its place in the culture of the age. In short, he is an authentic devil's disciple and represents on earth those powers of intellectual equivocation which, by debasing the value of the word, turn language into an empty gesture, a mask, and a hollow pretense. Incidentally, he is also the most perfect embodiment of what Hesse called "The Age of the Feuilleton" in opposition to which the Castalian ideal of discipline and meditation grew to perfection.

The most articulate of these impersonations of linguistic ambiguity is the Devil who, in his conversation with Leverkühn, supplies the composer with formulas of utmost explicitness, designed to assist him in overcoming whatever doubts and reservations he might still harbor in his headlong plunge into "barbarism". When he first appears before him in the twilight room at Palestrina, he looks "an ugly customer, a bully, a *strizzi*, a rough". His voice is that of an actor, and so indeed is his eloquence. He changes his personal appearance thrice in the course of the conversation. Only the voice remains the same, the trained elocution of an actor, "nasal, distinct, cultivated, pleasing". If his appearance is fluid, the identity of his articulation never remains in doubt. Whether as "the unspeakable losel, the cheezy rapscallion in the cap, with the red eyes" or as "a member of the intelligensia, writer on art, on music for the ordinary press, a theoretician and critic", or, finally, as an academic of some distinction indulging in small talk while "riding *légèrement*, half-sitting, on the curved arm of the sofa, his fingertips crossed in his lap and both thumbs spread out", he never pretends to be anything else than what he is, in part a projection of Leverkühn's own intellectual curiosity, in part an embodiment of the composer's unadmitted and inadmissible desire for musical synthesis, for the fusion of "strict" composition with expressiveness, itself the result of "osmotic pressure", which characterizes the age which he so eloquently represents. Words never fail him. He is at home in theology as well as in the history of music, in chemistry as well as in medicine; he discusses the archaic components with no less eloquence than the most contemporary tendencies in twentiety-century musical creation. Only once during his talk with Leverkühn does he admit his failure to clothe in words that which is inexpressible—the life of the damned after death, for "one can really not speak of it at all, because the actual is beyond what by word can be declared" and because hell "lies aside from and outside of speech, language has naught to do with and no connection with it."[38] It is not even certain, the Devil observes, in what tense to speak of it, if speak you must, whether in the past, the present, or the future, and where to place it, for the ladder that leads "down" to it is the same that ascends towards heaven, so that the way down is identical with the way up, and the only way to reach hell is by way of heavenly illumination. What indeed can language say about the dimension of the timeless and the beyond-space: even the Devil cannot articulate the intangible, the unsubstantial, and unimaginable.

There are other voices tempting Leverkühn to give artistic expression to the psychologically ambiguous, especially when the language used can be understood on several levels simultaneously. This certainly applies to Shakespeare and Blake, who, throughout Leverkühn's career as a composer, exercise a profound, though somewhat equivocal, attraction on his mind. Shakespeare's sonnets, for instance, were always with him, not, so far as is known, for their quality as poetry but for the human predicament they so eloquently illustrate. It is the dilemma of the artist who, in his inability to come to terms with healthy, normal life, requires the services of a "friend" to woo for him as his deputy, and who finds himself betrayed by that same friend when he discovers that the woman whom he was supposed to court in his name, has been seduced by the very man to whom he had entrusted the task. The situation which is merely hinted at in Shakespeare's sonnets, is dealt with in several of his comedies in a light-hearted, if not actually frivolous, manner. Leverkühn, in conversations with Zeitblom and others, jocularly quotes from these plays without their being aware of it. Thus, we hear him say, in all seriousness, "My liege, your highness now may do me good", followed by "she will attend it better in thy youth/ Than in a nuncio of more grave aspect", and, quite literally quoting, "Who should be trusted now, when one's right hand/ Is perjured to the bosom?"[39] Leverkühn's identification with some of Shakespeare's most preposterous characters, comic without really causing laughter, self-defeating without arousing compassion, is of some interest. No Lear, no Othello, no Macbeth, are ever quoted or even mentioned. Their overlife-size portrayal lacks the ironic dimension, is too unequivocally tragic, to attract Leverkühn's intellectual curiosity. Instead of these giants in the art of suffering, he chooses Berowne, in *Love's Labour Lost*, as a congenial hero for the opera he bases on this early Shakespearean comedy.

Once more, Leverkühn's choice is determined by the opportunities offered by the text, and especially by Berowne's monologue, to create a musically grotesque atmosphere in which the world of knowledge is being parodied, while at the same time the plot hints at his own dilemma as an artist who has "foresworn" the love of women and yet cannot escape the fascination of the "natural" and the "barbarous". The whole opera is conceived as a musical caricature, witty as well as melancholy, "an intellectual achievement which deserved the name of heroic, something just barely possible, behaving like arrogant travesty."[40] Whatever else the extracts from the opera which Leverkühn plays out to his friends during his stay at Palestrina communicates, it is not a love-emotion transposed into music, but a persiflage of it, not a return to the world of nature and humanity, but an expression of contempt for both. The life of innocence as well as of experience are treated with equal ridicule. Shakespeare's use of language, his poetry, is here transformed into the "self-centered and completely cool esoteric", a more explicit parody of the absurdity of all human endeavor, whether through estheticism or barbarism, than Shakespeare had ever intended.

Leverkühn's absorption in Shakespeare's *The Tempest*, shortly before he composes his last work, the *Lamentation of Doctor Faustus*, is in tune with the general mood of his life story. He sets to music Ariel's songs, plays them out to his little nephew Nepomuk, also called Echo, and shares with the lovely and innocent child all the charm and grace of the spirit of the air who serves his master Prospero until he is given his freedom to become one with the elements. The composer's last attempt to save his soul before it is too late, acquires conspicuously literary overtones. By identifying with Prospero, he also wishes to "drown his books", to bury his staff "certain fathoms in the earth", and to abjure "this rough magic" which Prospero also calls his Art. Prospero's epilogue could, effectively, have been Leverkühn's own. Having forgiven all, he speaks with quiet resignation, hoping that his return to civilization will free him from the compulsions of his art and give him the strength to devote himself to prayer and to thoughts of death. Echo's death is the Devil's punishment meted out to the composer for having loved the pure and innocent. The death of the child is a fore-taste of hell.

Leverkühn's choice of Blake's poems is more explicitly still a reflection of personal despair. Zeitblom mentions a number of them, "The Sick Rose", "A Poison Tree", "I saw a Chapel all of Gold", and "Silent, Silent Night". In contrast to Shakespeare's amusing equivocations, these poems express a horror of the human condition in which the composer must have found mir-rored his own awareness of the inevitability of evil polluting all that is innocent and beautiful, of disease attracted to what is most vulnerable, of the poison that lurks in the love-emotion itself. Yet, there is nothing morbid about Leverkühn's setting of Blakes' most life-denying poems to music. The simplicity of the language called for simple harmonies. Both are equally decep-tive. Just as Blake's produces an effect of "falseness", deliber-ately brought about by the use of the least equivocal of words, so the composer's music has a more "uncanny effect than the most daring harmonic tension, and made one actually experi-ence the common chord growing monstrous."[41]

The fusion of words and sounds leads to a "false" synthesis. It betrays the artist's desperate longing for the simple, the healthy, and the normal, a longing that can only be realized through the distorting medium of the intellect. The reader of Thomas Mann's novel—assuming he is sufficiently literate to recognize the hidden analogies established by the writer between the language of words and the language of music—is uncomfortably aware of the unfulfilled longing of the artist, and undoubtedly of Thomas Mann himself, for spiritual salvation in an age that offers little hope of redemption. The composer's invocation of the spoken work, as used by poets, symbolizes the novelist's own tribute to the power of words when subjected to the conscious will and discipline of a poet's creative thought. In German, after all, both the poet and the novelist, are called by the same name, *Dichter*. One may well be a *Dichter* in words as in sounds. Yet, there is little salvation to be found in visions of human frustration and absurdity, created by poets, either in a spirit of comic persiflage or as an expression of tragic awareness. Leverkühn's last work is also founded on "words", transmitted through primordial myth and legend, through primitive magic invocations or through the language of poetry, all of them using words expressive of man's ultimate anguish before his descent into hell. The language spoken by soloists or chorus, in Leverkühn's work, is a musical transposition on a gigantic scale of all the laments that have, throughout human history, reflected man's torment in the face of evil. However hard Zeitblom may try to convince the "future reader" of his book that his friend's *Lamentation* is a deeply religious work and that Faustus's plea to his companions to "sleep in peace" is "the conscious and deliberate reversal of the 'Watch with me' of Gethsemane,"[42] it is hard to be convinced by this loyal bourgeois optimist who discovers in the last of the sounds in this harrowing work, the high G of a cello, "a light in the night."[43] The end of his story, written by Thomas Mann in California, a few months after the end of the war and Germany's defeat at the hands of the Allies, promises no hopeful resurrection, no return to sanity. Zeitblom's words, addressed to the spirit of the age that has caused this madness to spread all over Europe, speaks of "a miracle beyond the power of belief", a miracle, Thomas Mann implies, which neither the language of words nor the language of music can be expected to perform.

Notes to Chapter Eight

1. Hesse completed the manuscript of *The Glass Bead Game* on April 29, 1942; the narrator of the story of Adrian Leverkühn starts his narrative on May 27, 1943 which, Thomas Mann informs the reader in his *Story of a Novel*, corresponds almost exactly to the actual date when he, Mann, began writing the novel, namely on May 23, 1943. The slight discrepancy in the dates remains unexplained.
2. Letter to Hermann Hesse, dated Pacific Palisades, California, 1550 San Remo Drive, 8 April 1945. *Letters of Thomas Mann, 1889–1955*, p. 349.
3. Thomas Mann, *The Story of a Novel*, p. 75.
4. *The Glass Bead Game*, pp. 337–338. For an exact identification of this passage from Burckhardt's posthumous writings, see Theodore Ziolkowski, *The Novels of Hermann Hesse*, pp. 314–315, footnote 39.

5. Hermann Hesse, letter of December 12, 1947, *Briefe (Letters)*, p. 247 (The translation is taken from Theodore Ziolkowski, *op. cit.*, pp. 306–307).

6. Letter dated "Beginning of March 1948", *Briefe (Letters)* (my own translation) p. 148. For a detailed analysis of the role of music in the work of the two German novelists see Klaus Mathias, *Die Musik bei Thomas Mann und Hermann Hesse*. Doctoral Dissertation, Kiel, 1956.

7. Thomas Mann, *Doctor Faustus*, p. 236.

8. *Ibid.*, p. 359. The Marxist literary critic Georg Lukàcs who has, on numerous occasions, shown greater insight into the social implications of *Doctor Faustus* than many other more academically inclined commentators, makes the following not altogether surprising observation: "By a remarkable coincidence (if coincidence it be) I had just finished reading *Doctor Faustus* when the central committee of the Communist Party of the Soviet Union published its decrees on modern music. In Thomas Mann's novel this decree finds its fullest intellectual and artistic confirmation, particularly in those parts which so brilliantly describe modern music as such." (*Essays on Thomas Mann*, p. 7) Whether this is an ironic reference to Leverkühn's flight from an exhausted estheticism into the "barbarism" of atonality or whether Lukàcs merely wishes to toe the party-line by encouraging "social realism" in musical composition is not clear. Lukàcs, for reasons of his own, had to keep on the right side of the fence, however disastrous the intellectual consequences of such a politically oriented attitude to art and music.

9. *Ibid.* p. 361.

10. The following quotation is of particular relevance since it is taken from a book dealing with both individual and collective suicide, so characteristic a feature of our age: "The response of the arts has been to reduce the pleasure principle to its most archaic forms— manic, naked, beyond culture. The new strategy of aesthetic sophistication is primitivism: tribal rhythms on every radio, fertility rites on the stage, real or improvised Gold Coast customs in the living room, concrete poets grunting and oinking beyond language and beyond expression, *avant-garde* musicians exploring the possibilities of random noise, painters immortalizing industrial waste, radical politicians modelling their behaviour on the clowns of a Roman Saturnalia, and a youth culture devoted to the gradual chronic suicide of drug addiction."(A.Alvarez,*The Savage God*,p.138).

11. *Doctor Faustus*, p. 267.

12. *Ibid.*, pp. 10 and 14.

13. *The Story of a Novel*, p. 30.

14. *Ibid.*,pp. 42–43.(The word "critical" is evidently a mistranslation. *Kritische Periode* may be translated either as "critical era" or as an "era of crisis." It is this latter meaning that Thomas Mann obviously has in mind in this passage). Lukàcs, in his interpretation of *Doctor Faustus*, sees in the figure of Adrian Leverkühn a form of

universality which "extends far beyond Germany's geographical and intellectual frontiers. Just as Nietzsche and Spengler, Freud and Heidegger, despite their immediate German characteristics, are international, indeed from an international standpoint the veriest signposts of the intellectual disasters of the imperialist period, so, too, is the imagined music of Adrian Leverkühn." *(Essays on Thomas Mann, p. 63).*

15. *Ibid.*, p. 88. Lukàcs, predictably, blames the novelist for having chosen as his mouthpiece a member of the German middle-class whose powerlessness in the face of political reaction is his most characteristic feature. In spite of all his reservations regarding Fascism and the disastrous war forced upon the German people by its leaders, Zeitblom feels himself bound to the 'national community' whose spiritual values he shares though he deeply distrusts the political chaos which it has created. Thus, Lukàcs concludes, Serenus Zeitblom "can find nothing positive to pit against the new intellectual world in which he clearly recognizes reaction and barbarism. In objecting he feels that he intrudes, that it behoves him better to keep quiet—which he does." *(Essays on Thomas Mann, p. 91).*

16. *Doctor Faustus*, pp. 258–266.

17. *Ibid.*, p. 98.

18. *Ibid.*, p. 49.

19. *Ibid.*, pp. 74–75.

20. *Ibid.*, p. 186. Thomas Mann himself had little sympathy with twentieth-century music. He actually admits as much: "I understood the New Music only very theoretically, though I know something of it, I cannot really enjoy and love it." (Letter of October 1951 to H. H. Stuckenschmidt, in the latter's *Arnold Schönberg*, quoted in Carnegy, *Faust as Musician*, p. 6). Stuckenschmidt, himself a composer, had expressed his admiration for *Doctor Faustus* in a letter to the distinguished conductor Klaus Pringsheim (a close relative of Thomas Mann) in which he admits that "this story has come to be a part of me, for it is set to a great extent in my most intimate surroundings, it portrays and pleads for my causes, and enunciates the ideas of my generation, the musical avant-garde." (Published in *Der Monat* 1 (1949), 89, and quoted in Gunilla Bergsten, *Thomas Mann's "Doctor Faustus"*, p. 74). More revealing than anything else is Thomas Mann's observation about Schubert's B flat major Trio to which he listened while writing the last pages of Doctor Faustus, "... meditated while I listened on the happy state of music that it represented, on the destiny of the musical art since then—a lost paradise." *(The Story of a Novel, p. 181).*

21. *Ibid.*, p. 367. For a discussion of the difference between Schönberg's theories and what Mann made of them, see Carnegy, *Faust as Musician*, Chapter IV. In a letter to Arnold Schönberg, Mann makes the following remark: "In a novel that attempts to give a picture of an epoch as a whole, I have taken an enormously

characteristic cultural phenomenon of the epoch and transferred it from its real author to a fictional artist, a representative and martyr of the age." This letter is dated February 17, 1948—*Letters of Thomas Mann, 1989–1955*, p. 397.

22. Lukàcs observes that this uncertainty regarding the time element in Mann's novel is representative of the writer's alienation from his own society and the refusal to acknowledge the historically significant processes which led to this alienation. The result of Mann's "montage technique" is, according to Lukàcs, "the destruction of the unity and process of epic totality. If the opposition between experienced and real time is stressed, if the difference in tempo between them (where experience turns minutes into eternities and years into brief moments) are made into principles of composition to 'prove' the deadness, inferiority, or unreality of objective time, when the whole crumbles under the excessive weight of the moments." *(Essays on Thomas Mann*, p. 80).

23. Thomas Mann's observations about Palestrina and Pfitzner's opera can be found in his *Betrachtungen eines Unpolitischen*, pp. 398–419, written in 1917.

24. For more details see Patrick Carnegy, *Faust as Musician*, Chapter VI, pp. 79–80.

25. Quoted in Guinilla Bergsten. *op. cit.,* p. 111.

26. The letter is quoted in *The Story of a Novel*, pp. 151–152.

27. *The Story of a Novel*, p. 54.

28. *Doctor Faustus*, pp. 65-70.

29. *Ibid.*, p. 234.

30. The Devil, not altogether surprisingly, supplies the formula, "Everything comes from osmosis, my friend," he tells Leverkühn, "in whose teasing manifestations you so early diverted yourself." The Devil refers specifically to those chemical processes produced by syphilitic infection and the relation between what he calls "fluid diffusion, the proliferation process", leading to venereal meningitis and the creative act. For, after having made quite clear to the composer that this is the disease that will drag him down to "hell", he continues, "That creative genius-giving disease that rides on high horse over all hindrances, and springs with drunken daring from peak to peak, is a thousand time dearer to life than plodding healthiness." (pp. 228 and 235). Thomas Mann invariably identifies the creativity of the human spirit with disease. As early as in 1922, in his essay "Goethe and Tolstoy", he observes, "in spirit, then, in disease, resides the dignity of man; and the genius of disease is more human than the genius of health." (Quoted in Joseph Gerard Brennan, *Thomas Mann's World*, p. 70). More explicit still, in 1948, he observes, "it depends who is diseased, an average fool from whose sickness the elements of spirit and culture are absent, or a Nietzsche, a Dostoyevsky" *(Neue Studien*, 1948, p. 90; my own translation). In his Goethe novel, published in 1939, he makes Goethe think, "Maybe the pathological teaches us most about the

norm; it comes to me sometimes that by setting out boldy on the track of disease we might best pierce the darkness of living forms." (*The Beloved Returns*, p. 334). Goethe who provided German literature with "the norm" is here, manifestly, of the devil's party. One of his precursors is Dr. Krokowski, the residing psychologist in the Sanatorium in *The Magic Mountain*, according to whom "symptoms of disease are nothing but a disguised manifestation of the power of love..." (p. 61). Osmotic pressure, then, appears to be the foundation of the love-impulse, no less than of artistic creativity.

31. *Doctor Faustus*, p. 475.
32. *Ibid.*, p. 485.
33. *Ibid.*, pp. 465–466. Zeitblom's reference to Monteverdi occurs in the same passage: "The return to Monteverdi and the style of his time is what I meant by 'the reconstruction of expressiveness in its first and original manifestation....'" (p. 468). Actually Monteverdi's position in the history of music is an ambivalent as that of Thomas Mann's fictitious composer. For expressiveness, in the words of a twentieth-century musicologist, could be achieved by him only when "he passed the boundary lines of the new tonality already visible at that time.... "Thus," continues the writer, "the first composer to bring the new theory to its climax injected into it the poison that was to cause its death almost before he had attained his purpose." (E. Krenek, *Music Here and Now*, p. 120).
34. *Ibid.*, p. 195.
35. *Ibid.*, pp. 271–273.
36. *Ibid.*, p. 383.
37. *Ibid.*, pp. 385–386.
38. *Ibid.*, p. 238.
39. *Much Ado About Nothing*, I, i, 292. *Twelfth Night*, I, 4, 27–28. *Two Gentlemen of Verona*, V, 4, 67–68.
40. *Doctor Faustus*, p. 211.
41. *Ibid.*, p. 255.
42. *Ibid.*, p. 470.

IX
The Intellect That Failed

1

Whether Thomas Mann wanted the reader to think of Adrian Leverkühn's progressive isolation in the world of art and society as being the cause or the effect of the breakdown of all traditional musical norms remains an open question. The hell to which he is consigned at the end of the novel is certainly of his own making. Though the devil comes to bargain for his soul uninvited he appeals to the composer's innate tendency towards the exhilarating and the grotesque. Nauseated by the devil's ostentatious vulgarity, Leverkühn is attracted by his caustic humor and his sharp wit. Like Marlowe's Faustus the composer also inquires about the after-life "in the Dragon's Den". Unlike Mephisto in Marlowe's play, the devil in Mann's novel keeps the secret of damnation to himself. Hell "is", he says, it just happens when one least expects it. But as it will be a composer's hell, the devil, an expert in the dissonances of serial music, provides sufficient hints about the kind of music which will resound "inside these echoless walls" to make one's hair stand on end. Leverkühn's hell will resemble and carry to its logical conclusion his own last composition. Music, finally, will cease to be itself. For hell will be filled "with screeching and beseeching, gurgling and groaning, with yauling and bauling and caterwauling, with horrid winding and grinding and racking ecstasies of anguish . . . the thick-clotted diapason of thrills and chirps lured from this everlasting dispensation of the unbelievable combined with the irresponsible."[1]

Leverkühn, repelled and fascinated, is given his twenty-four years of "high-flying time" which, according to the devil, will be a time of "illumination", "an ecstatie of delirium" provided he shuns other human beings and will, for the rest of his earthly existence, be impervious to human warmth, affection, and love. For, as the devil is not slow to point out, "Cold we want you to be, that the fire of creation shall be hot enough to warm yourself in."[2] The price to be paid for the ultimate musical "break-through" is the artist's unredeemable solitude and final madness. Living among men he will yet not be one of them. Speaking their language he will not be understood by any. If and when he loves he will infect the object of his love with the germs of disease. His creative fire will burn to ashes the very fabric of his compositions. Tenderness and compassion will find no place in his music as it will be absent from his life. But he will not be permitted to perish. An eternity of madness and dying will be his lot. Just as the common chord in his last composition "grows monstrous" so will his mind. He will have nothing else to communicate but the monstrosity which is his inner illumination.

While Thomas Mann was at work writing the history of his fictitious composer he read a great deal. A considerable number of books which attracted his particular attention dealt with *Hues*, a form of pestilence of mostly syphilitic origin. Others again were biographies of great musicians among whom the name of Hugo Wolf appears more than once, a composer who spent the last years of his life in a mental home. Nietzsche's life and final breakdown features prominently in the very extensive list of biographies. Also Dostoyevsky is mentioned a number of times. Thomas Mann's interest in disturbances of the mind, just as his preoccupation with music, was centered in nineteenth-century attempts at interpreting the mind of the genius in psycho-pathological and purely medical terms.

Thus he looked in the life history of men of outstanding gifts for inner tensions and pressures which, according to the biographies he was studying at that time, were open to rational explanation. Whatever medical science had to say about the pathology of the mind, its origin, growth, and final consummation in madness, especially as it applies to the artist, served as the raw material in Thomas Mann's description of Leverkühn's final breakdown. It was no haphazard decision on his part that made him choose the most rational of nineteenth-century humanists as the narrator of Leverkühn's tragic story. His admission of final defeat is indeed part of Mann's message. As the tragedy unfolds itself on two levels simultaneously, the individual-artistic and the national-politic, Mann's concern with madness extends from the very core of this violent upheaval, the eye of the storm, the composer himself, to the circumference, the bombing of German cities during the Second World War, the battle for Stalingrad, and Germany's final unconditional surrender.

The socio-political level serves the purpose of a counterpoint. It may, indeed, be rationally explained. The pathology of men's political enterprise, then, merely reflects on a gigantic scale the pathology of the artist's creative enterprise. The "irrationality" of Leverkühn's music (as it appeared to most of his hearers) thus becomes a matter of artistic, social, and medical significance. His "illumination" is—like that of the German people as a whole—a fever of the mind, a sickness affecting art no less than politics. The humanist's helplessness in the face of this form of self-destructive "ecstasis" is only too evident. It seems doubtful whether Thomas Mann believed in the availability of remedies to cure this deadly ill. As the artist has to be sacrificed for the sake of his artistic integrity, neither can the people be redeemed from hell. Goethe, in the wisdom of his old age, created a new Faustus, corresponding to nineteenth-century ideas of social reform. By redeeming the people among whom he lives he freed his soul from its subjection to the powers of darkness. Thomas Mann's twentieth-century perspective perceived a growing variety of damnations all equally indicative of the defeat of the regulating mind and the victory of chaos.

Twentieth-century attitudes to madness have undergone profound and significant changes since Mann wrote his novel. The emphasis falls less heavily on pathological symptoms than on social pressures. Individual susceptibility to mental disturbances followed by states of complete irrationality are explained in less medically-oriented language, with fewer references to remedial devices such as shock-treatment, psychoanalytical investigation, or cold-water cures. The first sentence in the Introduction to Michel Foucault's *Madness and Civilization* hints at a new evaluation of madness itself. "Madness has in our age become some sort of lost truth", says the writer in whose opinion "madness is a form of vision that destroys itself by its own choice of oblivion in the face of existing forms of social tactics and strategy." According to David Cooper, Foucault "makes it quite clear that the invention of madness as a disease is in fact nothing less than a peculiar disease of our civilization."[3]

The impact of the musical experience on the mind of the hearer, susceptible to intense emotional arousal, may indeed produce symptoms of mental alienation not dissimilar from those commonly associated with various forms of insanity— withdrawal from society, intense introspection or its opposite, a sense of utter vacuity, a fear of any kind of intimate contact with other human beings. At times, however, it may also lead to a recognition of the uniqueness of one's own being which may be the first step towards a realization of the true significance of one's Self. This discovery of inner time and inner space which music communicates more powerfully than any of the other arts is—as this study has shown on numerous occasions—looked upon by the socially well-adjusted with intense suspicion. Outer space and outer time—in so far as they are measurable and therefore communicable in clearly defined terms—have been for centuries officially sanctioned concepts. But the greater the inwardness of the musical experience, the more profound the silence surrounding the Self.

This is Patrick White's way of portraying Theodora, the protagonist of his novel *The Aunt's Story*, published in 1949, two years after Thomas Mann's *Doctor Faustus*. Patrick White may or may not have been familiar with Mann's novel. In all probability he read it shortly after it had been published in German. Possibly—and this is mere assumption—he was struck by the relation established between the impact of music on the mind and the utter inability of the intellect to master the experience in rational terms.

Though little enough is known about Patrick White's reading habits he must also have been familiar with Hermann Hesse's novels among which *The Glass Bead Game*, published in 1943, embodies some of the musical ideas which will reappear, though in considerably modified form, in *The Aunt's Story*. Fundamentally Patrick White's novels, those written before and after 1950, are part of the European heritage in fiction writing. The Australian background, more often than not, is a deliberate satire on middle-class society wherever it may be found, the absurdity of its social prejudices and moral superstitions.

His novels are concerned with the individual's struggle to

maintain his integrity in the face of a commonplace and thus indifferent, if not actually hostile, environment. What, from one novel to the next, compels the reader's attention is the novelist's growing realization that spiritual survival does not depend on introspective intellectualism nor on a capacity for rational analysis of the causes which threaten man with disintegration. In these novels the leveling process, characteristic of democratically organized societies, is repeatedly portrayed as inevitably creating the lowest common denominator of spiritual commonplaceness. It is this fatal, disintegrative tendency towards intellectual conformism that threatens the individual's sense of wholeness and his dedication to a life of acceptance and humility outside the inhibiting dictates of intellectual compulsion. "The intellect has failed us", exclaims one of White's "riders in the chariot,"[4] after having undergone all the indignities that society holds in store for the simple in spirit; another, no less afflicted character in the same novel, remembers, after a life of complete spiritual isolation which resembles, in the eyes of commonplace people, a state of utter mental alienation, that "in the end, if not always, truth was a stillness and a light."[5] It is in this same spirit that one more of Patrick White's guileless fools, in a moment of intense, almost unbearable self-recognition, wishes to destroy "the great monster Self" in order to achieve "that desirable state ... which resembles, one would imagine, nothing more than air and water."[6] This state towards which the whole novel in which this passage occurs moves is, later on, described as one of humility, anonymity, and pureness of being. It is achievable only by those who free themselves from the shackles of the intellect. Judged by commonplace standards of conduct, this is a state bordering on madness. To the one who has accepted the essence of things, reason is no longer a valid criterion for action. And when "the desirable state" is achieved "above the disintegrating world", nothing remains but "light and silence" eating into "the hard, resisting barriers of reason, hinting at some ultimate moment of clear vision."[7]

The literary historian may well consider man's intellect, his capacity to analyze, to understand, and to judge, the foundation upon which human civilizations are built. Every one of Patrick White's novels disproves this assumption. A civilization built upon reason and a standardized command of words defines itself by its own commplaceness; for what is being insisted upon is the intellect of those who follow their "great monster Self" and use words in order to hide their ignorance or their unwillingness to face the ultimate truth about themselves.[8] Yet the final vision is that of a reality in which stillness and light predominate. This may be either the reality of air and water, but also the more tangible reality of substantial things which do not articulate anything because they are devoid of speech. "There is perhaps no more complete a reality than a chair and a table,"[9] thinks Theodora Goodman while sitting in the hall of the Hôtel du Midi waiting for the receptionist to come and speak to her. Many pages later she makes what may appear a cryptic statement but which fits in well enough with her gradual insight into deeper levels of reality than those whom she addresses are aware of. " 'Only chairs and tables,' she said, 'are sane.' "[10]

The dividing line between sanity and insanity, it appears, corresponds to what commonplace people consider to be the limits of human reason. According to them, Mary Hare, another of the riders in the chariot, "was quite mad, quite contemptible, of course, by standards of human reason," and the author adds his own sardonic comment on the vulnerability of such a standard. For remembering what people sometimes are led to do to escape the fragmentary nature of their intellect and its articulation through words, he continues, "Reason finally holds a gun at its head—and does not always miss."[11] The desirable state resembling that of stillness and light, air and water, and, if everything else fails, chairs and tables, is, in effect, a state of sanity beyond the frontiers of the rationalizing intellect. To attain this awareness of the real which transcends all commonplace reality, one must walk among the fires of hell where "the wretched light of the intellect is of no avail,"[12] a state of recognition from which the "monster Self" has been excluded and which, Blake reminds us, "to Angels look[s] like torment and insanity."[13]

2

The failure of the intellect to come to terms with life characterizes Patrick White's preoccupation with music and the musical experience. This is invariably true of those occasions when the individual finds himself placed within a crowd of commonplace listeners whose musical expectations are restricted by social attitudes of unthinking assent. The alien and the quester, repelled by the hypocritical and self-conscious solemnity of the occasion, surrounded, indeed suffocated, by commonplace listeners, the anonymous majority of concert-goers, is the object of half-ironic comment (as if observed in the light of commonplace reason) in three of White's novels. On the other hand, the intellectually insecure invariably looks upon this majority with a mixture of awe, contempt, and admiration. In one of White's earliest novels, *The Living and the Dead*, Eden, observing her mother while listening to music, envies her "the immense satisfaction of the face, the half-closed eyes, whether this satisfaction was sincere, springing from the music itself, or merely from being in the right *milieu*. But her mother, bogus or not, sat in the firm protection of her own established envelope. Succinct, satisfied, proof against any physical or emotional disturbance. . . ."[14]

As Patrick White's art increases in depth of observation and insight, symbolic significances are emphasized, while naturalistic descriptions are given less prominence. The concert-halls are metamorphosed into commonplace infernos where instead of soaring fires consuming the living and the dead, dust settles comfortably on things and people. Sanity, however, is bestowed upon the chairs, at least as long as they remain unoccupied. It is a somewhat elusive symbolism but quite intelligible to one who reads the novel as if it were a poem and grasps the symbols as part of a total vision of life. In *The Aunt's Story* the protagonist undergoes a traumatic musical experience in such a symbolic setting, described with a subtle emphasis on commonplace naturalistic details. "At the concert, as at all concerts, everyone was rounded and well fed. Music filled out their lines and emphasized banality. It is not possible to listen to music without the body becoming a hump on a chair. Over the hall a great grey dumb organ hung and brooded, as it had over other similarly irrelevant occasions, of civic pomposity, or the paper folly of charity balls. Now an orchestra, playing an overture of a Russian, made the dust dance dimly on the organ's face, stirred the dinners in stomachs on chairs. Some of the chairs were still empty, the chairs of smarter people, who ate longer, later dinners."[15]

THE INTELLECT THAT FAILED

At a still later stage White's description of concert-halls and its *habitués*, performers as well as listeners, takes on an air of quiet and resigned detachment, as if the collective musical experience were some kind of esoteric magic ritual to which one has to submit in order to be accepted as a well-functioning member of society, in full command of his mental and emotional powers of coordination. Yet the descriptions increasingly stress the incipient loss of such equilibrium. Thus, in *The Vivisector*, at a concert which has an equally traumatic effect on the protagonist of this story, "a young man, the paler for his black, sank his teeth in Boris and couldn't get them out again, chin struck alarmingly, your own chin straining with his; because by now every agony was yours."[16] What else there was at this concert is summed up in Rachmaninov's "sticky ecstasies" and the fake "orgasm" of Liszt's "Quasi-adagio" in his Piano Concerto in E-flat Major. It is only when the main performer, a young pianist, transcends the awkward banality of the occasion, "because she willed it, from the quivering shoulders to the toe of her arrogant shoe", the members of the audience experience a shock of dismay. For what they witness is "too unrestrained a display of 'artistic temperament' in a hitherto normal, young Australian girl."[17] While they could accept the morbidly erotic implications of the "Quasi-adagio", they are bewildered by the genuine commitment of the artist to the work she is performing. Evidently, the clash between commonplace musical responses, predictable because conforming to social expectation as to how far the performer as well as the listener may surrender to musical arousal without losing face, and the trauma experienced by an alien in his isolation, profoundly aware of the wounds that music may inflict on the insecure and unprotected, furnishes Patrick White's musical episodes with moments of increasing distress and anguish.

Each one of these three concerts ends with the escape of the protagonist, usually even before the concert is over, an escape from the traumatic effect of the musical performance and the commonplaceness of the applause and the trivial remarks overheard during the concert. Having become aware of her mother's complacent and unruffled acceptance of musical ideas, her unquestioning surrender to conformist artistic criteria as regulated by the social establishment, the moral code of which she respects above anything else, Eden, listening to a Brahms concerto, all of a sudden realizes that "the clarinet had lost control. It ricocheted among the strings." And as the tension within her grows she has only one wish, to escape the suffocating dust of the Royal Albert Hall, the rustling of program sheets, her mother's self-possessed mask. Even though, "in the doorway the misery of violins fell upon her head" and "a long echoing of horns" followed her down the concrete tunnel of the stairs, she somehow reaches the street and finds herself standing on the pavement, "with the irrelevance of one anonymous star among many" looking down upon her. Escape is only partial salvation. It is merely the first step in an attempt to look for freedom from compulsion when the musical experience itself has become a prison, and consciousness a windowless and dark prison-cell, enclosing your "monster Self" in the waves of music, "the heavy, dusty waves, as if it were pinned down round the edges of the room, as if your hands could not reach out to rescue a phrase from the heavy fold of its own frustrated passion."[18] Whether the frustration is Eden's own or an intrinsic element in Brahms's music is hardly relevant for an understanding of this episode. Possibly it was she, the immature and emotionally vulnerable listener, who projected her own unfulfilled longings into "the heavy, dusty waves" of the Brahms concerto. The music provided no release from torment but merely a growing sense of alienation.

In the second novel, *The Aunt's Story*, the traumatic experience at the concert is more intense still and thus requires an even greater commitment to the music being played on the stage. The integration between music and listener is free of all intellectual rationalization. Theodora Goodman's consciousness is, as it were, blocked out the moment the music begins. Indeed, even her sense impressions are kept in abeyance for the duration of the concert. She, quite literally, ceases to exist on the level of commonplace reality. Her flight from this trauma of nonbeing sets in as soon as the concert is over. Before the applause has died down, she goes towards the open night-sky "into the trams. She walked some distance, the other side of the screeching trams, without seeing much. Her hollow body vibrated still with all she had experienced. Now it was as empty as hollow wood." Her mother finds Theodora's mood after the concert "rather immoral, the strange, withdrawn mood that one could not share". Failing to find the appropriate words, her "old, soft, fed stomach grizzled and complained".[19] If words fail to express the commonplace sentiments her mother would like to convey to her after her flight from the concert-hall, how much more does Theodora feel the need to escape into silence and light after "the suave forest of violins" and "the slabs of music piled one upon the other" which, together with the cellist's playing, constitute a level of reality unbearably poignant in its magnitude for the simple soul of the pure listener in an impure world.

In *The Vivisector*, the aging painter, Hurtle Duffield, who had gone to listen to the playing of his former mistress, an initially quite commonplace young woman who had succeeded in rising "above a vulgar situation", being in control of the music, herself transformed into "an archetypal figure he could no longer recognize", takes flight from the "roaring" audience the moment the pianist ceases playing. "He got up and started clambering out, past stubborn knees, trailing his overcoat across the laps of resentful strangers. Here and there he trod on the spongy insteps of seemingly dropsical women, who didn't scream, but moaned in harmony with his own painfully throbbing silence.

"What mattered was to escape the trauma of Kathy's performance, and more particularly this new Kathy, herself escaping in the direction she had chosen."[20]

The escape from the shattering impact of the musical experience accompanies the reader of Patrick White's novels across the thirty years that elapse between the writing of *The Living and the Dead*, published in 1941, and *The Vivisector*, published in 1970. It describes an archetypal situation, recreated by the novelist in a variety of settings, embodied in figures that have little else in common but a distrust of the intellect and a sense of alienation from the commonplaceness of the average listener's response to music. To all three of them alike the musical experience intimates a sense of freedom from the self-centeredness of an unregenerated ego. Surrounded by "light and silence" when the music ends, their precipitate flight from the concert-hall resembles a drowning man's desperate attempt to keep his head above water before the waves swallow him.

It is in this sense that in Patrick White's novels these listeners to music achieve an insight into suffering, regardless whether such music expresses this suffering or not. For even music which is filled with life-affirming joy, transcending the commonplace harmonies of everyday giving and taking, carries within it the germs of some future anguish, a foreknowledge of suffering to come. Such foreknowledge may be either a blessing or a curse, both equally unbearable, to the one who is so deeply immersed in the particular music of the present moment that flight alone can save him from drowning. But the silence into which these listeners escape is full of the echoes of music. To achieve a state of complete stillness—the stillness of "tables and chairs" which are deprived of all musical associations—requires the closing of all doors, if this were possible, the shutting out of all echoes, the return to a nothingness from which even the consciousness of suffering would be excluded. A singularly revealing passage in *The Aunt's Story* attempts to describe such a process of gradual withdrawal from knowledge. "The voice blurred, as the music doubled on its underwater shelf, with the glistening purity of snow water, a bluish white, joyful and perpetual as mountain water. Katina Pavlou lifted her hands and the music fell, sure and pure, and painfully transparent. So that any possible disaster of age or experience must drown in music. Disasters, the music implied, are reserved for observers, the drowning drown. Caught in the iciness of music, Theodora felt the breath stop in her throat. She went inside the little wintergarden and closed the door."

" 'It is difficult to escape from music. Music pursues,' " observes one of the more eccentric inhabitants of the hotel in which this scene takes place, and adds, " 'you must realize . . . that you cannot close doors.' "[21]

The most musical of Patrick White's novels in which these words are spoken, the story of the spinster Theodora Goodman, contemplates the closing of many doors until all echoes are swallowed in stillness and light. The consciousness of the protagonist increasingly resembles that desirable state which is "nothing more than air and water." The freedom thus achieved is indeed a freedom from "the monster Self", brought about by flight, more complete than in any other novel previously dealt with in this study, from the least tangible, least definable, yet most self-contained of all esthetic structures. The escape *from* music is, in effect, the novelist's last attempt to reformulate the meaning of reality in terms that already take the intellect's defeat for granted. The escape becomes a fulfillment, and the new reality is outside any musical context and no longer definable as pertaining to harmony or disharmony experienced by a commonplace mind on an average day.

3

Theodora Goodman has none of the ingredients that go to the making of an artist. She does not pretend to intellectual distinction. Her musical taste is not determined by study or experience. It is, indeed, doubtful whether she could distinguish one musical style from another. To call her a "musical" character is to burden her with an understanding of music she does not possess and with a sense of musical discrimination she has never aspired to cultivate. All the reader is given to know about her—when she is still an adolescent—is set down in a farewell speech, never delivered, by the mistress of the boarding-school who had occasion to observe her and thus formed a judgment about her which the reader is not meant to forget. Miss Spofforth who had more wisdom in her than "her squat body and her heavy face" indicated, would have liked to tell Theodora this: "But there is much that you will experience. You will see clearly, beyond the bone. You will grow up probably ugly, and walk through life in sensible shoes. Because you are honest, and because you are barren, you will be both honored and despised. You will never make a statue, nor write a poem. Although you will be torn by all the agonies of music, you are not creative. You have not the artist's vanity which is moved finally to express itself in objects. But there will be moments of passing affection, through which the opaque world will become transparent."[22] Beyond this passage which looks at Theodora from the outside, through the eyes of a sympathetic adult, the reader follows her development from the realization of her false self to her final commitment to an establishment for the mentally disturbed with which the novel ends. The reader also participates in a "stream of consciousness" which reveals the existence of conflict situations of which scarcely anything can be seen from the outside. Thus when she recognizes the intensity of her repugnance towards her mother, she thinks, "Then it is I . . . I have a core of evil in me that is altogether hateful."[23] On another occasion she realizes the inability of speech, based as it is on the assumption of rational articulation among human beings, to destroy "the great monster Self".

She achieves her final recognition that she is still a discord, a "black note", in the "solemnity of living and of days", expressed by the "flowing corn song" through which the train is passing which carries her away from "the violence of personality" to a place where her commonplace identity would no longer matter.[24] When she tears out her name "by the roots", throws away her rail and steamship tickets, actions "which had sprung out from some depth she could not fathom", she learns to accept life, hers and that of others she has met on the way, as an illusion of reality which does not greatly differ from the reality of an illusion conveyed to her most forcefully by her meeting with the cellist Moraïtis, before and during the concert she attends and from which she escapes, having undergone that metamorphosis she had been waiting for all her life. When the novel ends and the ordeal of freeing herself from her consciousness is over, she is no longer alone, for "there was no end to the lives of Theodora Goodman. These met and parted, met and parted, movingly . . . And in the same way that the created lives of Theodora Goodman were interchangeable, the lives into which she had entered, making them momently dependent for love or hate, owing her this portion of their fluctuating personalities . . . These were the lives of Theodora Goodman, these too."[25]

At the very center of this spiritual ordeal occurs the musical experience, preceded by the encounter with the musician. That Moraïtis should be a cellist seems both natural and necessary. Among all instruments the cello resembles the human voice most closely, the playing of the cello involves not merely the hands but the whole body, the musical message it evokes possesses some of the solid quality of the wood and its hollowness within which the air vibrates transforming silence into sound. There is indeed an intimation of physical union between the player and the instrument which, in the imagination of the listener, resembles the bodily union of two lovers.[26]

Moraïtis himself represents the very quintessence of the music he is playing. Withdrawn within himself, a man of few words, holding things in his hands "with humility", he comes from "a country of bones", his native Greece, where "it is not necessary to see things . . . if you know."[27] His eyes are veiled and do not seem to see anything at all. Thinking and feeling, his hands move from object to object, somewhat in the manner of a blind man whose understanding of life is rooted in a delicate and innate sense of touch. Thus Theodora Goodman realizes that when Moraïtis sits down with his cello between his legs to play whatever concerto it is he is supposed to be playing, "he saw and did not see"; yet, a few minutes later, she knew that his veiled eyes saw beyond his own integrity of innocence, "threatened with destruction by the violins", beyond his own isolation and his unconcern with those for whom he was playing. Moraïtis, embracing his cello with his whole body and moving the bow across the strings, "saw with the purity of primitive vision". He closed his eyes, "as if his faith would not allow", that faith, hinted at in his short conversation with Theodora, in the integrity of the bones which presume to be more than the skeleton of living things, and in "naked rooms" in which to practice on his instrument. Though Theodora points out that "bare" would be a more suitable word, she and the 'cellist agree that a state of nakedness would be the ultimate fulfilment for both player and instrument. The final transformation of the cello into a living vibrating being, simultaneously responding to the "thinking" hands of the cellist and transmitting his thoughts to the listener's consciousness, the dark womb of its cavity a willing receptable of the seed from which the player's vision of purity and simplicity will grow and expand in the minds of those who can see, their eyes closed, and who are thus able to know the essence of things.

Theodora Goodman experiences all this as if performer, instrument, the concert-hall itself, exist for her alone. Moraïtis's isolation becomes hers as well. His playing on the cello is transmitted to her mind through the echoing vibrations of her body. The bow in his hands gliding across the strings of the instrument seems to move across her flesh, stroking it, punishing it, purifying it. "She was herself the first few harsh notes that he struck out of his instrument . . ." And later on, while the music lasts, "he could breathe into her mouth. He filled her mouth with long aching silences, between the deeper notes that reached down into her body . . ." When the playing is over, Theodora's "hollow body vibrated still with all she had experienced."[28]

It is the trauma of this experience which haunts Theodora for the rest of her life, although Patrick White no more than hints at the ultimate effect of this musical conception. That Theodora conceives, as it were, *in* the flesh as well as "above" the flesh is made clear by the description of Moraïtis's playing which, at first, "was more tactile than the hot words of lovers spoken on a wild nasturtium bed", while the final emphasis is clearly not so much on the physical sensation aroused by the music as on the sense of complete fulfillment which Theodora experiences after the concert, indeed an inner illumination which, however, is neither an artist's nor a mother's. For she knows she can experience neither. But for the time being the fulfillment is complete, "she had waited for something to happen. Now existence justified itself."[29]

When Theodora, finally, divests herself of her false identity, her "monster Self", it is to the accompaniment of musical themes that this process is initiated. While the train which carries her all through America passes through the "trumpeting corn", "the white pizzicato of telephone wires", and "a counterpoint of houses", Theodora retreats "into her own distance", away from "the frills of flutes" into a solitude which is beyond all the music of passing days, a sense of being which is a kind of grace, lifting her up above the continuity of time and the irrelevancies of the ticking of clocks. When, in the separateness of her private vision, she meets the man Holstius who comes out of the timeless forest to give her the final instructions for what remains to be accomplished, it is a musical image, once more, that flashes across her mind. Actually it is her own mind that creates the musical image. For Theodora, having reached the end of her journey, waiting for Holstius, a nonmusical reincarnation of Moraïtis, to visit her for the last time, realizes that "the struggle to preserve her own instrument for some final, if also fatal, music that Holstius must play, had been at times difficult and unpleasant, but at least it was preserved."[30] The 'cello has remained undamaged, still speaking with the voice of some final vision of purity. Since, in its final analysis, this music is indeed "beyond the flesh", it has also preserved the innocence of its sound. Nothing remains now but man, man in his commonplace impurity, to disturb the humble anonymity of its being.

The "white room" to which she is taken belongs to an institution reserved for people of her kind. It is meant to make her feel "comfortable" in a commonplace sort of way. The doctor who has been called to bring her down from her mountain isolation in order to save her from the excesses of her madness very wisely remarks, "Lucidity . . . isn't necessarily a perpetual ailment,"[31] implying that not all hope is lost and that, finally, Theodora Goodman may be brought back to her senses. He does not know, as indeed he cannot, that in cases such as hers, insanity is a foretaste of that bliss which makes her "accept the pathetic presumption of the white room" without a shudder of revulsion. The bare room of the asylum is a good place "to practice" in, to transform a reality which has become irrelevant into an illusion which is the only truth that matters. Even the music within her is stilled. She no longer vibrates together with the strings of the cello. There is now only stillness and light around her, and the comfortable words spoken by that mild man who has come to save her from his speechless lucidity.

It is through man's disintegrating mind, whether as musician in Thomas Mann's novel or as listener in Patrick White's story, that either heaven or hell are made visible. Insanity as ecstasy and surrender to chaos or as a desirable state of ultimate lucidity is the choice laid before the reader. In both novels personal identity is seen to be a burden too heavy to carry. In Mann's portrayal of the helplessness of the intellect to cope with reality we sense a fatalistic awareness of the end of all things. Recognizing the expanding scope of inner space and time, Patrick White represents man's consciousness as freeing itself from the distracting intellect in readiness for the final vision of innocence, humility and anonymity.

4

Patrick White's last word on music as the only illusion worth preserving in a work of fiction is spoken in *The Vivisector*. As this is a novel dealing with the rise of a painter from commonplace suburban conformity to the impenetrable isolation of the creative artist looking for ways of self-expression through color and design, the musical aspect of the novel inevitably calls for visual interpretation. For when Hurtle Duffield, the painter, meets Katherine Volkov who, at the age of fourteen is possessed by the ambition to become a concert pianist one day, and makes her for a few hours his mistress, he experiences a sudden urge to transform the apparently casual encounter into a painting. The elderly painter, a stranger to society and thus unconcerned with the vagaries of public taste, begins to draw his "Girl at Piano" in a fairly realistic manner, as if it were merely a question of translating the spatial relationship between the sloping lines of an old upright piano and the straight lines of the young girl's back into a formal design "in which any light must flow from a suggestion of the girl's face." At a later stage he introduces a hermaphroditic element into the as yet unfinished picture. The young girl's shadow is shown to fall across "the boy of sinewy thighs and starfish breasts" so that the illusion is created as if "the boy's mouth was Kathy's."[32]

This is merely the first draft. After having destroyed it, he begins anew. Instead of the "sweaty schoolgirl of vulgar lapses, touchingly tentative aspirations, and at times brutal unconscious sensuality", Hurtle Duffield now transforms Kathy into what he desires her to be, "almost a woman, of studied ice and burning musical passion, who was daring him to transfer his own passion to the primed board". In the course of the painting he realizes that such a transference from one art form to another is in danger of being defeated by the different means used by the artists. For the greatest difficulty, indeed the problem that is beyond all solution, is not to "paint" the music or the musician, but the instrument on which she is playing. To bring the piano to life is beyond all esthetic speculation. Though a cello may be imagined as resembling the human body, the straight, unmoving lines of a piano resist the aging painter's urge to transform the girl's naïve sensuality into significant form. So he gives up what he has so thoughtlessly undertaken.

The final illumination occurs at Kathy's second concert, when she is, in effect, twenty years old and plays, not Liszt, but an early concerto by Mozart (K. 271), itself dedicated to a young girl-pianist. Her playing has become that of an accomplished artist; yet it lacks that perfection which Moraïtis, the cellist, possessed, the wisdom that sees "beyond the bones" and transcends the commonplace knowledge of man. At the concert the old painter who has, reluctantly, gone to listen to what he secretly hopes would be a promise fulfilled and a vision accomplished, experiences that sense of oneness between performer and listener which is the only valid test for the true meaning of a musical experience; for "his mistress Katherine Volkov played to delight her lover in a room empty except for themselves" and he, the painter, "recognized the milky lustre, the spurts of black fire as theirs: dark tragedies hinted at resolved themselves in limpid strength." Kathy has, finally, "exorcised herself". It is a revelation of "pure joy they shared, both then, and tonight." The visual associations no longer matter. Even Mozart's musical lucidity is merely a means to an end; for "innocence hides nothing; and perfection bears looking on."[33]

Kathy is aware of the presence of her former lover in the audience. But it is she who has the upper hand now, she who, under Mozart's guidance transforms the reality of the flesh into the illusion of pure being. She remembers him and their early encounter in his studio while she was still a child during her performance and tosses him back and forth between the two extremes of the real and the illusory, flesh and spirit, definable musical pattern and undefinable inner illumination. Her knowledge is less mature than his, because still attached to the commonplace joys of living and loving and being loved. Though it seems to him that her "heart were a simple cupboard one simply had to open", he no longer has the key; or rather, the only key he still has is his art.

After Hurtle Duffield's first stroke he attempts, once more, to translate the illusion of music onto canvas. Yet it is no longer he who is doing the painting. He is being "worked on" by a power he no longer can control. Thus, the pattern of lines and blocks of color are not his own, are unrelated, unintended, not corresponding to any sense of reality which he can still touch with his unparalysed hand. Looking for what, unknowingly, he has created on the canvas and realizing that his hands moved "round the edges of totality", he, for the first and last time in his life, "experienced a curious sense of grace."[34] For what he is trying to paint is no longer Kathy playing her Mozart concerto, but this sense of grace radiating from the illusion of lucidity created by Mozart's music and its incomplete reflection in color and design, an unpaintable illusion in search of an invisible reality. The painter's disintegrating mind experiences this grace as a color beyond all colors—one that would combine both auditory and visual perfection; he calls it his "indigo blue". When he makes his last attempt to transfer Mozart's Andantino and Kathy's playing of it on the unfinished canvas he suffers his second stroke.

There are few scenes in the literature of our time that so movingly portray the final illumination of an artist's consciousness and his acceptance of the "cloud of unknowing" as the ultimate gift of some unearthly grace. The extinction of the intellect is a necessary last step in the artist's development from the failure of reason to furnish adequate explanations for the ordeal of creation, to the vain attempt of the irrational to supply valid analogies that could be expressed through language and speech. For neither reason nor unreason are adequate criteria for an interpretation of the artist's function in our civilization.

The last pages of *The Vivisector* are written in similarly blurred speech as the last pages of Adrian Leverkühn's address to his invited guests before he sits down at the piano to play his "Lamentations of Doctor Faustus". In both novels individual identity is seen to be a burden too heavy for the artist to carry. The final stroke comes when, mercifully, expression through art is found to be beyond the means put at the artist's disposal. Adrian Leverkühn's dismal "lamentations" are as real as Hurtle Duffield's ultimate vision of "indigo blue" standing for an unalloyed affirmation of life. The reader's final choice lies between the acceptance of the reality of insanity as ecstasy and surrender to chaos or the dawning awareness that what people call madness may merely be a desirable state of ultimate lucidity transcending all commonplace formulas as to what man's intellect may or may not accomplish. The artist's disintegrating mind, be he painter or musician, is the medium through which either hell or heaven are made visible. Both novelists turn to music as the great liberator from intellectual conceit and as, possibly, the sole intimation of grace that is bestowed upon man in those rare moments when self-recognition can no longer be expressed through the language of words and their unavailing search for meaning.

Notes to Chapter Nine

1. Thomas Mann, *Doctor Faustus*, p. 238.
2. *Ibid.*, p. 242.
3. From the Introduction by David Cooper to Michel Foucault's *Madness and Civilization, A History of Insanity in the Age of Reason*, Tavistock Publications, London, 1971 (first published in England in 1967 and in France in 1961), pp. vii-ix. This may be compared with the following: "There is no such condition as 'Schizophrenia', but the label is a social fact and the social fact a *political* event. This political event, occurring in the civic order of society, imposes definitions and consequences on the labelled person. It is a social prescription that rationalizes a set of social actions whereby the labelled person is annexed by others, who are legally sanctioned, medically empowered, and morally obliged, to become responsible for the person labelled." (R.D. Laing, *The Politics of Experience*, Penguin Books, 1967, p. 100).
4. Patrick White, *The Riders in the Chariot*, 1961, p. 211. The social outcast, the nonconformist, the rebel against all forms of hypocrisy, and, not least, the willing victim of ironic circumstances, is most likely to be considered "mad" in the eyes of the commonplace. Thus Theodora Goodman, when still a child, experiences a strange feeling of kinship when she encounters "the man who was given his dinner". Listening to his silence rather to his words, she thinks, "that perhaps the man was a little bit mad, but she loved him for his madness even, for it made her warm." (*The Aunt's Story*, p. 47).
5. *The Riders in the Chariot*, p. 422.
6. *The Aunt's Story*, p. 134.
7. *Ibid.*, p. 286.
8. In Patrick White's novels words "whether written or spoken, [are] at most frail slate bridges over chasms." (*The Aunt's Story*, p. 134). He himself admitted in an interview the difficulty of expressing what he wishes to say "in a naturalistic medium"; referring in particular to the age in which he is writing, he observed, "I feel you can do far more with paint and music; I am hobbled by words . . . I find words frustrating as I sit year in year out reeling out an endless deadly grey . . . I wish I had been a painter or composer." (" A Conversation with Patrick White", in *Southerly, A Review of Australian Literature*, No. 2 (July 1973), 138–139).
9. *The Aunt's Story*, p. 141.
10. *Ibid.*, p. 175.
11. *The Riders in the Chariot*, p. 37.
12. At the time of writing *The Aunt's Story*, White visited a large exhibition of Paul Klee's work. According to Geoffrey Dutton (*Patrick White, Australian Writers and Their Work*, ed. G. Dutton, Melbourne, Oxford University Press, revised ed. 1963, p. 9) "parts of Klee's

credo ('in the highest circle an ultimate mystery lurks behind the mystery, and the wretched light of the intellect is of no avail') are profoundly relevant to White's own work."

13. William Blake, *The Marriage of Heaven and Hell.*
14. *The Living and the Dead,* p. 161. In this novel music is also part of cultural decadence as witnessed in pre-war London. Thus, in the "'marble waste land" of a Lyons Corner House, people exchange confidences over a cup of tea to the accompaniment of "the spun caramel of violins, a drawn-out Massenet" or "a rheumatic pizzicato that was Grieg". (p. 312).
15. *The Aunt's Story,* p. 114. In *The Vivisector* the concert audience is given these lines: "Along the rows the intellectual public servants and unassimilated Europeans were sitting tensed by the Andantino ... The ladies from the right suburbs loved to doze, but only to the right accompaniment ... For the time being, at least, the waves on which they were rising and falling wouldn't suck them down into some horrid abyss, or so they believed; they were riding safe in their own opalescent radiance." (p. 551).
16. *The Vivisector,* p. 521.
17. *Ibid.,* p. 523.
18. *The Living and the Dead,* pp. 161–163.
19. *The Aunt's Story,* pp. 116–117.
20. *The Vivisector,* pp. 524–525.
21. *The Aunt's Story,* pp. 244–5. Many pages earlier, in a non-musical context, occurs the following: "(Theodora Goodman) closed doors, and he was left standing on his handsome mahogany interior, which was external, fatally external, outside Theodora Goodman's closed door." (p. 113).
22. *Ibid.,* p. 66.
23. *Ibid.,* p. 123.
24. *Ibid.,* p. 270. A detailed analyis of the relation between music and life in *The Aunt's Story* from a metaphysical point of view, is found in the (as yet unpublished) doctoral dissertation by James Warner *The Development of Patrick White's Metaphysic: a Study of Three Novels,* The Hebrew University, Jerusalem, 1974, pp. 73–77.
25. *Ibid.,* p. 295. This, of course, is one of Patrick White's leitmotifs in most of his novels. In *The Living and the Dead,* the following sentence is repeated twice, at the beginning and at the end of the novel. It refers to the hero of the novel, Elyot, a figure out of T. S. Eliot's *Waste Land,* a Prufrock who can dimly perceive a way out of chaos and alienation: "Alone, he was yet not alone, uniting as he did the themes of many other lives." (p. 18 and p. 357).
26. Compare the following three passages:
   a. "Watching father carve the mutton it was like somebody with music, someone with a 'cello in his hands." (p. 49).
   b. "Moraïtis sat down and put his 'cello between his legs, and now you could see that his isolation fitted him closely, aptly, like an armour, which would protect him some moments that were too delicate to expose." (p. 115).

c. "The young man ... his face shaped like a scooped bone, though seen flat it was not unlike a 'cello." (p. 159).

27. *Ibid.*, p. 113. Theodora Goodman, already in her childhood, knew that hands can do more than merely touch. Playing Chopin, under her mother's insensitive supervision, she observes what happens to the *Nocturne* under her mother's hands: "She took possession of the piano, she possessed Chopin, they were hers while she wanted them, until she was ready to put them down. Only, watching the hands of Mother, which always did what they wanted to, Theodora was not moved. The music had lost its meaning . . ." (p. 29). Later on, after an unsuccessful attempt, to imitate her sister's self-possessed and artificial playing of Chopin, "she looked at her hands, that were never moved to do the things that Fanny did. But her hands touched, her hands became the shape of rose, she knew it in its utmost intimacy. Or she played the nocturne, as it was never meant, expressing some angular agony that she knew." (p. 32).

28. *Ibid.*, p. 116.

29. *Ibid.*, p. 117. Similar musical illuminations occur in a number of Patrick White's novels. One never-to-be-forgotten experience of this kind occurs when Mrs. Godbold, in *The Riders of the Chariot*, as a young child, listens for the first time, to Bach being played on the cathedral organ. "But there was no fire, only bliss, surging and rising, as she herself climbed upon the heavenly scaffolding and placed still other ladders, to reach higher. Her courage failed before the summit, at which she must either step right off into space . . . or be lifted out of sight for ever." (p. 236).

31. *Ibid.*, p. 297.

32. *The Vivisector*, pp. 489–490. The relation between painting and music has been mentioned before in this study, in particular in connection with D.H. Lawrence's attitude to both arts. See chapter IV above, pp. 106–108.

33. *Ibid.*, pp. 550–552. Musical images instead of abstractions are constantly used in White's novels to describe states of the soul. Thus, in *The Solid Mandala*, innocence is "a ceremony of white notes falling exactly into place", while isolation resembles "the twisted ropes of dark music." (p. 265).

34. *Ibid.*, p. 639.

X
Coda

No novelist in this study had undergone systematic musicological training. None among them was sufficiently versed in musicological disciplines to evaluate, in the language of musicology, past musical traditions or to pass considered judgment on contemporary musical experiments. This applies even to Thomas Mann who, after exhaustive conversations with Schönberg, ventured to introduce atonal music into *Doctor Faustus*. Fully aware of the cultural implications of atonality, he remained a stranger to Schönberg's musical theories and practice. Significantly, his detailed descriptions of Leverkühn's experiments with a new musical idiom are given by the musically conservative and somewhat unimaginative narrator of the story. He neither pretends to understand nor does he feel qualified to judge what he considers to be subversive musical deviation. It is Thomas Mann himself who speaks through the narrator's timid and simple-minded comments on a music he evidently does not approve of. The novelist's sympathy is with the classics, Bach, Mozart, and Beethoven. He never fails to respond to the simplicity of revelation, through joy or sorrow, in Schubert's chamber music or vocal compositions. For the writer of *Doctor Faustus*, the harmonious modulations of eighteenth and nineteenth century music provide the only criterion by which musical continuity can be measured. The musical present, and doubtless the future as well, has, in the words of the Devil in the novel, undergone a process of liberation. Musicology as expounded by Mephisto has opened the doors to the archaic and the primitive. It speaks the language of primordial Hell. From now on, the Devil tells the composer (and, of course, Leverkühn knew it all beforehand), everything will be permitted because no traditional restraints will be imposed on musical expression. Instead of nostalgically remembered harmonies, dissonance, chromaticism and dislocated rhythms will reign supreme. Although Thomas Mann wrote the most revolutionary musical novel of our time he remained a musical conservative in his predilection for the simple tune (as in Schubert's *Der Lindenbaum*), the operatic aria (as in Verdi's *Aida* or Bizet's *Carmen*), for the chamber music of the early nineteenth century.

There was much courage of despair in his fictitious life history of a contemporary composer. Yet in musical upbringing and taste he was not different from the other novelists dealt with in this study. Not only was he averse to contemporary music but he was candid enough to admit that he had tears in his eyes when listening to Schubert's Trio for piano, violin and cello, opus 99. As in the case of E. M. Forster, a novelist who does not easily lend himself to comparisons of this kind, music, in the words of a recent reviewer in the *Times Literary Supplement*, meant "uninhibited passion". At Forster's eightieth birthday a concert was given in which, in accordance with his wishes, pieces by Brahms, Franck, Wolf, and Strauss were played.[1] Thomas Mann, on the corresponding occasion—his eightieth birthday— suggested the following programme: Wagner's Prelude to *Lohengrin*, César Franck's Symphony, Debussy's *L'Après-midi d'un faune*, three *Lieder*—Schubert's *Im Dorf* and *Der Lindenbaum* and Schumann's *Zwielicht*—Schubert's Trio, opus 99, and lastly Beethoven's Leonore Overture No. 3.[2] Mann's response to music was, like Forster's determined by the emotional content of romantic and post-romantic symphonies and concertos, or by the use of musical evocation through the *leitmotif* in nineteenth-century opera.

The novelist's choice of a piece of music, whether it is an imaginary compound of various melodies as reassembled in Proust's musical memory, his "petite phrase", or whether it is a Beethoven quartet as in Huxley's *Point Counter Point* or a Mozart opera as in Hesse's *Steppenwolf*, is endowed with a significance transcending the novelist's creation of a fictitious universe. For the music has a reality of its own which the writer of fiction may search in vain to recapture. At times it is, in effect, the only meaningful reality which the characters in a work of fiction are aware of. Music in the novel is, in the most literal sense of the term, "taken from life"; it finds its place in the story where plot and character are all the novelist's own invention. Music alone pertains to the experience of reality as it occurs outside the novel. The music of Bach, Mozart and Beethoven does not have to be "invented". It was there before the novelist set to work to tell his story. Thus the composer's concern with inner time and the novelist's tale of outer time complement one another. Occasionally the inner and the outer require no clear-cut distinction. Whenever the two intermingle musical texture is translated into plot, melodic associations are transmuted into a "stream of consciousness" and a series of successive sounds is transposed into a "character".

Each novelist incorporates the musical experience into his novel in a different way, not as a mere structural analogy but as an equivalent or correlative for a variety of inner experiences. The novelist's concern with inner time and space determines the kind of music which conveys this introspective element best of all. Thus when Tolstoy chooses Beethoven's "Kreutzer Sonata", Huxley a Suite for flute and strings by Bach, and Thomas Mann in one of his stories the Prelude to *Tristan*, they adapt their musical preferences to the demands imposed by the psychological complexity of the character who either performs or listens. Virginia Woolf's predilection for chamber music characterizes much of her writing. Her novels and stories possess the intimacy and close texture of a small number of instruments playing in unison. The same composer may fulfill different functions in various novels; thus at times contradictory aspects of Beethoven's music are emphasized in the stories of Tolstoy, Huxley, Forster, and Thomas Mann. The same is true of Bach's compositions; they produce a diversity of echoes in Huxley's novels, in Hesse and in Patrick White.[3]

The response evoked by Mozart's *Don Giovanni* in the minds of various writers is of particular interest. Kierkegaard and Hesse, as part of their own musical development, heard the same music and were equally overwhelmed by its lyricism and its demonic power; yet it threatened to destroy the spiritual equilibrium of the former while curing the latter of a singularly severe form of mental alienation. On the other hand, in Thomas Mann's *Doctor Faustus* it is the devil who quotes Kierkegaard's essay with malicious approval. Again, in Joyce's *Ulysses* where

references to *Don Giovanni* abound, Mozart's opera provides the
novelist with a musical transmutation of the poetic myth upon
which the novel itself is founded. Side by side with the *Odyssey*
and *Hamlet*, the father-son relationship which lies at the core of
Joyce's novel forms part of a musical no less than of a literary
continuity. It is Stephen rather than Leopold Bloom who defines
this relationship in musical terms. What happens, at the end of
Mozart's opera, the return of the Commendatore, the solemn
rhythm of the terrifying octave leaps when he interrupts Don
Giovanni's celebration, presage a demonic, indeed a Faustian,
recognition of Self. Remembering Mozart's use of the octave,
Stephen thinks, "... the fundamental and the dominant are
separated by the greatest possible interval ... the ultimate return. The Octave ... What went forth to the ends of the world
to traverse not itself. God, the sun, Shakespeare, a commercial
traveller, having itself traversed in reality itself, becomes that
self ... Self which it itself was ineluctably preconditioned to
become." (p. 494). The "ultimate return" is the end of all
wandering: Ulysses' home-coming accompanied by his son Tel-
emachus, the meeting between the ghost of Hamlet's father and
his son on the platform at Elsinore, the Commendatore's final
encounter with Don Giovanni before his descent into hell,
Bloom's and Stephen's peregrination across Dublin towards
Eccles Street and restful sleep after a night of hallucinations and
chaos.

In an earlier episode Bloom's imagination is haunted by the
encounter between the seducer and the seduced. He quotes
from Mozart's opera

> Don Giovanni, a cenar teco
> M'invitasti,

and provides his own translation followed by the leaping and
ominous octaves,

> Don Giovanni, thou hast me invited
> To come to supper tonight,
> The rum the rumdrum. (p. 177)

But Bloom does not merely think of himself as the revenger. He
also is Ottavio, the rightful betrothed, the tenor defeated by the
baritone; he is also Masetto when he remembers that Boylan is
just then paying a visit to his wife to rehearse with her the duet

between Don Giovanni and Zerla "La ci darem la mano"; he is, finally, the silent listener at the Ormond Hotel to Bob Cowley playing the minuet from *Don Giovanni* on the piano (p. 277). A few minutes later he becomes Don Giovanni himself when he composes a letter to Martha, a more subtle form of adultery than the one that is taking place at that very moment at Eccles Street. On the way back from the red-light district Bloom and Stephen, in a spirit of placid exhaustion, exchange a few random remarks about music. Bloom admits to a temperamental aversion to Wagner whom he finds "a bit too heavy and hard to follow at the first go-off" but expresses a preference for "light opera of the *Don Giovanni* description" (p. 645).

Mozart's opera, then, exists on many different levels in Joyce's work. It expresses in musical terms the process of self-discovery which haunts Stephen's mind; it conveys an image of the tragedy of the human condition where a finer sensibility is defeated by the more robust sexuality of an unscrupulous rival; ultimately it adds a musical dimension to the archetypal dichotomy between father and son, the old and the young, the past and the future, the underworld where the ghosts of the departed dwell and the upper world of the living where innocence and experience meet in the greatest possible interval, the octave, the ultimate return. Although the Homeric and the Shakespearean analogies have been stressed by all commentators, Mozart's opera, its gaiety and its tragedy, constitutes one of the subtler ingredients in Joyce's thematic structure in his writing of *Ulysses*. References to it are less obvious than in the Devil's quotations from Kierkegaard's essay in Thomas Mann's *Doctor Faustus*, less explicit than in Hesse's story of resurrection through the body in his *Steppenwolf*. It encapsulates the whole of the Joycean universe as portrayed in *Ulysses*, from the most trivial to the most sublime.[4]

James Joyce who, on more than one occasion, has been called a "master-musician" used language the way Adrian Leverkühn composed music. The catalyst who, predictably, though without Joyce's knowledge or authority, provided the common denominator was Schönberg and his musical theories. Two years before Thomas Mann finished writing *Doctor Faustus*, he himself established an analogy between Joyce and Schönberg in a letter addressed to Bruno Walter, among the most eminent conductors in pre-Hitler Germany who had also emigrated to

California before the outbreak of the war. "But Joyce for example," writes Mann, "to whom I am closer in some ways, than might appear, is quite as outrageous to the mind trained in the classical, romantic, realistic traditions as Schönberg and his followers."[5] Such a statement is based on the assumption that the artist's attempts at portraying reality, whether through language or through music, has reached a dead end. What is being questioned here is the narrator's art itself insofar as it takes chronological time and traditional semantics for granted. For in order to cope with twentieth-century reality it must—in the words of a distinguished contemporary humanist writing on Thomas Mann's novel—"load the tangible with so many levels of meaning that the complete work really becomes an orchestral score requiring a conductor,"[6] a statement with which many readers of *Finnegans Wake* would agree. The novelist himself is "drawn into a kind of polyphonic soliloquy" expressive of the final retreat from the word and symbolizing the end of rational speech among men.

One of the most revealing remarks made by Adrian Leverkühn to his narrator-friend after having composed a piece of chamber music reflects the contemporary novelist's concern with the relationship between language and reality. " 'I have' ", says Leverkühn, " 'not wanted to write a sonata but a novel.' " The narrator's own comment on this hypothetical "novel" as musical score is significant on several accounts. "If I am to sum up the whole impression: it is as though one were lured from a firm and familiar setting—out into ever-remoter regions—everything seems contrary to expectation."[7] It is perfectly in keeping with the general tone of *Doctor Faustus* to imagine Adrian Leverkühn writing a "novel" in the spirit of Schönberg's musical theories. Would this "novel" have been, one is tempted to ask, in any notable way different from *Finnegans Wake*?

To the musicologist, however, Joyce's experiments with words may appear as intellectually coherent and inevitable as Schönberg's experiments with sounds. According to Wilfred Mellers who writes as a musicologist, Joyce's last novel, in effect, owes a debt to Schönberg. But, in Meller's opinion, "Schönberg's music has demonstrated how the glimmer of faith is to be attained only by the relinquishment of consciousness, of corporal rhythm, of thematic definition and of harmonious volition."[8]

That "glimmer of faith", though discernible in Joyce's night-vision of man's pilgrimage across the earth, is conspicuously absent from Mann's despairing cry at the end of *Doctor Faustus*. The possibility that Mann misunderstood Schönberg's musical message and saw cultural chaos and disintegration where others discovered a new musical vocabulary tending towards coherence and affirmation is not to be dismissed lightly. Even Adrian Leverkühn's "breakthrough", as Thomas Mann calls it, the resurrection of Monteverdi's naïve polyphonic harmonies in the last of Leverkühn's works, is merely one more remembrance of things past which has lost its meaning in an age so profoundly devoid of innocence and so agonizingly aware of discord as ours.

Though the musical experience may be conveyed in the modern novel in a spirit of frivolity or seriousness, in anguish or in hope, in denial or in affirmation, it acquires a more than passing significance when measured by criteria of coherence and proportion. The Pythagorean music of the spheres provides a common denominator however remote in time it may appear to be. Its echo reaches us across millennia of undiminished human dissonance. It constitutes a counterpoint of simplicity in the story of man's aspiration from the complexity of social compulsion to the discovery of inner time and space through harmonious sound. The glimmer of faith has not been extinguished in spite of—or perhaps because of—the musician's exploration of unchartered territories where, in Hesse's prophetic description, the world of numbers and that of sounds are once again shown to meet, "so that it became possible to combine astronomical and musical formulas, to reduce mathematics and music to a common denominator."[9]

Hesse's use of the past tense is somewhat misleading. He refers in this sentence to an imagined future where the synthesis of appearance and reality, of numerical symbolism and of musical proportion, will have been accomplished in a "game" in which the master-players of the province of Castalia achieve some final integration of all the arts. The novelist who during the war-years "invented" the game and put it all on paper is himself one of them. By writing in the past tense of a future still to come he places himself in the ineluctable present. His "game", like that of all the novelists discussed in this study, is the telling of stories. The discipline he applies to the playing of the game is that of art. His assumption that the perfect work of art will be created by the "master of the game" in whom is vested the authority of organizing all the arts, from the simplest to the most complex, into one satisfying whole is shared by all the novelists dealt with in this study. Although mathematics and astronomy, architecture and painting, are all ingredients of that final proportion which is reflected in the novelist's portrayal of reality, the interplay between consonance and dissonance can only be found at the still centre of the work.

Notes to Chapter Ten

1. Noël Annan in a review of P.N. Furbank's *E.M. Forster: A Life*, vol. II, in *The Times Literary Supplement*, March 24, 1978, pp. 334ff.
2. In a letter dated Kilchberg am Zürchersee, May 3, 1954, addressed to Dr. Jancke. *Briefe (Letters)*, vol. III, 1965, p. 335.
3. In the emotionally charged prose of Romain Rolland's *Jean Christophe*, a fugue by Bach, heard by two lovers, evokes a considerable degree of self-pity: "They wept silently as they sat listening to the music . . . There are moments where music summons forth all the sadness woven into the woof of a human being's destiny." (vol. III, "Journey's End", p. 35).
4. For a detailed discussion of the part played by Mozart's opera in Joyce's *Ulysses* see Frederic W. Sternfeld, "Poetry and Music– Joyce's *Ulysses*," in *Sound and Poetry*, English Institute Essays, 1956, edited with an introduction by Northrop Frye, Columbia University Press, N.Y. and London.
5. Letters of Thomas Mann, 1889–1955, p. 345, dated 1 March 1945. Schönberg's atonal music has frequently been compared to Joyce's asemantic use of language in *Finnegans Wake*. See Gordon Epperson's *The Musical Symbol, A Study of the Philosophic Theory of Music*. p. 257.
6. Erich Kahler, *The Orbit of Thomas Mann*, p. 20.
7. Thomas Mann, *Doctor Faustus*, p. 438.
8. Wilfrid Mellers, *Caliban Reborn*, pp. 44–51; quoted in Patrick Carnegy, *Faust as Musician*, p. 135.
9. Hermann Hesse, *The Glass Bead Game*, p. 38.

BIBLIOGRAPHY

1. *Primary Sources:*

Bellow, Saul, *Dangling Man* (1944), A Signet Book, 1965

Forster, E. M., *A Room with a View* (1908), Penguin Books, Harmondsworth, 1962

_____ *Howards End* (1910), Edward Arnold, London, 1960

_____ *A Passage to India* (1924), Penguin Books, Harmondsworth, 1963

_____ *Aspects of the Novel* (1927), Harcourt, Brace & Co., New York, n.d.

Gide, André, *The Counterfeiters* (1925), translated by Dorothy Bussy, Cassel, London, 1952

Hesse, Hermann, *Demian, The Story of Emil Sinclair's Youth* (1919), Introduction by Thomas Mann, translated by Michael Roloff & Michael Lebeck, Bantam Books, New York, 1970

_____ *Steppenwolf* (1927), translated by Basil Creighton, revised by Walter Sorrell, Penguin Books, Harmondsworth, 1973

_____ *Die Morgenlandfahrt* (The Journey to the East) (1932), Suhrkamp, Frankfurt/Main, 1963

_____ *The Glass Bead Game* (1943), translated by Richard & Clara Winston, Penguin Books, Harmondsworth, 1972

_____ *Briefe (Letters)*, Suhrkamp Verlag, Frankfurt/Main, 1964

Hesse, Hermann–Mann, Thomas, *Briefwechsel* (Correspondence), Suhrkamp Verlag, Frankfurt/Main, 1968

Huxley, Aldous, *Antic Hay* (1923), Modern Library, New York, 1932

_____ *Point Counter Point* (1928), Chatto & Windus, London, 1947

_____ *On Art and Artists*, Meridian Books, New York, 1960

"Music at Night" (1931); "The Rest is Silence" (1931); "The Doors of Perception" (1954); "Gesualdo: Variations on a Musical Theme" (1956)

———— *Letters*, Edited by Grover Smith, Chatto & Windus, London, 1969

James, Henry, *The Art of the Novel, Critical Prefaces*, with an introduction by Richard P. Blackmur, Charles Scribner's Sons, New York, London, 1953

Joyce, James, *Giacomo Joyce* (probably completed in July/August 1914), with an introduction by Richard Ellmann, Faber & Faber, London, 1968

———— *Dubliners* (1916), The Modern Library, New York, n.d.

———— *A Portrait of the Artist as a Young Man* (1916), The Modern Library, New York, 1928

———— *Ulysses* (1922), The Modern Library, New York, 1934

———— *Selected Letters*, edited by Richard Ellmann, Faber & Faber, London, 1975

Lawrence, D. H., *The Trespasser* (1912), Penguin Books, Harmondsworth, 1961

———— *Aaron's Rod* (1922), William Heinemann, London, 1948

———— "Pornography and Obscenity" (1929), in *Selected Literary Criticism*, edited by Anthony Beal, The Viking Press, New York, 1966

Mann, Thomas, *Buddenbrooks* (1901), translated by H. T. Lowe-Porter, Vintage Books, Random House, New York, 1952

———— *Stories of a Lifetime*, vol. 1, Mercury Books, London, 1961 *Tristan* (1902); *Tonio Kröger* (1903); *The Blood of the Walsung* (1921)

———— *Betrachtungen eines Unpolitischen* (1918), S. Fischer, Frankfurt/Main, 1956

———— *The Magic Mountain* (1924), translated by H. T. Lowe-Porter, Knopf, New York, 1967

———— *Doctor Faustus, The Life of the German Composer Adrian Leverkühn As Told by a Friend* (1947), translated by H. T. Lowe-Porter, Penguin Books, Harmondsworth, 1971

———— *Adel des Geistes*, Berman-Fischer Verlag, Stockholm, 1948

———— *The Story of a Novel. The Genesis of 'Doctor Faustus'*, translated by Richard & Clara Winston, Knopf, New York, 1961 (first published 1949)

———— "The Making of *The Magic Mountain*" (1953), in *The*

Magic Mountain, translated by H. T. Lowe-Porter, Knopf, New York, 1967

_____ *Briefe (Letters)*, vols. 1–3, S. Fischer Verlag, Frankfurt/ Main, 1962–1965

_____ *Letters of Thomas Mann, 1889–1955*, selected and translated by Richard & Clara Winston, Vintage Books, Random House, New York, 1975, (first published 1970)

Proust, Marcel, *Remembrance of Things Past* (1913–1927), translated by C. K. Scott Moncrieff, Chatto & Windus, London, 1941

_____ *On Art and Literature* (1896–1914), translated by Sylvia Townsend Warner, Delta Books, Dell Publishing, New York, 1958

Rolland, Romain, *Jean Christophe* (1904–1912), translated by Gilbert Cannan, The Modern Library, New York, n.d.

Sartre, Jean-Paul, *Nausea* (1938), translated by Lloyd Alexander, New Direction Paperback, New York, 1964

_____ *Words* (1964), translated by Irene Clephane, Hamish Hamilton, London, 1964

_____ *The Psychology of Imagination*, translated by Bernard Frechtman, Washington Square Press, New York, 1966 (first published 1940)

Tolstoy, Leo, *What is Art?* (1897), translated by Aylmer Maude, Worlds Classics, Oxford University Press, 1950

_____ "The Kreutzer Sonata" (1889) in *The Death of Ivan Ilych and other Stories*, translated by Louise and Aylmer Maude, Signet, New York, 1960

White, Patrick, *The Living and the Dead* (1941), Penguin Books, Harmondsworth, 1967

_____ *The Aunt's Story* (1948), Penguin Books, Harmondsworth, 1965

_____ *The Riders in the Chariot* (1961), Penguin Books, Harmondsworth, 1964

_____ *The Solid Mandala* (1966), Penguin Books, Harmondsworth, 1972

_____ *The Vivisector*, Jonathan Cape, London, 1970

Woolf, Virginia, "The String Quartet" (probably 1921) in *A Haunted House and Other Stories*, Hogarth Press, London, 1944

_____ *The Waves* (1931), Hogarth Press, London, 1946

———— *The Common Reader* ("Modern Fiction") (1925), First Series, Hogarth Press, London, 1948

2. *On Individual Authors:*
E. M. Forster:
Bradbury, Malcolm, (ed.), *E. M. Forster, 'A Passage to India'*, *A Casebook*, Macmillan, London, 1970
Burra, Peter, Introduction to the Everyman edition of *A Passage to India*, Dent, London, 1942
Kermode, Frank, *Puzzles and Epiphanies: Essays and Reviews 1958–1961*, Chilmark Press, New York, 1962
Wilde, Alan, *Art and Order. A Study of E. M. Forster*, New York University Press, 1964

Hermann Hesse:
Boulby, Mark, *Hermann Hesse. His Mind and Art*, Cornell University Press, 1967
Volke-Michels, (ed.), *Materialien zu Hermann Hesse's 'Der Steppenwolf'*, Suhrkamp Taschenbuchverlag, Frankfurt/Main, 1972
Serrano, Miguel, *C. G. Jung and Herman Hesse, A Record of Two Friendships*, translated by Frank MacShane, Schocken Books, New York, 1966
Ziolkowski, Theodore, *The Novels of Hermann Hesse. A Study in Theme and Structure*, Princeton University Press, 1965

James Joyce:
Adams, Robert Martin, *Surface and Symbol, the Consistency of James Joyce's 'Ulysses'*, Oxford University Press, New York, 1967
Deming, Robert H., (ed.), *James Joyce. The Critical Heritage*, Vols. 1 and 2, Routledge & Kegan Paul, London, 1970
Ellmann, Richard, *James Joyce*, Oxford University Press, 1966
———— *Ulysses on the Liffey*, Faber & Faber, London, 1972
Gilbert, Stuart, *James Joyce's Ulysses. A Study*, (1930), Vintage Books, Random House, New York, 1952
Levin, Harry, *James Joyce. A Critical Introduction*, New Directions Books, Norfolk, Conn., 1941
Litz, A. Walton, *The Art of James Joyce, Method and Design in 'Ulysses' and 'Finnegan's Wake'*, Oxford University Press, London, 1961

Sternfeld, Frederick W., "Poetry and Music—Joyce's *Ulysses*", in *Sound and Poetry*, English Institute Essays, Columbia University Press, 1956

D. H. Lawrence:
Hough, Graham, *The Dark Sun: A Study of D. H. Lawrence* (1956), Penguin Books, Harmondsworth, 1961
Moore, Harry T., *The Intelligent Heart: The Story of D. H. Lawrence* (1955), Penguin Books, Harmondsworth, 1960
Sagan, Keith, *The Art of D. H. Lawrence*, Cambridge University Press, 1966

Thomas Mann:
Baumgart, Reinhard, *Das Ironische und die Ironie in den Werken Thomas Manns*, Karl Hanser Verlag, Munich, 2nd edition, 1966
Bergsten, Gunilla, *Thomas Mann's 'Doctor Faustus'. The Sources and Structure of the Novel* (1963), translated by Krishna Winston, University of Chicago Press, 1969
Brennan, Joseph Gerard, *Thomas Mann's World*, Columbia University Press, 1942
Hatfield, Henry, (ed.), *Thomas Mann. A Collection of Critical Esays*, Prentice-Hall, Englewood Cliffs, 1964
Carnegy, Patrick, *Faust as Musician. A Study of Thomas Mann's Novel 'Doctor Faustus'*, Chatto & Windus, London, 1973
Jung, Ute, *Die Musikphilosophie Thomas Manns*, Kölner Beitrage zur Musikforschung, Vol. 3, Gustav Bosse Verlag, Regensburg, 1969
Kahler, Erich, *The Orbit of Thomas Mann*, Princeton University Press, 1969
Lukács, Georg, *Thomas Mann*, Aufbau-Verlag, Berlin, 1953
—————— *Essays on Thomas Mann*, translated by Stanley Mitchell, Universal Library, Grosset & Dunlap, New York, 1964
Putz, Heinz Peter, *Kunst und Künstlerexistenz bei Nietzsche und Thomas Mann. Zum Problem des Aesthetischen Perspektivismus in der Moderne*, Bonner Arbeiten zur Literatur, Bruno von Wiese (ed.), Vol. 6, H. Bouvier Verlag, Bonn, 1963
Marcel Proust:
Beckett, Samuel, *Proust and Three Dialogues* (1931), John Calder, London, 1965

Benoist-Mechin, *La Musique et l'Immortalité dans l'oeuvre de Marcel Proust*, Simon Kra, Paris, 1926

Bersoni, Leo, *Marcel Proust. The Fictions of Life and of Art*, Oxford University Press, New York, 1965

Brée, Germaine, *The World of Marcel Proust*, Riverside Studies in Literature, Houghton Mifflin, Boston, 1966

Brincourt, André & Jean, *Les Oeuvres et les Lumières*, La Table Ronde, 1955

Butor, Michel, *Les Oeuvres d'Art Imaginaires chez Proust*, Athlone Press, University of London, 1964

Graham, Victor E., *The Imagery of Proust*, Blackwell, Oxford, 1966

Hindus, Milton, *The Proustian Vision*, Southern Illinois University Press, 1954

Jean-Paul Sartre:

Bauer, George Howard, *Sartre and the Artist*, University of Chicago Press, 1969

McMahon, Joseph H., *Humans Being. The World of Jean-Paul Sartre*, University of Chicago Press, 1971

Leo Tolstoy:

Simmons, Ernest J., *Leo Tolstoy*, Vol. 2 *The Years of Maturity*, Vintage Books, Random House, New York, 1960

Tolstoy, Sergei, *Tolstoy Remembered—By his Son*, translated by Moura Budberg, Weidenfeld & Nicolson, London, 1961

Patrick White:

Mackenzie, Manfred, "Patrick White's Later Novels: A Generic Reading", *Southern Review*, I.3.5–17, 1965

Morley, Patricia A., *The Mystery of Unity. Theme and Technique in the Novels of Patrick White*, McGill Queen's University Press, 1972

Warner, James, *The Development of Patrick White's Metaphysic: A Study of Three Novels*, unpublished doctoral dissertation, The Hebrew University, Jerusalem, 1974

Wilkes, J. A., (ed.), *Ten Essays on Patrick White*, selected from *Southerly* (1964–1967), Angus & Robertson, Sydney, 1970

3. *Varieties of Musical Experience:*

Beardsley, M. C., *Aesthetics*, Harcourt, Brace & World, New York, 1958

Bergson, Henri, *Creative Evolution* (1907), translated by Arthur Mitchell, Modern Library, New York, 1944

———— *Time and Free Will. An Essay on the Immediate Data of Consciousness* (1889), translated by F. C. Pogson, Allen & Unwin, London, 1950

————"Laughter" (published in 1900), in *Comedy*, introduced and edited by Wylie Sypher, Doubleday Anchor Books, New York, 1956

Bloch, Ernst, *Das Prinzip Hoffnung*, vol. 3 Part 5/51, "Musik", Suhrkamp Verlag, Frankfurt/Main, 1968

Kierkegaard, Søren, "The Immediate Stages of the Erotic, or, The Musical Erotic" in *Either/Or*, vol. 1 (1845), Anchor Books, Doubleday, New York, 1959

Nietzsche, Friedrich, *The Birth of Tragedy from the Spirit of Music* (1872) in *The Philosophy of Nietzsche*, translated by C. P. Fadison, Modern Library, New York, 1954

———— *Attempt at a Self-Criticism* (1886), translated with commentary by Walker Kaufman, Vintage Books, Random House, New York, 1967

———— *The Case of Wagner. A Musician's Problem. Turinese Letter of May 1888*, translated with commentary by Walter Kaufman, Vintage Books, Random House, New York, 1967

Rougemont, Denis de, *Passion and Society*, translated by Montgomery Belgion, Faber & Faber, London, 1962

———— *The Myths of Love*, translated by Richard Howard, Faber & Faber, London, 1964

Schopenhauer, Arthur, "On the Metaphysic of Music" (1883), in *The World as Will and Idea*, translated by B. Haldane & J. Kemp, Routledge & Kegan Paul, London, 1964

4. *Literary and Musical Correspondences:*

Alvarez, A., *The Savage God, A Study of Suicide*, Penguin Books, Harmondsworth, 1974

Baudelaire, Charles, *Critique Littéraire et Musicale*, Claude Pichois (ed.), Librarie Armand Colin, Paris, 1961

Brown, Calvin S., *Music and Literature. A Comparison of the Arts*, University of Georgia Press, Athens, 1948

———— *Tones into Words. Musical Composition as Subjects of Poetry*, University of Georgia Press, Athens, 1953

Brown, E. K., *Rhythm in the Novel*, University of Toronto Press, 1963

Eliot, T. S. "The Music of Poetry" in *On Poetry and Poets*, Noonday Press, Farrar, Straus & Giroux, New York, 1967

Falk, Eugene H., *Types of Thematic Structure. The Nature and Function of Motifs in Gide, Camus, and Sartre*, University of Chicago Press, 1967

Foss, Martin, *Symbol and Metaphor*, University of Nebraska Press, 1964

Foucault, Michel, *Madness and Civilization, A History of Insanity in the Age of Reason*, translated by Richard Howard, Tavistock, London, 1971

French, Richard F., (ed.), *Music and Criticism. A Symposium*, Harvard University Press, 1948

Frye, Northrop, *Anatomy of Criticism*, Princeton University Press, 1957

Garden, Edward, "Tchaikovsky and Tolstoy" in *Music and Letters*, 55.3 (July 1974)

Howes, Frank, *Man, Mind, and Music*, Secker & Warburg, London, 1948

Humphrey, Robert, *Stream of Consciousness in the Modern Novel*, University of California Press, 1954

Jung, C. G., *Memories, Dreams, Reflections*, Aniela Jaffé (ed.), translated by Richard & Clara Winston, Vintage Books, Random House, New York, 1965

Laing, Ronald D., *The Politics of Experience*, Penguin Books, Harmondsworth, 1967.

Langer, Susanne K., *Philosophy in a New Key, A Study in the Symbolism of Reason, Rite and Art* (1942), Harvard University Press, 1969

———— *Feeling and Form. A Theory of Art developed from "Philosophy in a New Key"*, Routledge & Kegan Paul, London, 1953

Mendilov, A. A., *Time and the Novel*, Peter Nevill, London, 1952

Meyers, Jeffrey, *Painting and the Novel*, Manchester University Press, 1975

Richards, I. A., *Principles of Literary Criticism* (1924), Kegan Paul, Trench, Trubner, London, 1945

Steiner, George, *Language and Silence, Essays 1958–1966*, Faber & Faber, London, 1967

Wilson, Edmund, *Axel's Castle. A Study in the Imaginative Literature of 1870–1930*, Charles Scribner's Sons, New York, 1931

5. *Musicological and Allied Studies:*

Adorno, Theodor W., *Dissonanzen. Musik in der Verwalteten Welt*, Vanderhoeck & Ruprecht, Göttingen, 1956

——— *Einleitung in die Musiksoziologie*, Suhrkamp Verlag, Frankfurt/Main, 1962 and 1968

Beethoven, Ludwig v., *Letters, Journals and Conversations*, edited and translated by Michael Hamburger, Thames & Hudson, London, 1951

Carpentier, Alejo, "A Feeling for Music", in *The Times Literary Supplement*, September 22, 1972, pp. 1097–1099

Cooke, Deryck, *The Language of Music*, Oxford University Press, 1959

Copland, Aaron, *Music and Imagination*, Mentor Books, New American Library, New York, 1959

Cott, Jonathan, *Stockhausen. Conversations with the Composer*, Pan Books, London, 1974

Crossley-Holland, Peter, "India", in *The Pelican History of Music*, Alec Robertson & Denis Stevens (eds.), Penguin

Diserens, Charles M., *A Psychology of Music. The Influence of Music on Behaviour*, The College of Music, Cincinnati, 1939

Epperson, Gordon, *The Musical Symbol. A Study of the Philosophic Theory of Music*, Iowa State University Press, 1967

Farnsworth, Paul R., *The Social Psychology of Music*, Iowa State University Press, 1969

Hindemith, Paul, *A Composer's World*, Harvard University Press, 1952

Longhet-Higgins, H. C., "The Language of Music" in *The Times Literary Supplement*, November 20, 1970 pp. 1151–1152

Mellers, Wilfrid, *Music and Society. England and the European Tradition*, Denis Dobson, London, 1946

―――― *Harmonious Meeting. A Study of the Relationship between English Music, Poetry and Theatre, 1600–1900*, Denis Dobson, London, 1965

Meyer, Leonard B., *Emotion and Meaning in Music*, University of Chicago Press, 1956

―――― *Music, the Arts, and Ideas. Patterns and Predictions in Twentieth Century Culture*, University of Chicago Press, 1967

Middleton, Richard, "Stravinsky's Development: A Jungian Approach", in *Music and Letters*, 54.3 (July 1973) p. 289ff

Mitchell, Donald, *The Language of Modern Music*, Faber & Faber, London, 1963

Sessions, Roger, *The Musical Experience of Composer, Performer, Listener*, Princeton University Press, 1950

Shaw, Bernard, "The Perfect Wagnerite" (1898) & "The Sanity of Art" (1895) in *Major Critical Essays*, Constable, London, 1948

Storr, Anthony, "The Meaning of Music", in *The Times Literary Supplement*, November 20, 1970 pp. 1363–1364

Zuckerkandl, Victor, *Sound and Symbol. Music and the External World*, translated by William R. Trask, Bollingen Series XLIV, Pantheon Books, New York, 1959

6. *Music and Synesthesia:*

Arnheim, Rudolf, *Towards a Psychology of Art, Collected Essays*, Faber & Faber, London, 1967

Balzac, Honoré de, *Gambara* (1837–1839) in *Pleasures of Music. A Reader's Choice of Great Writing about Music from Cellini to Bernard Shaw*, edited with introduction by Jacques Barzun, Viking Press, New York, 1951

Goldwater, Robert & Treves, Marco, (eds.), *Artists on Art*, Pantheon Books, New York, 1945

Gombrich, E. H., *Art and Illusion, A Study in the Psychology of Pictorial Representation*, Phaidon, London, 1959

―――― *Symbolic Images, Studies in the Art of the Renaissance*, Phaidon, London, 1972

Holt, Elizabeth G., *A Documentary History of Art*, vol. 1, Anchor Books, Doubleday, New York, 1957

Huysman, J. K., *Against Nature* (1884), translated by Robert Baldick, Penguin Books, Harmondsworth, 1959

Lévi-Strauss, Claude, *L'Homme Nu*, Mythologiques IV, Plon, Paris, 1972

Mallarmé, Stéphane, "Divagations Premières" (1893), in *Vers et Prose*, Perrin, Paris, 1935

_____ "La Musique et les Lettres" in *Oeuvres Complètes*, Bibliothèque de la Pléiade, Paris, 1945

Matthiessen, F. O., *The Achievement of T. S. Eliot*, Oxford University Press, 1959

Pater, Walter, "The School of Giorgione" (1877) in *The Renaissance*, The Modern Library, New York, n.d.

Richter, J. R. & I. A., *The Literary Works of Leonardo da Vinci*, Oxford University Press, 1939

Spender, Stephen, *Eliot*, Frank Kermode (ed.), Fontana, Glasgow & London, 1957

Symons, Arthur, *The Symbolist Movement in Literature* (1899), Richard Ellmann (ed.), Dutton, New York, 1958

Yeats, W. B., *Essays and Introductions*, Macmillan, London, 1961

_____ *Explorations*, selected by Mrs. W. B. Yeats, Macmillan, London, 1962

Index

his transmutation of words into sounds, 45–46; and pure sound, 140; disintegration of at the end of *Doctor Faustus*, 203–204; in Patrick White's novels, 235 n4

Stravinsky, Igor: on the powerlessness of music to express anything at all, 58; described as exploring the unconscious, 59; his own comment, 63 n42

Structural analogies: between musical compositions and fiction writing, xii, 12, 65–68 *passim*; established by Forster in his *Aspects of the Novel*, 28–29; Thomas Mann's insistence on musical structure in writing his novels, 32; *Finnegans Wake* as an instance of musical structure, 60–61

Swann (in Proust's novel): as listener to music, 74

Synesthesia: 8–12, in Joyce's *Portrait*, 45–46

Synge, John: on literature and life as a symphony, 11

Theodora (in Patrick White's *The Aunt's Story*): listening to music xiii, 224–225; her individuation, 219, 226–227, 227–231 *passim*; her attitude to reality, 221; her escape from the concert hall, 224–225

Time: in music and language, 19–20; in the stream of consciousness considered as a musical score, 52–56 *passim*; and pure sound, 140; in Hesse's *Glass Bead Game*, 164–165; in Thomas Mann's *Doctor Faustus*, 198–199, 214 n22

Tolstoy, Leo N.: on Beetho-

ven, 91; quoting Kant on music, 93; his "Kreutzer Sonata", 93–94; on Wagner's music, 94; his married life, 108 n9

Verdi, Giuseppe: Hans Castorp listening to *Aida* in *The Magic Mountain*, 81

Vinci, Leonardo da: on the relation between music and painting, 6

Vinteuil (in Proust's novel): as fictitious composer, xii; Swann's and Marcel's response to his "petite phrase", 22–24, 113–114; their response to his Septet, 24; erotic ambiguities in his music, 117–119 *passim*; musical transcendence, 141–143

Wagner, Richard: Baudelaire's response to his operas, 10; the Prelude to *Tristan* in psychological terms, 64 n44; *Tristan* symbolizing the end of a civilization, 70; on Beethoven, 91; moral equivocation of his music, 94–96; his influence on modern novelists, 96; D.H. Lawrence on *Tristan*, 97; Tonio Kröger on *Tristan*, 100; on the effect of *Tristan* in Thomas Mann's story "Tristan", 100–102; the effect of *The Valkyrie* in one of Mann's early stories, 102–103; Denis de Rougemont on *Tristan*, 109 n15

Whistler, James A. McNeill: on the relation between music and painting, 6

White, Patrick: his concern with individuation through the musical experience,